The Structural Transformation
of the Public Sphere

The Structural Transformation of the Public Sphere

An Inquiry into a Category of Bourgeois Society

Jürgen Habermas

translated by Thomas Burger
with the assistance of Frederick Lawrence

The MIT Press, Cambridge, Massachusetts

Twelfth printing, 2001

First MIT Press paperback edition, 1991

This translation © 1989 Massachusetts Institute of Technology.
This work originally appeared in German under the Title *Strukturwandel der Öffentlicheit*, © 1962 Hermann Luchterhand Verlag, Darmstadt and Neuwied, Federal Republic of Germany.

This book was typeset by DEKR Corporation and was printed and bound in the United States of America.

Library of Congress Cataloging-in-Publication Data

Habermas, Jürgen.
  The structural transformation of the public sphere.

  (Studies in contemporary German social thought)
  Translation of: Strukturwandel der Öffentlichkeit.
  Bibliography: p.
  Includes index.
  1. Sociology—Methodology. 2. Social Structure.
3. Middle classes. 4. Political sociology. I. Title.
II. Series.
HM24.H2713 1989   305   88-13456
ISBN 0-262-08180-6 (hardcover) 0-262-58108-6 (paperback)

To Wolfgang Abendroth in gratitude

Contents

III Political Functions of the Public Sphere

IV The Bourgeois Public Sphere: Idea and Ideology

V The Social-Structural Transformation of the Public Sphere

Contents

VI The Transformation of the Public Sphere's Political Function

VII On the Concept of Public Opinion

Introduction

There is no good reason why *Strukturwandel der Öffentlichkeit*, one of Habermas's most influential and widely translated works, should not have appeared in English sooner. That would likely have facilitated the reception of his thought among Anglo-American scholars by showing how the more abstract and theoretical concerns of his later work arose out of the concrete issues raised in this study. *The Structural Transformation of the Public Sphere* is a historical-sociological account of the emergence, transformation, and disintegration of the bourgeois public sphere. It combines materials and methods from sociology and economics, law and political science, and social and cultural history in an effort to grasp the preconditions, structures, functions, and inner tensions of this central domain of modern society. As a sphere between civil society and the state, in which critical public discussion of matters of general interest was institutionally guaranteed, the liberal public sphere took shape in the specific historical circumstances of a developing market economy. In its clash with the arcane and bureaucratic practices of the absolutist state, the emergent bourgeoisie gradually replaced a public sphere in which the ruler's power was merely represented *before* the people with a sphere in which state authority was publicly monitored through informed and critical discourse *by* the people.

Habermas traces the interdependent development of the literary and political self-consciousness of this new class, weaving together accounts of the rise of the novel and of literary and political journalism and the spread of reading societies, salons, and coffee houses into a *Bildungsroman* of this "child of the eighteenth century." He notes the contradiction between the liberal public sphere's constitutive catalogue of "basic rights of man" and their de facto restriction to a certain class of men. And he traces the tensions this occasioned as, with the further development of capitalism, the public body expanded beyond the bourgeoisie to include groups that were systematically disadvantaged by the workings of the free market and sought state regulation and compensation. The consequent intertwining of state and society in the late nineteenth and the twentieth centuries meant the end of the liberal public sphere. The public sphere of social-welfare-state democracies is rather a field of competition among conflicting interests, in which organizations representing diverse constituencies negotiate and compromise among themselves and with government officials, while excluding the public from their proceedings. Public opinion is, to be sure, taken into account, but not in the form of unrestricted public discussion. Its character and function are indicated rather by the terms in which it is addressed: "public opinion research," "publicity," "public relations work," and so forth. The press and broadcast media serve less as organs of public information and debate than as technologies for managing consensus and promoting consumer culture.

While the historical structures of the liberal public sphere reflected the particular constellation of interests that gave rise to it, the idea it claimed to embody—that of rationalizing public authority under the institutionalized influence of informed discussion and reasoned agreement—remains central to democratic theory. In a post-liberal era, when the classical model of the public sphere is no longer sociopolitically feasible, the question becomes: can the public sphere be effectively reconstituted under radically different socioeconomic, political and cultural conditions? In short, is democracy possible? One could do worse than to view Habermas's work in the twenty-five years since *Strukturwandel* through the lens of this question. That is not, however, the only or the best reason for publishing this English edition now. The contingencies of intellectual history have placed us in a situation that is particularly well disposed to its appearance:

• Feminist social theorists, having identified institutional divisions between the public and the private as a thread running through the history of the subordination of women will find here a case study in the sociostructural transformation of a classic form of that division.

• Political theorists, having come to feel the lack of both large-scale social analysis and detailed empirical inquiry in the vast discussion centering around Rawls's normative theory of justice, will appreciate this empirical-theoretical account of the network of interdependencies that have defined and limited the democratic practice of justice.

• Literary critics and theorists who have grown dissatisfied with purely textual approaches will be interested in Habermas's cultural-sociological account of the emergence of the literary public sphere and its functioning within the broader society.

• Comparative-historical sociologists will see here an exemplary study that manages to combine a macroanalysis of large-scale structural changes with interpretive access to the shifting meanings by and to which actors are oriented.

• Political sociologists will discover that familiar problems of democratic political participation, the relation of economy to polity, and the meaning of public opinion are cast in a new light by Habermas's theoretical perspective and historical analysis.

• Communications and media researchers will profit not only from Habermas's account of the rise of literary journalism and the subsequent transformation of the press into one of several mass media of a consumer society, but also from the framework for future research that this account suggests.

• Legal theorists will discover here a way of critically analyzing the gaps between claim and reality which avoids the dead end of pure deconstruction.

In all of these areas, to be sure, significant work has been done since Habermas first published this study. But I think it fair to say that no single work, or body of work, has succeeded in fusing these disparate lines of inquiry into a unified whole of comparable insight and power. In this respect it remains paradigmatic.

Thomas McCarthy
Northwestern University

Translator's Note

Habermas's *The Structural Transformation of the Public Sphere* contains a number of terms that present problems to the translator. One of these, *Öffentlichkeit*, which appears in the very title of the book, may be rendered variously as "(the) public," "public sphere," or "publicity." Whenever the context made more than one of these terms sensible, "public sphere" was chosen as the preferred version.

Habermas distinguishes several types of *Öffentlichkeit*:

politische Öffentlichkeit: "political public sphere" (or sometimes the more cumbersome "public sphere in the political realm")

literarische Öffentlichkeit: "literary public sphere" (or "public sphere in the world of letters")

repräsentative Öffentlichkeit: "representative publicness" (i.e., the display of inherent spiritual power or dignity before an audience)

Another troublesome term is *bürgerlich*, an adjective related to the noun *Bürger*, which may be translated as "bourgeois" or "citizen." *Bürgerlich* possesses both connotations. In expressions such as "civil code," "civil society," "civic duty," "bourgeois strata," and "bourgeois family" the German term for "civil," "civic," and "bourgeois" is *bürgerlich*. *Bürgerlich* also means "middle class" in contrast to "noble" or "peasant." *Bürgerliche Öffentlichkeit* thus is difficult to translate adequately. For better or worse, it is rendered here as "bourgeois public sphere."

Intimsphäre denotes the core of a person's private sphere which by law, tact, and convention is shielded from intrusion; it is translated here as "intimate sphere."

Thomas Burger

Author's Preface

This investigation endeavors to analyze the type "bourgeois public sphere" (*bürgerliche Öffentlichkeit*). Its particular approach is required, to begin with, by the difficulties specific to an object whose complexity precludes exclusive reliance on the specialized methods of a single discipline. Rather, the category "public sphere" must be investigated within the broad field formerly reflected in the perspective of the traditional science of "politics."[1] When considered within the boundaries of a particular social-scientific discipline, this object disintegrates. The problems that result from fusing aspects of sociology and economics, of constitutional law and political science, and of social and intellectual history are obvious: given the present state of differentiation and specialization in the social sciences, scarcely anyone will be able to master several, let alone all, of these disciplines.

The other peculiarity of our method results from the necessity of having to proceed at once sociologically and historically. We conceive bourgeois public sphere as a category that is typical of an epoch. It cannot be abstracted from the unique developmental history of that "civil society" (*bürgerliche Gesellschaft*) originating in the European High Middle Ages; nor can it be transferred, idealtypically generalized, to any number of historical situations that represent formally similar constellations. Just as we try to show, for instance, that one can properly speak of public opinion in a precise sense only with regard to late-seventeenth-century Great Britain and eighteenth-century

France, we treat public sphere in general as a historical category. In this respect our procedure is distinguished *a limine* from the approach of formal sociology whose advanced state nowadays is represented by so-called structural-functional theory. The sociological investigation of historical trends proceeds on a level of generality at which unique processes and events can only be cited as examples—that is, as cases that can be interpreted as instances of a more general social development. This sociological procedure differs from the practice of historiography strictly speaking in that it seems less bound to the specifics of the historical material, yet it observes its own equally strict criteria for the structural analysis of the interdependencies at the level of society as a whole.

After these two methodological preliminaries, we would also like to record a reservation pertaining to the subject matter itself. Our investigation is limited to the structure and function of the *liberal* model of the bourgeois public sphere, to its emergence and transformation. Thus it refers to those features of a historical constellation that attained dominance and leaves aside the *plebeian* public sphere as a variant that in a sense was suppressed in the historical process. In the stage of the French Revolution associated with Robespierre, for just one moment, a public sphere stripped of its literary garb began to function—its subject was no longer the "educated strata" but the uneducated "people." Yet even this plebeian public sphere, whose continued but submerged existence manifested itself in the Chartist Movement and especially in the anarchist traditions of the workers' movement on the continent, remains oriented toward the intentions of the bourgeois public sphere. In the perspective of intellectual history it was, like the latter, a child of the eighteenth century. Precisely for this reason it must be strictly distinguished from the plebiscitary-acclamatory form of regimented public sphere characterizing dictatorships in highly developed industrial societies. Formally they have certain traits in common; but each differs in its own way from the literary character of a public sphere constituted by private people putting reason to use—one is illiterate, the other, after a fashion, post-literary. The similarity with certain aspects of plebiscitary form cannot conceal the fact that these two variants of the public sphere of bourgeois society (which in the context of the present investigation will be equally neglected) have also been charged with different political functions, each at a distinct stage of social development.

Our investigation presents a stylized picture of the liberal elements of the bourgeois public sphere and of their transformation in the social-welfare state.

I am grateful to the Deutsche Forschungsgemeinschaft for generous support. This work, with the exception of sections 13 and 14, was presented to the Philosophical Faculty at Marburg as my *Habilitationsschrift*.

J. H.
Frankfurt, Autumn 1961

The Structural Transformation of the
Public Sphere

I

Introduction: Preliminary Demarcation of a Type of Bourgeois Public Sphere

1 The Initial Question

The usage of the words "public" and "public sphere" betrays a multiplicity of concurrent meanings. Their origins go back to various historical phases and, when applied synchronically to the conditions of a bourgeois society that is industrially advanced and constituted as a social-welfare state, they fuse into a clouded amalgam. Yet the very conditions that make the inherited language seem inappropriate appear to require these words, however confused their employment. Not just ordinary language (especially as it bears the imprint of bureaucratic and mass media jargon) but also the sciences—particularly jurisprudence, political science, and sociology—do not seem capable of replacing traditional categories like "public" and "private," "public sphere," and "public opinion," with more precise terms. Ironically, this dilemma has first of all bedeviled the very discipline that explicitly makes public opinion its subject matter. With the application of empirical techniques, the object that public-opinion research was to apprehend has dissolved into something elusive;[1] nevertheless sociology has refused to abandon altogether these categories; it continues to study public opinion.

We call events and occasions "public" when they are open to all, in contrast to closed or exclusive affairs—as when we speak of public places or public houses. But as in the expression "public building," the term need not refer to general accessibility; the building does not even have to be open to public traffic. "Public buildings" simply house state institutions and as such are "public." The state is the "public authority." It owes this attribute to its task of promoting the public or common welfare of its rightful members. The word has yet another meaning when one speaks of a "public [official] reception"; on such occasions a powerful display of representation is staged whose "publicity" contains an element of public recognition. There is a shift in meaning again when we say that someone has made a name for himself, has a public reputation. The notion of such personal prestige or renown originated in epochs other than that of "polite society."

None of these usages, however, have much affinity with the meaning most commonly associated with the category—expressions like "public opinion," an "outraged" or "informed public," "publicity," "publish," and "publicize." The subject of this publicity is the public as carrier of public opinion; its function as a critical judge is precisely what makes the public character of proceedings—in court, for instance—meaningful. In the realm of the mass media, of course, publicity has changed its meaning. Originally a function of public opinion, it has become an attribute of whatever attracts public opinion: public relations and efforts recently baptized "publicity work" are aimed at producing such publicity. The public sphere itself appears as a specific domain—the public domain versus the private. Sometimes the public appears simply as that sector of public opinion that happens to be opposed to the authorities. Depending on the circumstances, either the organs of the state or the media, like the press, which provide communication among members of the public, may be counted as "public organs."

A social-historical analysis of the syndrome of meanings possessed by "public" and "publicity" could uncover the essential sociological characteristics of the various historical language strata. The first etymological reference to the public sphere is quite revealing. In German the noun *Öffentlichkeit* was formed from the older adjective *öffentlich* during the eighteenth century,[2] in analogy to *"publicité"* and "publicity"; by the close of the century the word was still so little used that Heynatz could consider it objectionable.[3] If the public sphere did not require a name of its own before this period, we may assume that this sphere first emerged and took on its function only at that time, at least in Germany. It was specifically a part of "civil society," which at the same time established itself as the realm of commodity exchange and social labor governed by its own laws. Notions concerning what is "public" and what is not—that is, what is "private"—however, can be traced much further back into the past.

We are dealing here with categories of Greek origin transmitted to us bearing a Roman stamp. In the fully developed Greek city-state the sphere of the *polis*, which was common (*koine*) to the free citizens, was strictly separated from the sphere of the *oikos*; in the sphere of the *oikos*, each individual is in his own realm (*idia*). The public life, *bios politikos*, went on in the market place (*agora*), but of course this did not mean that it occurred necessarily only in this specific locale. The public sphere was constituted in discussion (*lexis*), which could also assume the forms of consultation and of sitting in the court of law, as well as in common action (*praxis*), be it the waging of war or competition in athletic games. (Strangers were often called upon to legislate, which was not properly one of the public tasks.) The political order, as is well known, rested on a patrimonial slave economy. The citizens were thus set free from productive labor; it was, however, their private autonomy as masters of households on which their participation in public life depended. The private sphere was attached to the house not by (its Greek) name only. Movable wealth and control over labor power were no more substitutes for being the master of a household and of a family than, conversely, poverty and a lack of slaves would in themselves prevent admission to the *polis*. Exile, expropriation, and the destruction of the house amounted to one and the same thing. Status in the *polis* was therefore based upon status as the unlimited master of an *oikos*. The reproduction of life, the labor of the slaves, and the service of the women went on under the aegis of the master's domination; birth and death took place in its shadow; and the realm of necessity and transitoriness remained immersed in the obscurity of the private sphere. In contrast to it stood, in Greek self-interpretation, the public sphere as a realm of freedom and permanence. Only in the light of the public sphere did that which existed become revealed, did everything become visible to all. In the discussion among citizens issues were made topical and took on shape. In the competition among equals the best excelled and gained their essence—the immortality of fame. Just as the wants of life and the procurement of its necessities were shamefully hidden inside the *oikos*, so the *polis* provided an open field for honorable distinction: citizens indeed interacted as equals with equals (*homoioi*), but each did his best to excel (*aristoiein*). The virtues, whose catalogue was codified by Aristotle, were ones whose test lies in the public sphere and there alone receive recognition.

Since the Renaissance this model of the Hellenic public sphere, as handed down to us in the stylized form of Greek self-interpretation, has shared with everything else considered "classical" a peculiarly normative power.[4] Not the social formation at its base but the ideological template itself has preserved continuity over the centuries—on the level of intellectual history. To begin with, throughout the Middle Ages the categories of the public and the private and of the public sphere understood as *res publica* were passed on in the definitions of Roman law. Of course, they found a renewed application meaningful in the technical, legal sense only with the rise of the modern state and of that sphere of civil society separated from it. They served the political self-interpretation as well as the legal institutionalization of a public sphere that was bourgeois in a specific sense. Meanwhile, however, for about a century the social foundations of this sphere have been caught up in a process of decomposition. Tendencies pointing to the collapse of the public sphere are unmistakable, for while its scope is expanding impressively, its function has become progressively insignificant. Still, publicity continues to be an organizational principle of our political order. It is apparently more and other than a mere scrap of liberal ideology that a social democracy could discard without harm. If we are successful in gaining a historical understanding of the structures of this complex that today, confusedly enough, we subsume under the heading "public sphere," we can hope to attain thereby not only a sociological clarification of the concept but a systematic comprehension of our own society from the perspective of one of its central categories.

2 Remarks on the Type of Representative Publicness

During the Middle Ages in Europe the contrast drawn in Roman law between *publicus* and *privatus*[5] was familiar but had no standard usage. The precarious attempt to apply it to the legal conditions of the feudal system of domination based on fiefs and manorial authority (*Grundherrschaft*) unintentionally provides evidence that an opposition between the public and private spheres on the ancient (or the modern) model did not exist. Here too an economic organization of social labor caused all relations of domination to be centered in the lord's household. Nevertheless, the feudal lord's position within the process of production was not comparable to the "private" authority of the *oikodespotes* or of the *pater familias*. While manorial authority (and its derivative, feudalism) as the quintessence of all lordly particular rights might be conceived of as a *jurisdictio*, it could not be fitted readily into the contrast between private dominion (*dominium*) and public autonomy (*imperium*). There were lower and higher "sovereignties," eminent and less eminent prerogatives; but there was no status that in terms of private law defined in some fashion the capacity in which private people could step forward into a public sphere. In Germany manorial authority, fully developed in the High Middle Ages, was transformed into private landed property only in the eighteenth century as part of the liberation of the peasants and the clearing of land holdings from feudal obligations. The domestic authority of the head of a household is not the same as private dominion, whether in the sense of classical law or in that of modern civil law. When the latter's categories were transferred to social conditions providing no basis for division between the public sphere and the private domain, difficulties arose:

If we think of the land as the public sphere, then the house and the authority exercised by its master must simply be considered a public authority of the second order: it is certainly private in relation to that of the land to which it is subordinated, but surely in a sense very different from how the term is understood in modern private law. Thus it seems quite intelligible to me that "private" and "public" powers are so fused together into an indivisible unity that both are emanations from a single unified authority, that they are inseparable from the land and can be treated like legitimate private rights.[6]

It should be noted, however, that the tradition of ancient Germanic law, through the categories "*gemeinlich*" and "*sunderlich*," "common" and "particular," did generate a contrast that corresponded somewhat to the classical one between "*publicus*" and "*privatus*." That contrast referred to communal elements to the extent to which they survived under the feudal conditions of production. The commons was public, *publica*; for common use there was public access to the fountain and market square—*loci communes, loci publici*. The "particular" stood opposed to this "common," which etymologically is related to the common or public welfare (common wealth, public wealth). This specific meaning of "private" as "particular" reverberates in today's equation of special interests with private interests. Yet one should note that within the framework of feudalism the particular *also* included those who possessed special rights, that is, those with immunities and privileges. In this respect the particular (i.e., what stood apart), the exception through every sort of exemption, was the core of the feudal regime and hence of the realm that was "public." The original parallelism of Germanic and Roman legal categories was reversed as soon as they were absorbed by feudalism—the common man became the private man. A linguistic reminder of this relationship is the use of "private" in the sense of "common" soldier—the ordinary man without rank and without the particularity of a special power to command interpreted as "public." In medieval documents "lordly" and "*publicus*" were used synonymously; *publicare* meant to claim for the lord.[7] The ambivalence in the meaning of "*gemein*" (common) as "communal," that is, (publicly) accessible to all and "ordinary," that is, without special right (namely, lordly prerogative) and without official rank in general still reflects the integration of elements of communal (*genossenschaftlich*) organization into a social structure based on manorial authority.[8]

Sociologically, that is to say by reference to institutional criteria, a public sphere in the sense of a separate realm distinguished from the private sphere cannot be shown to have existed in the feudal society of the High Middle Ages. Nevertheless it was no accident that the attributes of lordship, such as the ducal seal, were called "public"; not by accident did the English king enjoy "publicness"[9]—for lordship was something publicly represented. This *publicness* (or *publicity*) *of representation* was not constituted as a social realm, that is, as a public sphere; rather, it was something like a status attribute, if this term may be permitted. In itself the status of manorial lord, on whatever level, was neutral in relation to the criteria of "public" and "private"; but its incumbent represented it publicly. He displayed himself, presented himself as an embodiment of some sort of "higher" power.[10] The concept of representation in this sense has been preserved down to the most recent constitutional doctrine, according to which representation can "occur only in public . . . there is no representation that would be a 'private' matter."[11] For representation pretended to make something invisible visible through the public presence of the person of the lord: ". . . something that has no life, that is inferior, worthless, or mean, is not representable. It lacks the exalted sort of being suitable to be elevated into public status, that is, into existence. Words like excellence, highness, majesty, fame, dignity, and honor seek to characterize this peculiarity of a being that is capable of representation." Representation in the sense in which the members of a national assembly represent a nation or a lawyer represents his clients had nothing to do with this publicity of representation inseparable from the lord's concrete existence, that, as an "aura," surrounded and endowed his authority. When the territorial ruler convened about him ecclesiastical and wordly lords, knights, prelates, and cities (or as in the German Empire until 1806 when the Emperor invited the princes and bishops, Imperial counts, Imperial towns, and abbots to the Imperial Diet), this was not a matter of an assembly of delegates that was someone else's representative. As long as the prince and the estates of his realm "were" the country and not just its representatives, they could represent it in a specific sense. They represented their lordship not for but "before" the people.

The staging of the publicity involved in representation was wedded to personal attributes such as insignia (badges and arms), dress (clothing and coiffure), demeanor (form of greeting and poise) and rhetoric (form of address and formal discourse in general)[12]—in a word, to a strict code of "noble" conduct. The latter crystallized during the High Middle Ages into the system of courtly virtues, a Christianized form of the Aristotelian cardinal virtues, which subdued the heroic to form the chivalrous and courteous. Characteristically, in none of these virtues did the physical aspect entirely lose its significance, for virtue must be embodied, it had to be capable of public representation.[13] Especially in the joust, the replica of the cavalry battle, this representation came into its own. To be sure, the public sphere of the Greek *polis* was no stranger to a competitive display of *arete*; but the publicity of courtly-knightly representation which, appropriately enough, was fully displayed on feast days, the "high holy days," rather than on court days was completely unlike a sphere of political communication. Rather, as the aura of feudal authority, it indicated social status. This is why it had no particular "location": the knightly code of conduct was common as a norm to all nobles, from the king down to the lowliest knight standing just above the peasants. It provided orientation not merely on definite occasions at definite locales (say, "in" a public sphere) but constantly and everywhere, as representative of their lordly rights.

Only the ecclesiastical lords had, in addition to the occasions that were part of the affairs of the world, a specific locale for their representation: the church. In church ritual, liturgy, mass, and processions, the publicity that characterized representation has survived into our time. According to a well-known saying the British House of Lords, the Prussian General Staff, the French Academy, and the Vatican in Rome were the last pillars of representation; finally only the Church was left, "so utterly alone that those who see in it no more than an external form cannot suppress the epigrammatic joke that it no longer represents anything except representation itself."[14] For all that, the relationship of the laity to the priesthood illustrates how the "surroundings" were part and parcel of the publicity of representation (from which they were nevertheless excluded)—those surroundings were private in the sense in which the private soldier was excluded from representation and from military honor, even though he had to be "part." The complement of this exclusion was a secret at the inner core of publicity: the latter was based on an *arcanum*; mass and the Bible were read in Latin rather than in the language of the people.

The representation of courtly-knightly publicity attained its ultimate pure form at the French and Burgundian courts in the fifteenth century.[15] The famous Spanish ceremonial was the petrified version of this late flowering and in this form survived for several centuries at the courts of the Hapsburg. A new form of the representative publicness, whose source was the culture of the nobility of early capitalist northern Italy, emerged first in Florence and then in Paris and London. It demonstrated its vigor, however, in its assimilation of bourgeois culture, whose early manifestation was humanism; the culture of humanism became a component of courtly life.[16] However, following the activities of the first tutors to princes (i.e., as early as around 1400) humanism—which developed the art of philological criticism only in the course of the sixteenth century— became the vehicle for reshaping the style of courtly life itself. Under the influence of the *Cortegiano* the humanistically culti- vated courtier replaced the Christian knight. The slightly later notions of the gentleman in Great Britain and of the *honnête homme* in France described similar types. Their serene and eloquent sociability was characteristic of the new "society" cen- tered in the court.[17] The independent provincial nobility based in the feudal rights attached to the land lost its power to represent; publicity of representation was concentrated at the prince's court. The upshot of this was the baroque festivity in which all of its elements were united one more time, sensation- ally and magnificently.

In comparison to the secular festivities of the Middle Ages and even of the Renaissance the baroque festival had already lost its public character in the literal sense. Joust, dance, and theater retreated from the public places into the enclosures of the park, from the streets into the rooms of the palace. The castle park made its first appearance in the middle of the seventeenth century but then spread rapidly over Europe along with the architecture of the French Century. Like the baroque palace itself, which was built around the grand hall in which the festivities were staged, the castle park permitted a courtly life sealed off from the outside world. However, the basic pattern of the representative publicness not only survived but became more prominent. Mademoiselle de Scudéry reported in her *Conversations* the stress of the grand festivities; these served not so much the pleasure of the participants as the demonstration of grandeur, that is, the grandeur of the host and guests. The common people, content to look on, had the most fun.[18] Thus even here the people were not completely excluded; they were ever present in the streets. Representation was still dependent on the presence of people before whom it was displayed.[19] Only the banquets of bourgeois notables became exclusive, taking place behind closed doors:

> The bourgeois is distinguished from the courtly mentality by the fact that in the bourgeois home even the ballroom is still homey, whereas in the palace even the living quarters are still festive. And actually, beginning with Versailles, the royal bedroom develops into the palace's second center. If one finds here the bed set up like a stage, placed on a platform, a throne for lying down, separated by a barrier from the area for the spectator, this is so because in fact this room is the scene of the daily ceremonies of *lever* and *coucher*, where what is most intimate is raised to public importance.[20]

In the etiquette of Louis XIV concentration of the publicity of representation at the court attained the high point of refinement.

The aristocratic "society" that emerged from that Renaissance society no longer had to represent its own lordliness (i.e., its manorial authority), or at least no longer primarily; it served as a vehicle for the representation of the monarch. Only after national and territorial power states had arisen on the basis of the early capitalist commercial economy and shattered the feudal foundations of power could this court nobility develop the framework of a sociability—highly individuated, in spite of its comprehensive etiquette—into that peculiarly free-floating

but clearly demarcated sphere of "good society" in the eighteenth century.[21] The final form of the representative publicness, reduced to the monarch's court and at the same time
receiving greater emphasis, was already an enclave within a
society separating itself from the state. Now for the first time
private and public spheres became separate in a specifically
modern sense.

Thus the German word *privat*, which was borrowed from the
Latin *privatus*, can be found only after the middle of the sixteenth century,[22] having the same meaning as was assumed by
the English "private" and the French *privé*. It meant as much
as "not holding public office or official position,"[23] *ohne öffentliches Amt*,[24] or *sans emplois que l'engage dans les affaires publiques*.[25]
"Private" designated the exclusion from the sphere of the state
apparatus; for "public" referred to the state that in the meantime had developed, under absolutism, into an entity having
an objective existence over against the person of the ruler. The
public (*das Publikum, le public*), was the "public authority" (*öffentliche Gewalt*) in contrast to everything "private" (*Privatwesen*).
The servants of the state were *öffentliche Personen*, public persons, or *personnes publiques*; they were incumbent in some official position, their official business was "public" (*öffentliches Amt,
service public*), and government buildings and institutions were
called "public." On the other hand, there were private individuals, private offices, private business, and private homes; Gott-
helf speaks of the *Privatmann* (private person). The authorities
were contrasted with the subjects excluded from them; the
former served, so it was said, the public welfare, while the
latter pursued their private interests.

The major tendencies that prevailed by the end of the eighteenth century are well-known. The feudal powers, the
Church, the prince, and the nobility, who were the carriers of
the representative publicness, disintegrated in a process of polarization; in the end they split into private elements, on the
one hand, and public ones, on the other. The status of the
Church changed as a result of the Reformation; the anchoring
in divine authority that it represented—that is, religion—became a private matter. The so-called freedom of religion historically secured the first sphere of private autonomy; the

Church itself continued to exist as one corporate body among others under public law. The first visible mark of the analogous polarization of princely authority was the separation of the public budget from the territorial ruler's private holdings. The bureaucracy, the military (and to some extent also the administration of justice) became independent institutions of public authority separate from the progressively privatized sphere of the court. Out of the estates, finally, the elements of political prerogative developed into organs of public authority: partly into a parliament, and partly into judicial organs. Elements of occupational status group organization, to the degree that they were already involved in the urban corporations and in certain differentiations within the estates of the land, developed into the sphere of "civil society" that as the genuine domain of private autonomy stood opposed to the state.

Excursus: The Demise of the Representative Publicness Illustrated by the Case of Wilhelm Meister

Forms of the representative publicness, to be sure, remained very much in force up to the beginning of the nineteenth century; this held true especially for economically and politically backward Germany, in which Goethe wrote the second version of his *Wilhelm Meister*. This novel contains a letter[26] in which Wilhelm renounces the world of bourgeois activity embodied by his brother-in-law Werner. Wilhelm explains why it is that the stage means all the world to him. Namely, it meant the world of the nobility, of good society—the public sphere as publicity of representation—as he states in the following passage:

A burgher may acquire merit; by excessive efforts he may even educate his mind; but his *personal qualities* are lost, or worse than lost, let him struggle as he will. Since the nobleman frequenting the society of the most polished, is compelled to give himself a polished manner; since this manner, neither door nor gate being shut against him, grows at last an unconstrained one; since, in court or camp, his *figure*, his *person*, are a part of his possessions, and it may be, the most necessary part,—he has reason enough to put some value on them, and to show that he puts some.

The nobleman was authority inasmuch as he made it present. He displayed it, embodied it in his cultivated personality; thus "He is a *public person*; and the more cultivated his movements, the more sonorous his voice, the more staid and measured his whole being is, the more perfect is he; . . . and whatever else there may be in him or about him, capacities, talents, wealth, all seem gifts of supererogation." Goethe one last time caught the reflection of the representative publicness whose light, of course, was refracted in the French rococo court and refracted yet again in its imitation by the petty German princes. The different hues emerged all the more preciously: the appearance of the "lord," who was "public" by virtue of representation, was stylized into the embodiment of gracefulness, and in this publicity he ceremoniously fashioned an aura around himself. Goethe again used "public person" in the traditional sense of public representation, although in the language of his age it had already taken on the more recent meaning of a servant of public authority or of a servant of the state. The "person," however, was immediately modified into the "cultured personality." Strictly speaking, the nobleman in the context of this letter served as something of a pretext for the thoroughly bourgeois idea of the freely self-actualizing personality that already showed the imprint of the neohumanism of the German classical period. In our context Goethe's observation that the bourgeoisie could no longer represent, that by its very nature it could no longer create for itself a representative publicness, is significant. The nobleman was what he represented; the bourgeois, what he produced: "If the nobleman, merely by his personal carriage, offers all that can be asked of him, the burgher by his personal carriage offers nothing, and can offer nothing. The former has a right to *seem*: the latter is compelled to *be*, and what he aims at seeming becomes ludicrous and tasteless." The representative bearing that the nouveau riche wanted to assume turned into a comical make-believe. Hence, Goethe advised not to ask him "'What art thou?' but only: 'What hast thou? What discernment, knowledge, talent, wealth?'" This is a statement which Nietzsche's later aristocratic pretensions adopted: a man proved himself not by what he could do, but by who he was.

Wilhelm confesses to his brother-in-law the need "to become a public person and to please and influence in a larger circle." Yet since he is no nobleman and as a bourgeois also does not want to make the vain effort merely to appear to be one, he seeks out the stage as a substitute, so to speak, for publicity. Here lies the secret of his theatrical mission: "On the boards a polished man appears in his splendor with personal accomplishments, just as he does so in the upper classes of society." It may well be that it was the secret equivocation of the "cultured personality" ("the necessity I feel to cultivate my mental faculties and tastes"), the bourgeois intention in the figure projected as a nobleman, that permitted the equation of theatrical performance with public representation. But in turn the perception of the disintegration of the representative publicness in bourgeois society was so much on the mark and the inclination to belong to it nevertheless so strong that there must be more to the matter than a simple equivocation. Wilhelm came before his public as Hamlet, successfully at first. The public, however, was already the carrier of a different public sphere, one that no longer had anything in common with that of representation. In this sense Wilhelm Meister's theatrical mission had to fail. It was out of step, as it were, with the bourgeois public sphere whose platform the theatre had meanwhile become. Beaumarchais's Figaro had already entered the stage and along with him, according to Napoleon's famous words, the revolution.

3 On the Genesis of the Bourgeois Public Sphere

With the emergence of early finance and trade capitalism, the elements of a new social order were taking shape. From the thirteenth century on they spread from the northern Italian city-states to western and northern Europe and caused the rise first of Dutch centers for staple goods (Bruges, Lüttich, Brussels, Ghent, etc.) and then of the great trade fairs at the crossroads of long-distance trade. Initially, to be sure, they were integrated without much trouble by the old power structure. That initial assimilation of bourgeois humanism to a noble courtly culture, as we observe it paradigmatically during the rise of Florentine Renaissance society, must also be seen against this background. Early capitalism was conservative not only as regards the economic mentality so vividly described by Sombart (a characteristic way of doing business typified by "honorable" gain[27]) but also as regards politics. As long as it lived from the fruits of the old mode of production (the feudal organization of agricultural production involving an enserfed peasantry and the petty commodity production of the corporatively organized urban craftsmen) without transforming it,[28] it retained ambivalent characteristics. On the one hand this capitalism stabilized the power structure of a society organized in estates, and on the other hand it unleashed the very elements within which this power structure would one day dissolve. We are speaking of the elements of the new commercial relationships: the *traffic in commodities and news* created by early capitalist long-distance trade.

The towns, of course, had local markets from the beginning. In the hands of the guilds and the corporations, however, these remained strictly regulated, serving more as instruments for the domination of the surrounding areas than for free commodity exchange between town and country.[29] With the rise of long-distance trade, for which—according to Pirenne's observations—the town was only a base of operations, markets of a different sort arose. They became consolidated into periodic trade fairs and, with the development of techniques of capitalist financing (it is known that letters of credit and promissory notes were in use at the trade fairs of the Champagne as early as the thirteenth century), were established as stock exchanges. In 1531 Antwerp became a "permanent trade fair."[30] This commercial exchange developed according to rules which certainly were manipulated by political power; yet a far-reaching network of horizontal economic dependencies emerged that in principle could no longer be accommodated by the vertical relationships of dependence characterizing the organization of domination in an estate system based upon a self-contained household economy. Of course, the political order remained unthreatened by the new processes which, as such, had no place in the existing framework, as long as the members of the old ruling stratum participated in them only as consumers.

When they earmarked an increasing portion of what was produced on their lands for the acquisition of luxury goods made available through long-distance trade, this by itself did not bring traditional production—and hence the basis of their rule—into dependence on the new capital.

The traffic in news that developed alongside the traffic in commodities showed a similar pattern. With the expansion of trade, merchants' market-oriented calculations required more frequent and more exact information about distant events. From the fourteenth century on, the traditional letter carrying by merchants was for this reason organized into a kind of guild-based system of correspondence for their purposes. The merchants organized the first mail routes, the so-called ordinary mail, departing on assigned days. The great trade cities became at the same time centers for the traffic in news;[31] the organization of this traffic on a *continuous* basis became imperative to the degree to which the exchange of commodities and of securities became continuous. Almost simultaneously with the origin of stock markets, postal services and the press institutionalized regular contacts and regular communication. To be sure, the merchants were satisfied with a system that limited information to insiders; the urban and court chanceries preferred one that served only the needs of administration. Neither had a stake in information that was public. What corresponded to their interests, rather, were "news letters," the private correspondences commercially organized by newsdealers.[32] The new sector of communications, with its institutions for a traffic in news, fitted in with the existing forms of communication without difficulty as long as the decisive element—publicness—was lacking. Just as, according to Sombart's definition, one could speak of "mail" only when the regular opportunity for letter dispatch became accessible to the general public,[33] so there existed a press in the strict sense only once the regular supply of news became public, that is, again, accessible to the general public. But this occurred only at the end of the seventeenth century.[34] Until then the traditional domain of communication in which publicity of representation held sway was not fundamentally threatened by the new domain of a public sphere whose decisive mark was the published word.

There was as yet no publication of commercially distributed news; the irregularly published reports of recent events were not comparable to the routine production of news.[35]

These elements of early capitalist commercial relations, that is, the traffic in commodities and news, manifested their revolutionary power only in the mercantilist phase in which, simultaneously with the modern state, the national and territorial economies assumed their shapes.[36] When in 1597 the German Hanse was definitively expelled from London, and when a few years later the Company of Merchant Adventurers established itself in Hamburg, this signified not merely the economic and political ascendancy of Great Britain but an altogether new stage of capitalism. From the sixteenth century on merchant companies were organized on an expanded capital basis; unlike the old traders in staple goods, they were no longer satisfied with limited markets. By means of grand expeditions they opened up new markets for their products.[37] In order to meet the rising need for capital and to distribute the growing risks, these companies soon assumed the form of stock companies. Beyond this, however, they needed strong political guarantees. The markets for foreign trade were now justly considered "institutional products"; they resulted from political efforts and military force. The old home towns were thus replaced as bases of operations by the state territory. The process that Heckscher describes as the nationalization of the town-based economy began.[38] Of course, within this process was constituted what has since been called the "nation"—the modern state with its bureaucracies and its increasing financial needs. This development in turn triggered a feedback that accelerated mercantilist policy. Neither private loans made to the prince by financiers nor public borrowing were sufficient to cover these needs; only an efficient system of taxation met the demand for capital. The modern state was basically a state based on taxation, the bureaucracy of the treasury the true core of its administration. The separation precipitated thereby between the prince's personal holdings and what belonged to the state[39] was paradigmatic of the objectification of personal relations of domination. Local administrations were brought under the control of the state, in Great Britain through the institution of the Justice of the Peace, on the continent, after the French model, with the help of superintendents.

The reduction in the kind of publicity involved in representation that went hand in hand with the elimination of the estate-based authorities by those of the territorial ruler created room for another sphere known as the public sphere in the modern sense of the term: the sphere of public authority. The latter assumed objective existence in a *permanent* administration and a *standing* army. Now continuous state activity corresponded to the continuity of contact among those trafficking in commodities and news (stock market, press). Public authority was consolidated into a palpable object confronting those who were merely subject to it and who at first were only negatively defined by it. For they were the private people who, because they held no office, were excluded from any share in public authority. "Public" in this narrower sense was synonymous with "state-related"; the attribute no longer referred to the representative "court" of a person endowed with authority but instead to the functioning of an apparatus with regulated spheres of jurisdiction and endowed with a monopoly over the legitimate use of coercion. The manorial lord's feudal authority was transformed into the authority to "police"; the private people under it, as the addressees of public authority, formed the public.

The relation between authorities and subjects took on a peculiar character as a result of mercantilist policies, policies formally oriented to the maintenance of an active balance of trade. It is a familiar story how the opening up and expansion of markets for foreign trade, in which the privileged companies managed to attain monopolistic control through political pressure—in a word, the new colonialism—step by step began to serve the development of a commercial economy at home. In parallel fashion the interests of capitalists engaged in manufacture prevailed over those engaged in trade. In this way one element of the early capitalist commercial system, the trade in commodities, brought about a revolution, this time in the structure of production as well. The exchange of imported raw materials for finished and semi-finished domestic goods must be viewed as a function of the process in which the old mode

of production was transformed into a capitalist one. Dobb remarks on how this shift was reflected in the mercantilist literature of the seventeenth century. Foreign trade no longer
counted per se as the source of wealth, but only insofar as it
aided the employment of the country's population—employment created by trade.[40] Administrative action was increasingly
oriented to this goal of the capitalist mode of production. The
privileges granted to occupation-based corporations characterizing the estate regime were replaced by royal grants of personal privileges and were aimed at transforming extant
manufacture into capitalist production or at creating new manufacturing enterprises altogether. Hand in hand with this went
the regulation of the process of production itself, down to the
last detail.[41]

Civil society came into existence as the corollary of a depersonalized state authority. Activities and dependencies hitherto
relegated to the framework of the household economy
emerged from this confinement into the public sphere. Schumpeter's observation "that the old forms that harnessed the
whole person into systems of supraindividual purpose had died
and that each family's individual economy had become the
center of its existence, that therewith a private sphere was born
as a distinguishable entity in contrast to the public"[42] only
captures one side of the process—the privatization of the process of economic reproduction. It glances over the latter's new
"public" relevance. The economic activity that had become
private had to be oriented toward a commodity market that
had expanded under public direction and supervision; the
economic conditions under which this activity now took place
lay outside the confines of the single household; for the first
time they were of general interest. Hannah Arendt refers to
this *private sphere of society that has become publicly relevant* when
she characterizes the modern (in contrast to the ancient) relationship of the public sphere to the private in terms of the rise
of the "social": "Society is the form in which the fact of mutual
dependence for the sake of life and nothing else assumes public
significance, and where the activities connected with sheer survival are permitted to appear in public."[43]

The changed conditions of the times were reflected in the

transformation of the economics handed down from antiquity into political economy. Indeed the term "economic" itself, which until the seventeenth century was limited to the sphere of tasks proper to the *oikodespotes*, the *pater familias*, the head of the household, now, in the context of a practice of running a business in accord with principles of profitability, took on its modern meaning. The duties of the household head were narrowed and "economizing" became more closely associated with thriftiness.[44] Modern economics was no longer oriented to the *oikos*; the market had replaced the household, and it became "commercial economics" (*Kommerzienwirtschaft*). Significantly, in eighteenth-century cameralism (whose name derives from *camera*, the territorial ruler's treasure chamber) this forerunner of political economy was part of "police-science," that is, of administrative science proper, together with the science of finance on the one hand and with agricultural technology on the other (which was becoming differentiated from traditional economics). This shows how closely connected the private sphere of civil society was to the organs of the public authority.

Within this political and social order transformed during the mercantilist phase of capitalism (and whose new structure found its expression precisely in the differentiation of its political and social aspects) the second element of the early capitalist commercial system, the press, in turn developed a unique explosive power. The first journals in the strict sense, ironically called "political journals", appeared weekly at first, and daily as early as the middle of the seventeenth century. In those days private correspondence contained detailed and current news about Imperial Diets, wars, harvests, taxes, transports of precious metals, and, of course, reports on foreign trade.[45] Only a trickle of this stream of reports passed through the filter of these "news letters" into printed journals. The recipients of private correspondence had no interest in their contents becoming public. On the one hand, therefore, the political journals responded to a need on the part of the merchants; on the other hand, the merchants themselves were indispensable to the journals. They were called *custodes novellarum* among their contemporaries precisely because of this dependence of public reporting upon their private exchange of news.[46] It was essentially news from abroad, of the court, and of the less important commercial events that passed through the sieve of the merchants' unofficial information control and the state administrations' official censorship. Certain categories of traditional "news" items from the repertoire of the broadsheets were also perpetuated—the miracle cures and thunderstorms, the murders, pestilences, and burnings.[47] Thus, the information that became public was constituted of residual elements of what was actually available; nevertheless, it requires explanation why at this particular time they were distributed and made generally accessible, made public at all. It is questionable whether the interests of those who made a living by writing news pamphlets would have provided a sufficiently strong impetus; still, they *did* have an interest in publication. For the traffic in news developed not only in connection with the needs of commerce; the news itself became a commodity. Commercial news reporting was therefore subject to the laws of the same market to whose rise it owed its existence in the first place. It is no accident that the printed journals often developed out of the same bureaus of correspondence that already handled handwritten newsletters. Each item of information contained in a letter had its price; it was therefore natural to increase the profits by selling to more people. This in itself was already sufficient reason periodically to print a portion of the available news material and to sell it anonymously, thus giving it publicity.

The interest of the new (state) authorities (which before long began to use the press for the purposes of the state administration), however, was of far greater import. Inasmuch as they made use of this instrument to promulgate instructions and ordinances, the addressees of the authorities' announcements genuinely became "the public" in the proper sense. From the very beginning, the political journals had reported on the journeys and returns of the princes, on the arrival of foreign dignitaries, on balls, "special events" (*Solennitäten*) at court, appointments, etc.; in the context of this news from the Court, which can be thought of as a kind of transposition of the publicity of representation into the new form of public sphere, there also appeared "sovereign ordinances in the subjects' best interest." Very soon the press was systematically made to serve the interests of the state administration. As late as March 1769 a press ordinance of the Vienna government witnessed the style of this practice: "In order that the writer of the journal might know what sort of domestic decrees, arrangements, and other matters are suitable for the public, such are to be compiled weekly by the authorities and are to be forwarded to the editor of the journal."[48] As we know from the letters of Hugo Grotius, then Swedish emissary in Paris, Richelieu already possessed a lively sense of the usefulness of the new instrument.[49] He was a patron of the *Gazette* established in 1631 by Renaudot, which served as the model for the *Gazette of London* that appeared from 1665 on under Charles II. Two years earlier the officially authorized *Intelligencer* had appeared in London, itself preceded by the *Daily Intelligencer of Court, City, and County* that sporadically appeared as early as 1643.[50] Everywhere these advertisers, which first arose in France as aids to address agencies or intelligence agencies, became the preferred instruments of governments.[51] Many times the intelligence agencies were taken over by governments, and the advertisers changed into official gazettes. According to an order of 1727 by the Prussian cabinet, this institution was intended "to be useful for the public" and to "facilitate communication." Besides the decrees and proclamations "in police, commerce, and manufacture" there appeared the quotations of the produce markets, of the taxes on food items, and generally of the most important prices of domestic and imported products; in addition, stock market quotations and trade reports and reports on water levels were published. Accordingly, the Palatine-Bavarian government could announce to the "commercial public" an advertiser "in the service of trade and the common man, so that he can inform himself both about the decrees that from time to time are issued by the King and about the prices of various commodities so that he can sell his merchandise at a better price."[52]

The authorities addressed their promulgations to "the" public, that is, in principle to all subjects. Usually they did not reach the "common man" in this way, but at best the "educated classes." Along with the apparatus of the modern state, a new stratum of "bourgeois" people arose which occupied a central position within the "public." The officials of the rulers' administrations were its core—mostly jurists (at least on the continent, where the technique of the received Roman law was adopted as an instrument for the rationalization of social organization). Added to them were doctors, pastors, officers, professors, and "scholars," who were at the top of a hierarchy reaching down through schoolteachers and scribes to the "people."[53]

For in the meantime the genuine "burghers," the old occupational orders of craftsmen and shopkeepers, suffered downward social mobility; they lost their importance along with the very towns upon whose citizens' rights their status was based. At the same time, the great merchants outgrew the confining framework of the towns and in the form of companies linked themselves directly with the state. Thus, the "capitalists," the merchants, bankers, entrepreneurs, and manufacturers (at least where, unlike in Hamburg, the towns could not maintain their independence from the territorial rulers) belonged to that group of the "bourgeois" who, like the new category of scholars, were not really "burghers" in the traditional sense.[54] This stratum of "bourgeois" was the real carrier of the public, which from the outset was a reading public. Unlike the great urban merchants and officials who, in former days, could be assimilated by the cultivated nobility of the Italian Renaissance courts, they could no longer be integrated *in toto* into the noble culture at the close of the Baroque period. Their commanding status in the new sphere of civil society led instead to a tension between "town" and "court," whose typical form in different nations will concern us later.[55]

In this stratum, which more than any other was affected *and* called upon by mercantilist policies, the state authorities evoked a resonance leading the *publicum*, the abstract counterpart of public authority, into an awareness of itself as the latter's opponent, that is, as the public of the now emerging *public sphere of civil society*. For the latter developed to the extent to which the public concern regarding the private sphere of civil society was no longer confined to the authorities but was considered by the subjects as one that was properly theirs. Besides the carriers of commercial and finance capitalism, a growing group of entrepreneurs, manufacturers, and factory owners became dependent upon measures taken by the state administration whose intent certainly was not merely that of controlling commercial-entrepreneurial activity but also of encouraging initiative through regulation. Mercantilism did not at all, as widespread prejudice would have it, favor state enterprise; rather, its commercial policy, albeit in a bureaucratic fashion, promoted the establishment and dissolution of private businesses run in a capitalist manner.[56] The relationship between the authorities and the subjects thereby assumed the peculiar ambivalence of public regulation and private initiative. In this way the zone in which public authority, by way of continuous administrative acts, maintained contact with private people, was rendered problematic. This in fact involved a wider circle of persons than those participating directly in capitalist production. To the degree to which the latter became pervasive, the number of self-sufficient economic units shrank and the dependence of local markets upon regional and national ones grew. Accordingly, broad strata of the population, especially in the towns, were affected in their daily existence as consumers by the regulations of mercantilist policy. Not the notorious dress codes but taxes and duties and, generally, official interventions into the privatized household finally came to constitute the target of a developing critical sphere. When there was a scarcity of wheat, bread cosumption on Friday evenings was prohibited by official decree.[57] Because, on the one hand, the society now confronting the state clearly separated a private domain from public authority and because, on the other hand, it turned the reproduction of life into something transcending the confines of private domestic authority and becoming a subject of public interest, that zone of continuous administrative contact became "critical" also in the sense that it provoked the critical judgment of a public making use of its reason. The public could take on this challenge all the better as it required merely a change in the function of the instrument with whose help the state administration had already turned society into a public affair in a specific sense—the press.

As early as in the last third of the seventeenth century journals were complemented by periodicals containing not primarily information but pedagogical instructions and even criticism and reviews. At first there were scholarly periodicals speaking to the circle of educated laymen: Denys de Sallo's *Journal des Savants* of 1665, Otto Mencken's *Acta Eruditorum* of 1682, and finally the famous *Monatsgespräche* of 1688 by Thomasius; these forged the model for an entire genre of periodicals. In the course of the first half of the eighteenth century, in the guise of the so-called learned article, critical reasoning made its way into the daily press. When, from 1729 on, the *Hallenser Intelligenzblatt*, besides the usual material contained in advertisers also published learned articles, book reviews, and occasionally "a historical report sketched by a professor and relevant to current events," the Prussian King was moved to take the development into his own hands. Even the use of one's own reason as such was subjected to regulation. All chaired professors of the faculties of law, medicine, and philosophy were to take turns in "submitting to the editor of the gazette, expeditiously and no later than Thursday, a special note, composed in a pure and clear style of writing."[58] In general "the scholars were to inform the public of useful truths." In this instance the bourgeois writers still made use of their reason at the behest of the territorial ruler; soon they were to think their own thoughts, directed against the authorities. In a rescript of Frederick II from 1784 one reads: "A private person has no right to pass *public* and perhaps even disapproving judgment on the actions, procedures, laws, regulations, and ordinances of sovereigns and courts, their officials, assemblies, and courts of law, or to promulgate or publish in print pertinent reports that he manages to obtain. For a private person is not at all capable of making such judgment, because he lacks complete knowledge of circumstances and motives."[59] A few years before the French Revolution, the conditions in Prussia looked like a static model of a situation that in France and especially in Great Britain had become fluid at the beginning of the century. The inhibited judgments were called "public" in view of a public sphere that without question had counted as a sphere of public authority, but was now casting itself loose as a forum in which the private people, come together to form a public, readied themselves to compel public authority to legitimate itself before public opinion. The *publicum* developed into the public, the *subjectum* into the [reasoning] subject, the receiver of regulations from above into the ruling authorities' adversary.

The history of words preserved traces of this momentous shift. In Great Britain, from the middle of the seventeenth century on, there was talk of "public," whereas until then "world" or "mankind" was usual. Similarly, in France *le public* began to denote what in the eighteenth century, according to Grimm's *Wörterbuch*, also gained currency throughout Germany as *Publikum* (its use spreading from Berlin). Until then one spoke of the "world of readers" (*Lesewelt*), or simply of the "world" (*Welt*) in the sense still used today: all the world, *tout le monde*. Adelung draws a distinction between the public that gathered as a crowd around a speaker or actor in a public place, and the *Lesewelt* (world of readers).[60] Both, however, were instances of a "critical (*richtend*) public." Whatever was submitted to the judgment of the public gained *Publizität* (publicity). At the end of the seventeenth century the English "publicity" was borrowed from the French *publicité*; in Germany the word surfaced in the eighteenth century. Criticism itself was presented in the form of *öffentliche Meinung*, a word formed in the second half of the eighteenth century in analogy to *opinion publique*. In Great Britain "public opinion" arose at about the same time; the expression "general opinion," however, had been in use long before.

II

Social Structures of the Public Sphere

4 The Basic Blueprint

The bourgeois public sphere may be conceived above all as the sphere of private people come together as a public; they soon claimed the public sphere regulated from above against the public authorities themselves, to engage them in a debate over the general rules governing relations in the basically privatized but publicly relevant sphere of commodity exchange and social labor. The medium of this political confrontation was peculiar and without historical precedent: people's public use of their reason (*öffentliches Räsonnement*). In our [German] usage this term (i.e., *Räsonnement*) unmistakably preserves the polemical nuances of both sides: simultaneously the invocation of reason and its disdainful disparagement as merely malcontent griping.[1] Hitherto the estates had negotiated agreements with the princes in which from case to case the conflicting power claims involved in the demarcation of estate liberties from the prince's overlordship or sovereignty were brought into balance.[2] Since the thirteenth century this practice first resulted in a dualism of the ruling estates and of the prince; soon the territorial estates alone represented the land, over against which stood the territorial ruler.[3] It is well known that where the prince's power was relatively reduced by a parliament, as in Great Britain, this development took a different course than it did on the continent, where the monarchs mediatized the estates. The third estate broke with this mode of balancing power since it was no longer capable of establishing itself as a *ruling* estate. A division of rule by parcelling out lordly rights (including the "liberties" of the estates) was no longer possible on the basis of a commercial economy, for the power of control over one's own capitalistically functioning property, being grounded in private law, was apolitical. The bourgeois were private persons; as such they did not "rule." Their power claims against the public authority were thus not directed against the concentration of powers of command that ought to be "divided"; instead, they undercut the principle on which existing rule was based. The principle of control that the bourgeois public opposed to the latter—namely, publicity—was intended to change domination as such. The claim to power presented in rational-critical public debate (*öffentliches Räsonnement*), which *eo ipso* renounced the form of a claim to rule, would entail, if it were to prevail, more than just an exchange of the basis of legitimation while domination was maintained in principle (section 7).

The standards of "reason" and the forms of the "law" to which the public wanted to subject domination and thereby change it in substance reveal their sociological meaning only in an analysis of the bourgeois public sphere itself, especially in the recognition of the fact that it was private people who related to each other in it as a public. The public's understanding of the public use of reason was guided specifically by such private experiences as grew out of the audience-oriented (*publikumsbezogen*) subjectivity of the conjugal family's intimate domain (*Intimsphäre*). Historically, the latter was the source of privateness in the modern sense of a saturated and free interiority. The ancient meaning of the "private"—an inevitability imposed by the necessities of life—was banned, or so it appears, from the inner region of the private sphere, from the home, together with the exertions and relations of dependence involved in social labor. To the degree to which commodity exchange burst out of the confines of the household economy, the sphere of the conjugal family became differentiated from the sphere of social reproduction. The process of the polarization of state and society was repeated once more within society itself. The status of private man combined the role of owner of commodities with that of head of the family, that of property owner with that of "human being" *per se*. The doubling of the private sphere on the higher plane of the intimate sphere (section 6) furnished the foundation for an identification of those two roles under the common title of the "private"; ultimately, the political self-understanding of the bourgeois public originated there as well.

To be sure, before the public sphere explicitly assumed political functions in the tension-charged field of state-society relations, the subjectivity originating in the intimate sphere of the conjugal family created, so to speak, its own public. Even before the control over the public sphere by public authority was contested and finally wrested away by the critical reasoning of private persons on political issues, there evolved under its cover a public sphere in apolitical form—the literary precursor of the public sphere operative in the political domain. It provided the training ground for a critical public reflection still preoccupied with itself—a process of self-clarification of private people focusing on the genuine experiences of their novel privateness. Of course, next to political economy, psychology arose as a specifically bourgeois science during the eighteenth century. Psychological interests also guided the critical discussion (*Räsonnement*) sparked by the products of culture that had become publicly accessible: in the reading room and the theater, in museums and at concerts. Inasmuch as culture became a commodity and thus finally evolved into "culture" in the specific sense (as something that pretended to exist merely for its own sake), it was claimed as the ready topic of a discussion through which an audience-oriented (*publikumsbezogen*) subjectivity communicated with itself.

The public sphere in the world of letters (*literarische Öffentlichkeit*) was not, of course, autochthonously bourgeois; it preserved a certain continuity with the publicity involved in the representation enacted at the prince's court. The bourgeois avant-garde of the educated middle class learned the art of critical-rational public debate through its contact with the "elegant world." This courtly-noble society, to the extent that the modern state apparatus became independent from the monarch's personal sphere, naturally separated itself, in turn, more and more from the court and became its counterpoise in the town. The "town" was the life center of civil society not only economically; in cultural-political contrast to the court, it designated especially an early public sphere in the world of letters whose institutions were the coffee houses, the *salons*, and the *Tischgesellschaften* (table societies). The heirs of the humanistic-aristocratic society, in their encounter with the bourgeois intellectuals (through sociable discussions that quickly developed into public criticism), built a bridge between the remains of a collapsing form of publicity (the courtly one) and the precursor of a new one: the bourgeois public sphere (section 5).

With the usual reservations concerning the simplification involved in such illustrations, the blueprint of the bourgeois public sphere in the eighteenth century may be presented graphically as a schema of social realms in the diagram:

Private Realm		Sphere of Public Authority
Civil society (realm of commodity exchange and social labor)	Public sphere in the political realm Public sphere in the world of letters (clubs, press)	State (realm of the "police")
Conjugal family's internal space (bourgeois intellectuals)	(market of culture products) "Town"	Court (courtly-noble society)

The line between state and society, fundamental in our context, divided the public sphere from the private realm. The public sphere was coextensive with public authority, and we consider the court part of it. Included in the private realm was the authentic "public sphere," for it was a public sphere constituted by private people. Within the realm that was the preserve of private people we therefore distinguish again between private and public spheres. The private sphere comprised civil society in the narrower sense, that is to say, the realm of commodity exchange and of social labor; imbedded in it was the family with its interior domain (*Intimsphäre*). The public sphere in the political realm evolved from the public sphere in the world of letters; through the vehicle of public opinion it put the state in touch with the needs of society.

5 Institutions of the Public Sphere

In seventeenth-century France *le public* meant the *lecteurs, spectateurs,* and *auditeurs* as the addressees and consumers, and the critics of art and literature;[4] reference was still primarily to the court, and later also to portions of the urban nobility along with a thin bourgeois upper stratum whose members occupied the loges of the Parisian theaters. This early public, then, comprised both court and "town." The thoroughly aristocratic polite life of these circles already assumed modern characteristics. With the Hôtel de Rambouillet, the great hall at court in which the prince staged his festivities and as patron gathered the artists about him was replaced by what later would be called the *salon.*[5] The hôtel provided the model for the *ruelles* (morning receptions) of the *précieuses,* which maintained a certain independence from the court. Although one sees here the first signs of that combination of the economically unproductive and politically functionless urban aristocracy with eminent writers, artists, and scientists (who frequently were of bourgeois origin) typical of the *salon* of the eighteenth century, it was still impossible, in the prevailing climate of *honnêteté,* for reason to shed its dependence on the authority of the aristocratic noble hosts and to acquire that autonomy that turns conversation into criticism and *bons mots* into arguments. Only with the reign of Philip of Orléans, who moved the royal residence from Versailles to Paris, did the court lose its central position in the public sphere, indeed its status *as* the public sphere. For inasmuch as the "town" took over its cultural functions, the public sphere itself was transformed.

The sphere of royal representation and the *grand goût* of Versailles became a facade held up only with effort. The regent and his two successors preferred small social gatherings, if not the family circle itself, and to a certain degree avoided the etiquette. The great ceremonial gave way to an almost bourgeois intimacy:

At the court of Louis XVI the dominant tone is one of decided intimacy, and on six days of the week the social gatherings achieve the character of a private party. The only place where anything like a court household develops during the Régence is the castle of the Duchess of Maine at Sceaux, which becomes the scene of brilliant, expensive, and ingenious festivities and, at the same time, a new centre of art, a real Court of the Muses. But the entertainments arranged by the Duchess contain the germ of the ultimate dissolution of court life: They form the transition from the old-style court to the *salons* of the eighteenth century—the cultural heirs of the court.[6]

In Great Britain the Court had never been able to dominate the town as it had in the France of the Sun King.[7] Nevertheless, after the Glorious Revolution a shift in the relationship between court and town can be observed similar to the one that occurred one generation later in the relationship between *cour* and *ville*. Under the Stuarts, up to Charles II, literature and art served the representation of the king. "But after the Revolution the glory of the Court grew dim. Neither the political position of the Crown, nor the personal temperament of those who wore it was the same as of old. Stern William, invalid Anne, the German Georges, farmer George, domestic Victoria, none of them desired to keep a Court like Queen Elizabeth's. Henceforth the Court was the residence of secluded royalty, pointed out from afar, difficult of access save on formal occasions of proverbial dullness."[8] The predominance of the "town" was strengthened by new institutions that, for all their variety, in Great Britain and France took over the same social functions: the coffee houses in their golden age between 1680 and 1730 and the *salons* in the period between regency and revolution. In both countries they were centers of criticism—literary at first, then also political—in which began to emerge, between aristocratic society and bourgeois intellectuals, a certain parity of the educated.

Around the middle of the seventeenth century, after not only tea—first to be popular—but also chocolate and coffee had become the common beverages of at least the well-to-do strata of the population, the coachman of a Levantine merchant opened the first coffee house. By the first decade of the eighteenth century London already had 3,000 of them, each with a core group of regulars.[9] Just as Dryden, surrounded by the new generation of writers, joined the battle of the "ancients and moderns" at Will's, Addison and Steele a little later convened their "little senate" at Button's; so too in the Rotary Club, presided over by Milton's secretary, Marvell and Pepys met with Harrington who here probably presented the republican ideas of his *Oceana*.[10] As in the *salons* where "intellectuals" met with the aristocracy, literature had to legitimate itself in these coffee houses. In this case, however, the nobility joining the upper bourgeois stratum still possessed the social functions lost by the French; it represented landed and moneyed interests. Thus critical debate ignited by works of literature and art was soon extended to include economic and political disputes, without any guarantee (such as was given in the *salons*) that such discussions would be inconsequential, at least in the immediate context. The fact that only men were admitted to coffee-house society may have had something to do with this, whereas the style of the *salon*, like that of the rococo in general, was essentially shaped by women. Accordingly the women of London society, abandoned every evening, waged a vigorous but vain struggle against the new institution.[11] The coffee house not merely made access to the relevant circles less formal and easier; it embraced the wider strata of the middle class, including craftsmen and shopkeepers. Ned Ward reports that the "wealthy shopkeeper" visited the coffee house several times a day,[12] this held true for the poor one as well.[13]

In contrast, in France the *salons* formed a peculiar enclave. While the bourgeiosie, for all practical purposes excluded from leadership in state and Church, in time completely took over all the key positions in the economy, and while the aristocracy compensated for its material inferiority with royal privileges and an ever more rigorous stress upon hierarchy in social intercourse, in the *salons* the nobility and the *grande bourgeoisie* of finance and administration assimilating itself to that nobility met with the "intellectuals" on an equal footing. The plebeian d'Alembert was no exception; in the *salons* of the fashionable ladies, noble as well as bourgeois, sons of princes and counts associated with sons of watchmakers and shopkeepers.[14] In the *salon* the mind was no longer in the service of a patron; "opinion" became emancipated from the bonds of economic dependence. Even if under Philip the *salons* were at first places more for gallant pleasures than for smart discourse, such discussion indeed soon took equal place with the *diner*. Diderot's distinction between written and oral discourse[15] sheds light on the functions of the new gatherings. There was scarcely a great writer in the eighteenth century who would not have first submitted his essential ideas for discussion in such discourse, in lectures before the *académies* and especially in the *salons*. The *salon* held the monopoly of first publication: a new work, even a musical one, had to legitimate itself first in this forum. The Abbé Galiani's *Dialogues on the Grain Trade* give a vivid picture of the way in which conversation and discussion were elegantly intertwined, of how the unimportant (where one had traveled and how one was doing) was treated as much with solemnity as the important (theater and politics) was treated *en passant*.

In Germany at that time there was no "town" to replace the courts' publicity of representation with the institutions of a public sphere in civil society. But similar elements existed, beginning with the learned *Tischgesellschaften* (table societies), the old *Sprachgesellschaften* (literary societies) of the seventeenth century. Naturally they were fewer and less active than the coffee houses and *salons*. They were even more removed from practical politics than the *salons*; yet, as in the case of the coffee houses, their public was recruited from private people engaged in productive work, from the dignitaries of the principalities' capitals, with a strong preponderance of middle-class academics. The *Deutsche Gesellschaften* ("German Societies"), the first of which was founded by Gottsched in Leipzig in 1727, built upon the literary orders of the preceding century. The latter were still convened by the princes but avoided social exclusiveness; characteristically, later attempts to transform them into knightly orders failed. As it is put in one of the founding documents, their intent was "that in such manner an equality and association among persons of unequal social status might be brought about."[16] Such orders, chambers, and academies were preoccupied with the native tongue, now interpreted as the medium of communication and understanding between people in their common quality as human beings and nothing more than human beings. Transcending the barriers of social hierarchy, the bourgeois met here with the socially prestigious but politically uninfluential nobles as "common" human beings.[17] The decisive element was not so much the political equality of the members but their exclusiveness in relation to the political realm of absolutism as such: social equality was possible at first only as an equality outside the state. The coming together of private people into a public was therefore anticipated in secret, as a public sphere still existing largely behind closed doors. The secret promulgation of enlightenment typical of the lodges but also widely practiced by other associations and *Tischgesellschaften* had a dialectical character. Reason, which through public use of the rational faculty was to be realized in the rational communication of a public consisting of cultivated human beings, itself needed to be protected from becoming public because it was a threat to any and all relations of domination. As long as publicity had its seat in the secret chanceries of the prince, reason could not reveal itself directly. Its sphere of publicity had still to rely on secrecy; its public, even as a public, remained internal. The light of reason, thus veiled for self-protection, was revealed in stages. This recalls Lessing's famous statement about Freemasonry, which at that time was a broader European phenomenon: it was just as old as bourgeois society—"if indeed bourgeois society is not merely the offspring of Freemasonry."[18]

The practice of secret societies fell prey to its own ideology to the extent to which the public that put reason to use, and hence the bourgeois public sphere for which it acted as the pacemaker, won out against state-governed publicity. From publicist enclaves of civic concern with common affairs they developed into "exclusive associations whose basis is a separation from the public sphere that in the meantime has arisen."[19] Other societies, in contrast (especially those arising in the course of the eighteenth century among bourgeois dignitaries), expanded into open associations access to which (through cooptation or otherwise) was relatively easy. Here bourgeois forms of social intercourse, closeness (*Intimität*), and a morality played off against courtly convention were taken for granted; at any rate they no longer needed affirmation by means of demonstrative fraternization ceremonies.

However much the *Tischgesellschaften, salons,* and coffee houses may have differed in the size and composition of their publics, the style of their proceedings, the climate of their debates, and their topical orientations, they all organized discussion among private people that tended to be ongoing; hence they had a number of institutional criteria in common. *First,* they preserved a kind of social intercourse that, far from presupposing the equality of status, disregarded status altogether. The tendency replaced the celebration of rank with a tact befitting equals.[20] The parity on whose basis alone the authority of the better argument could assert itself against that of social hierarchy and in the end can carry the day meant, in the thought of the day, the parity of "common humanity" (*"bloss Menschliche"*). *Les hommes,* private gentlemen, or *die Privatleute* made up the public not just in the sense that power and prestige of public office were held in suspense; economic dependencies also in principle had no influence. Laws of the market were suspended as were laws of the state. Not that this idea of the public was actually realized in earnest in the coffee houses, the *salons,* and the societies; but as an idea it had become institutionalized and thereby stated as an objective claim. If not realized, it was at least consequential.

Secondly, discussion within such a public presupposed the problematization of areas that until then had not been questioned. The domain of "common concern" which was the object of public critical attention remained a preserve in which church and state authorities had the monopoly of interpretation not just from the pulpit but in philosophy, literature, and art, even at a time when, for specific social categories, the development of capitalism already demanded a behavior whose rational orientation required ever more information. To the degree, however, to which philosophical and literary works and works of art in general were produced for the market and distributed through it, these culture products became similar to that type of information: as commodities they became in principle generally accessible. They no longer remained components of the Church's and court's publicity of representation; that is precisely what was meant by the loss of their aura of extraordinariness and by the profaning of their once sacramental character. The private people for whom the cultural product became available as a commodity profaned it inasmuch as they had to determine its meaning on their own (by way of rational communication with one another), verbalize it, and thus state explicitly what precisely in its implicitness for so long could assert its authority. As Raymond Williams demonstrates, "art" and "culture" owe their modern meaning of spheres separate from the reproduction of social life to the eighteenth century.[21]

Thirdly, the same process that converted culture into a commodity (and in this fashion constituted it as a culture that could become an object of discussion to begin with) established the public as in principle inclusive. However exclusive the public might be in any given instance, it could never close itself off entirely and become consolidated as a clique; for it always understood and found itself immersed within a more inclusive public of all private people, persons who—insofar as they were propertied and educated—as readers, listeners, and spectators could avail themselves via the market of the objects that were subject to discussion. The issues discussed became "general" not merely in their significance, but also in their accessibility: everyone had to *be able* to participate. Wherever the public established itself institutionally as a stable group of discussants, it did not equate itself with *the* public but at most claimed to act as its mouthpiece, in its name, perhaps even as its educator—the new form of bourgeois representation. The public of the first generations, even when it constituted itself as a specific circle of persons, was conscious of being part of a larger public. Potentially it was always also a publicist body, as its discussions did not need to remain internal to it but could be directed at the outside world—for this, perhaps, the *Diskurse der Mahlern*, a moral weekly published from 1721 on by Bodmer and Breitinger in Zurich, was one among many examples.

In relation to the mass of the rural population and the common "people" in the towns, of course, the public "at large" that was being formed diffusely outside the early institutions of the public was still extremely small. Elementary education, where it existed, was inferior. The proportion of illiterates, at least in Great Britain, even exceeded that of the preceding Elizabethan epoch.[22] Here, at the start of the eighteenth century, more than half of the population lived on the margins of subsistence. The masses were not only largely illiterate but also so pauperized that they could not even pay for literature. They did not have at their disposal the buying power needed for even the most modest participation in the market of cultural goods.[23] Nevertheless, with the emergence of the diffuse public formed in the course of the commercialization of cultural production, a new social category arose.

The court aristocracy of the seventeenth century was not really a reading public. To be sure, it kept men of letters as it kept servants, but literary production based on patronage was more a matter of a kind of conspicuous consumption than of serious reading by an interested public. The latter arose only in the first decades of the eighteenth century, after the publisher replaced the patron as the author's commissioner and organized the commercial distribution of literary works.[24]

In the same way as literature, the theater obtained a public in the strict sense of the word only when the theaters attached to court and palace, so typical of Germany, became "public." Of course in Great Britain and France the populace—the *Pöbel* (people), as they were called in contemporary sources—had been admitted even as far back as the seventeenth century to the Globe Theater and the *Comédie*. This included even domestic servants, soldiers, apprentices, young clerks, and a lumpenproletariat who were always ready for a "spectacle." But they were all still part of a different type of publicity in which the "ranks" (preserved still as a dysfunctional architectural relic in our theater buildings) paraded themselves, and the people applauded. The way in which the *parterre* (main floor) had to change to become the bourgeois public was indicated by the Parisian police ordinances that from the royal edict of 1641 on were issued to combat the noise and fighting and, indeed, killing. For before long it was not only the "society" seated in the loges and balconies that was to be protected from the *filous* but also a certain part of the main floor audience itself—the bourgeois part, whose first typical representatives were the *marchands de la rue St. Denis* (the owners of the new fashion and luxury shops: jewelers, opticians, music dealers, and glove makers). The main floor became the place where gradually the people congregated who were later counted among the cultured classes without, however, already belonging to the upper stratum of the upper bourgeoisie who moved in the *salons*. In Great Britain the change was more abrupt. The popular theater did not survive; at the time of Charles II a single theater managed to persist under the patronage of the court, "and even there it appealed not to the citizens, but [only to] . . . the fashionables of the Town."[26] Only in the post-revolutionary phase, marked by the transition from Dryden's comedies to the dramas of Congreve, were the theaters opened to an audience of which Gottsched in the sixties of the following century could finally say: "In Berlin the thing is now called *Publikum*."[27] For in 1766, as a consequence of the critical efforts of Gottsched and Lessing, Germany finally acquired a permanent theater, i.e., the "German National Theater" (*Deutsches Nationaltheater*).

The shift which produced not merely a change in the composition of the public but amounted to the very generation of the "public" as such, can be categorically grasped with even more rigor in the case of the concert-going public than in the case of the reading and theater-going public. For until the final years of the eighteenth century all music remained bound to the functions of the kind of publicity involved in representation—what today we call occasional music. Judged according to its social function, it served to enhance the sanctity and dignity of worship, the glamor of the festivities at court, and the overall splendor of ceremony. Composers were appointed as court, church, or council musicians, and they worked on what was commissioned, just like writers in the service of patrons and court actors in the service of princes. The average person scarcely had any opportunity to hear music except in church or in noble society. First, private *Collegia Musica* appeared on the scene; soon they established themselves as public concert societies. Admission for a payment turned the musical performance into a commodity; simultaneously, however, there arose something like music not tied to a purpose. For the first time an audience gathered to listen to music as such—a public of music lovers to which anyone who was propertied and educated was admitted.[28] Released from its functions in the service of social representation, art became an object of free choice and of changing preference. The "taste" to which art was oriented from then on became manifest in the assessments of lay people who claimed no prerogative, since within a public everyone was entitled to judge.

The conflict about lay judgment, about the public as a critical authority, was most severe in that field where hitherto a circle of connoisseurs had combined social privilege with a specialized competence: in painting, which was essentially painting for expert collectors among the nobility until here too the artists saw themselves forced to work for the market. To the same degree painters emancipated themselves from the constrictions of the guilds, the court, and the Church; craftsmanship developed into an *ars liberalis*, albeit only by way of a state monopoly. In Paris the Academy of Art was founded in 1648 under Le Brun; in 1677, only three years after Colbert granted it similar privileges as the Académie Française, it opened its first *salon* to the public. During the reign of Louis XIV at most ten such exhibitions took place.[29] They became regular only after 1737; ten years later La Font's famous reflections were published formulating for the first time the following principle: "A painting on exhibition is like a printed book seeing the day, a play performed on the stage—anyone has the right to judge it."[30] Like the concert and the theater, museums institutionalized the lay judgment on art: discussion became the medium through which people appropriated art. The innumerable pamphlets criticizing or defending the leading theory of art built on the discussions of the *salons* and reacted back on them—art criticism as conversation. Thus, in the first half of the eighteenth century the *amateurs éclairés* formed the inner circle of the new art public. To the extent to which the public exhibitions received wider attention and, going over the heads of the connoisseurs, presented works of art directly to a broader public, these could no longer maintain a position of control. Yet since their function had become indispensable, it was now taken over by professional art criticism. That the latter too had its proper origin in the *salon* is at once demonstrated by the example of its first and most significant representative. From 1759 on Diderot wrote his *Salon* (i.e., knowledgeable reviews of the periodic exhibitions at the *Académie*)[31] for Baron de Grimm's *Literary Correspondence*, a newsletter inspired by Madame de Epinay's famous *salon* and produced for its use.

In the institution of art criticism, including literary, theater, and music criticism, the lay judgment of a public that had come of age, or at least thought it had, became organized. Correspondingly, there arose a new occupation that in the jargon of the time was called *Kunstrichter* (art critic). The latter assumed a peculiarly dialectical task: he viewed himself at the same time as the public's mandatary and as its educator.[32] The art critics could see themselves as spokesmen for the public—and in their battle with the artists this was the central slogan—because they knew of no authority beside that of the better argument and because they felt themselves at one with all who were willing to let themselves be convinced by arguments. At the same time they could turn against the public itself when, as experts combatting "dogma" and "fashion," they appealed to the ill-informed person's native capacity for judgment. The context accounting for this self-image also elucidated the actual status of the critic: at that time, it was not an occupational role in the strict sense. The *Kunstrichter* retained something of the amateur; his expertise only held good until countermanded; lay judgment was organized in it without becoming, by way of specialization, anything else than the judgment of one private person among all others who ultimately were not to be obligated by any judgment except their own. This was precisely where the art critic differed from the judge. At the same time, however, he had to be able to find a hearing before the entire public, which grew well beyond the narrow circle of the *salons*, coffee houses, and societies, even in their golden age. Soon the periodical (the handwritten correspondence at first, then the printed weekly or monthly) became the publicist instrument of this criticism.

As instruments of institutionalized art criticism, the journals devoted to art and cultural criticism were typical creations of the eighteenth century.[33] "It is remarkable enough," an inhabitant of Dresden wrote in justified amazement, "that after the world for millenia had gotten along quite well without it, toward the middle of the eighteenth century art criticism all of a sudden bursts on the scene."[34] On the one hand, philosophy was no longer possible except as critical philosophy, literature and art no longer except in connection with literary and art criticism. What the works of art themselves criticized simply reached its proper end in the "critical journals." On the other hand, it was only through the critical absorption of philosophy, literature, and art that the public attained enlightenment and realized itself as the latter's living process.

In this context, the moral weeklies were a key phenomenon. Here the elements that later parted ways were still joined. The critical journals had already become as independent from conversational circles as they had become separate from the works to which their arguments referred. The moral weeklies, on the contrary, were still an immediate part of coffee-house discussions and considered themselves literary pieces—there was good reason for calling them "periodical essays."[35]

When Addison and Steele published the first issue of the *Tatler* in 1709, the coffee houses were already so numerous and the circles of their frequenters already so wide,[36] that contact among these thousandfold circles could only be maintained through a journal.[37] At the same time the new periodical was so intimately interwoven with the life of the coffee houses that the individual issues were indeed sufficient basis for its reconstruction. The periodical articles were not only made the object of discussion by the public of the coffee houses but were viewed as integral parts of this discussion; this was demonstrated by the flood of letters from which the editor each week published a selection. When the *Spectator* separated from the *Guardian* the letters to the editor were provided with a special institution: on the west side of Button's Coffee House a lion's head was attached through whose jaws the reader threw his letter.[38] The dialogue form too, employed by many of the articles, attested to their proximity to the spoken word. One and the same discussion transposed into a different medium was continued in order to reenter, via reading, the original conversational medium. A number of the later weeklies of this genre even appeared without dates in order to emphasize the trans-temporal continuity, as it were, of the process of mutual enlightenment. In the moral weeklies,[39] the intention of the self-enlightenment of individuals who felt that they had come of age came more clearly to the fore than in the later journals. What a little later would become specialized in the function of art critic, in these weeklies was still art and art criticism, literature and literary criticism all in one. In the *Tatler*, the *Spectator*, and the *Guardian* the public held up a mirror to itself; it did not yet come to a self-understanding through the detour of a reflection on works of philosophy and literature, art and science, but through entering itself into "literature" as an object. Addison viewed himself as a censor of manners and morals; his essays concerned charities and schools for the poor, the improvement of education, pleas for civilized forms of conduct, polemics against the vices of gambling, fanaticism, and pedantry and against the tastelessness of the aesthetes and the eccentricities of the learned. He worked toward the spread of tolerance, the emancipation of civic morality from moral theology and of practical wisdom from the philosophy of the scholars. The public that read and debated this sort of thing read and debated about itself.

6 The Bourgeois Family and the Institutionalization of a Privateness Oriented to an Audience

While the early institutions of the bourgeois public sphere originally were closely bound up with aristocratic society as it became dissociated from the court, the "great" public that formed in the theaters, museums, and concerts was bourgeois in its social origin. Around 1750 its influence began to predominate. The moral weeklies which flooded all of Europe already catered to a taste that made the mediocre *Pamela* the best seller of the century. They already sprang from the needs of a bourgeois reading public that later on would find genuine satisfaction in the literary forms of the domestic drama and the psychological novel. For the experiences about which a public passionately concerned with itself sought agreement and enlightenment through the rational-critical public debate of private persons with one another flowed from the wellspring of a specific subjectivity. The latter had its home, literally, in the sphere of the patriarchal conjugal family. As is well known, this family type—emerging from changes in family structure for which centuries of transformations toward capitalism paved the way—consolidated itself as the dominant type within the bourgeois strata.

To be sure, the urban nobility, especially that of the French capital which set the standards for the rest of Europe, still kept an open "house" and despised the bourgeois family life turned in on itself. The continuity of the family line, one with the inheritance of privileges, was sufficiently guaranteed by the name alone; not even a common household was required of the spouses who frequently enough lived each in his or her own *hôtel* and who in some cases met one another more often in the extrafamilial sphere of the *salon* than in the circle of their own family. The *maîtresse* was an institution and symptomatic of the fact that the fluctuating but nevertheless strictly conventionalized relations of "life in society" only rarely allowed for a private sphere in the bourgeois sense. A playful intimacy, where it managed to arise nevertheless, was distinct from the permanent intimacy of the new family life. The latter, in turn, contrasted with the older forms of communality in the extended family as they continued to be observed among the "people," especially in the countryside, until long after the eighteenth century. These forms were pre-bourgeois also in the sense that they did not fit the distinction between "public" and "private."

But already the seventeenth-century British gentry, becoming more bourgeois in orientation, appeared to have deviated from a life-style that in this manner involved the "whole house." The privatization of life can be observed in a change in architectural style: "Certain changes were taking place in the structure of the houses newly built. The lofty, raftered hall . . . went out of fashion. 'Dining rooms' and 'drawing rooms' were now built of one storey's height, as the various purposes of the old 'hall' were divided up among a number of different chambers of ordinary size. The courtyard . . . , where so much of the life of the old establishment used to go on, also shrank . . . , ; the yard was placed no longer in the middle of the house but behind it."[40] What Trevelyan reports here about the country seat of the British gentry held true on the continent for the bourgeois homes of the subsequent century:

In the modern private dwellings in the big cities, all rooms serving the "whole house" are limited to the extreme: the spacious vestibules are reduced to a scanty entrance way; instead of family and servants, only maids and cooks are left bustling about the profaned kitchen; in particular, however, the courtyards . . . have frequently become small, dank, smelly corners. . . . If we look into the interiors of our homes, what we find is that the "family room," the communal room for husband and wife and children and domestic servants, has become ever smaller or has completely disappeared. In contrast, the special rooms for the individual family members have become ever more numerous and more specifically furnished. The solitarization of the family members even within the house is held to be a sign of distinction.[41]

Riehl analyzes that process of privatization which, as he expresses it in one place, made the house more of a home for each individual, but left less room for the family as a whole.[42] The "public" character of the extended family's parlor, in which the lady of the house at the side of its master performed the representative functions before the domestic servants and neighbors, was replaced by the conjugal family's living room into which the spouses with their smaller children retired from the personnel. Festivities for the whole house gave way to social evenings; the family room became a reception room in which private people gather to form a public. "Those places and halls that are for everyone are reduced as much as possible. The most imposing room in the distinguished bourgeois home, in contrast, is reserved for a completely novel chamber: the *salon* . . . yet this *salon* does not serve the 'house'—but 'society'; and this *salon* society is by no means to be equated with the small intimate circle of friends of the house."[43] The line between private and public sphere extended right through the home. The privatized individuals stepped out of the intimacy of their living rooms into the public sphere of the *salon*, but the one was strictly complementary to the other. Only the name of *salon* recalled the origin of convivial discussion and rational-critical public debate in the sphere of noble society. By now the *salon*, as the place where bourgeois family heads and their wives were sociable, had lost its connection with that sphere. The privatized individuals who gathered here to form a public were not reducible to "society"; they only entered into it, so to speak, out of a private life that had assumed institutional form in the enclosed space of the patriarchal conjugal family.

This space was the scene of a psychological emancipation that corresponded to the political-economic one.[44] Although there may have been a desire to perceive the sphere of the family circle as independent, as cut off from all connection with society, and as the domain of pure humanity, it was, of course, dependent on the sphere of labor and of commodity exchange—even this consciousness of independence can be understood as flowing from the factual dependency of that reclusive domain upon the private one of the market. In a certain fashion commodity owners could view themselves as autonomous. To the degree that they were emancipated from governmental directives and controls, they made decisions freely in accord with standards of profitability. In this regard they owed obedience to no one and were subject only to the anonymous laws functioning in accord with an economic rationality immanent, so it appeared, in the market. These laws were backed up by the ideological guarantee of a notion that market exchange was just, and they were altogether supposed to enable justice to triumph over force. Such an autonomy of private people, founded on the right to property and in a sense also realized in the participation in a market economy, had to be capable of being portrayed as such. To the autonomy of property owners in the market corresponded a self-presentation of human beings in the family. The latter's intimacy, apparently set free from the constraint of society, was the seal on the truth of a private autonomy exercized in competition. Thus it was a private autonomy denying its economic origins (i.e., an autonomy *outside* the domain of the only one practiced by the market participant who believed himself autonomous) that provided the bourgeois family with its consciousness of itself. It seemed to be established voluntarily and by free individuals and to be maintained without coercion; it seemed to rest on the lasting community of love on the part of the two spouses; it seemed to permit that non-instrumental development of all faculties that marks the cultivated personality. The three elements of voluntariness, community of love, and cultivation were conjoined in a concept of the humanity that was supposed to inhere in humankind as such and truly to constitute its absoluteness: the emancipation (still resonating with talk of "pure" or "common" humanity) of an inner realm, following its own laws, from extrinsic purposes of any sort.

However, the conjugal family's self-image of its intimate sphere collided even within the consciousness of the bourgeoisie itself with the real functions of the bourgeois family. For naturally the family was not exempted from the constraint to which bourgeois society like all societies before it was subject. It played its precisely defined role in the process of the reproduction of capital. As a genealogical link it guaranteed a continuity of personnel that consisted materially in the accumulation of capital and was anchored in the absence of legal restrictions concerning the inheritance of property. As an agency of society it served especially the task of that difficult mediation through which, in spite of the illusion of freedom, strict conformity with societally necessary requirements was brought about. Freud discovered the mechanism of the internalization of paternal authority; his disciples have related it, in terms of social psychology, to the patriarchally structured conjugal family type.[45] At any rate, the independence of the property owner in the market and in his own business was complemented by the dependence of the wife and children on the male head of the family; private autonomy in the former realm was transformed into authority in the latter and made any pretended freedom of individuals illusory. Even the contractual form of marriage, imputing the autonomous declaration of will on the part of both partners, was largely a fiction, especially since a marriage, to the extent that the family owned capital, could not remain unaffected by considerations regarding the latter's preservation and augmentation. The jeopardy into which the idea of the community of love was thereby put, up to our own day, occupied the literature (and not only the literature) as the conflict between marriage for love and marriage for reason, that is, for economic and social considerations.[46] Finally, occupational requirements also contradicted the idea of a personal cultivation as its own end. Hegel soon grasped how cultivation at its core (which as bourgeois cultivation it could not acknowledge) remained tied to the socially necessary labor. The old contradiction continues on today in the conflict between a cultivation of the person, on the one hand, and a training that provides mere skills, on the other.

Although the needs of bourgeois society were not exactly kind to the family's self-image as a sphere of humanity-generating closeness, the ideas of freedom, love, and cultivation of the person that grew out of the experiences of the conjugal family's private sphere were surely more than just ideology. As an objective meaning contained as an element in the structure of the actual institution, and without whose subjective validity society would not have been able to reproduce itself, these ideas were also reality. In the form of this specific notion of humanity a conception of what existed was promulgated within the bourgeois world which promised redemption from the constraint of what existed without escaping into a transcendental realm. This conception's transcendence of what was immanent was the element of truth that raised bourgeois ideology above ideology itself, most fundamentally in that area where the experience of "humanity" originated:[47] in the humanity of the intimate relationships between human beings who, under the aegis of the family, were nothing more than human.[48]

In the intimate sphere of the conjugal family privatized individuals viewed themselves as independent even from the private sphere of their economic activity—as persons capable of entering into "purely human" relations with one another. The literary form of these at the time was the letter. It is no accident that the eighteenth century became the century of the letter:[49] through letter writing the individual unfolded himself in his subjectivity. In the initial stages of modern postal service—chiefly a carrier of news reports—the letter soon came to serve scholarly communication and familial courtesy. But even the "well worded" family letter of the seventeenth century, which before all else declared "married love and faithfulness" to the spouse and affirmed filial obedience to ̀Herr Vater and Frau Mutter, still had its mainstay in the dry communications, the news reports (Zeitungen), which had by then become a separate and distinct rubric. The bride of Herder, in contrast, was already afraid that "nothing but reports" might be contained in her letters and that "you may even be capable of considering me only a good news reporter."[50] In the age of sentimentality letters were containers for the "outpourings of the heart" more than for "cold reports" which, if they get mentioned at all, required an excuse. In the jargon of the time, which owed so much to Gellert, the letter was considered an "imprint of the soul," a "visit of the soul"; letters were to be written in the heart's blood, they practically were to be wept.[51] From the beginning, the psychological interest increased in the dual relation to both one's self and the other: self-observation entered a union partly curious, partly sympathetic with the emotional stirrings of the other I. The diary became a letter addressed to the sender, and the first-person narrative became a conversation with one's self addressed to another person. These were experiments with the subjectivity discovered in the close relationships of the conjugal family.

Subjectivity, as the innermost core of the private, was always already oriented to an audience (*Publikum*). The opposite of the intimateness whose vehicle was the written word was indiscretion and not publicity as such. Letters by strangers were not only borrowed and copied, some correspondences were intended from the outset for publication, such as those of Gellert, Gleim, and Goethe in Germany. An idiomatic expression current at the time described the well composed letter as "pretty enough to print." Thus, the directly or indirectly audience-oriented subjectivity of the letter exchange or diary explained the origin of the typical genre and authentic literary achievement of that century: the domestic novel, the psychological description in autobiographical form. Its early and for a long time most influential example, *Pamela* (1740), arose directly from Richardson's intention to produce one of the popular collections of model letters. Unawares, the plot used by the author as a vehicle then came to occupy center stage. *Pamela* in fact became a model, not indeed for letters, but for novels written in letters. Richardson himself, with *Clarissa* and *Sir Charles Grandison*, was not the only one to stay with the form once it was discovered. When Rousseau used the form of the novel in letters for *La Nouvelle Heloise* and Goethe for *Werthers Leiden*, there was no longer any holding back. The rest of the century reveled and felt at ease in a terrain of subjectivity barely known at its beginning.

The relations between author, work, and public changed. They became intimate mutual relationships between privatized individuals who were psychologically interested in what was "human," in self-knowledge, and in empathy. Richardson wept over the actors in his novels as much as his readers did; author and reader themselves became actors who "talked heart to heart." Especially Sterne, of course, refined the role of the narrator through the use of reflections by directly addressing the reader, almost by stage directions; he mounted the novel once more for a public that this time was included in it, not for the purpose of creating distance (*Verfremdung*) but to place a final veil over the difference between reality and illusion.[52] The reality as illusion that the new genre created received its proper name in English, "fiction": it shed the character of the *merely* fictitious. The psychological novel fashioned for the first time the kind of realism that allowed anyone to enter into the literary action as a substitute for his own, to use the relationships between the figures, between the author, the characters, and the reader as substitute relationships for reality. The contemporary drama too became fiction no differently than the novel through the introduction of the "fourth wall." The same Madame de Staël who in her house cultivated to excess that social game in which after dinner everyone withdrew to write letters to one another became aware that the persons themselves became *sujets de fiction* for themselves and the others.

The sphere of the public arose in the broader strata of the bourgeoisie as an expansion and at the same time completion of the intimate sphere of the conjugal family. Living room and *salon* were under the same roof; and just as the privacy of the one was oriented toward the public nature of the other, and as the subjectivity of the privatized individual was related from the very start to publicity, so both were conjoined in literature that had become "fiction." On the one hand, the empathetic reader repeated within himself the private relationships displayed before him in literature; from his experience of real familiarity (*Intimität*), he gave life to the fictional one, and in the latter he prepared himself for the former. On the other hand, from the outset the familiarity (*Intimität*) whose vehicle was the written word, the subjectivity that had become fit to print, had in fact become the literature appealing to a wide public of readers. The privatized individuals coming together to form a public also reflected critically and in public on what they had read, thus contributing to the process of enlightenment which they together promoted. Two years after *Pamela* appeared on the literary scene the first public library was founded; book clubs, reading circles, and subscription libraries shot up. In an age in which the sale of the monthly and weekly journals doubled within a quarter century, as happened in England after 1750,[53] they made it possible for the reading of novels to become customary in the bourgeois strata. These constituted the public that had long since grown out of early institutions like the coffee houses, *salons*, and *Tischgesellschaften* and was now held together through the medium of the press and its professional criticism. They formed the public sphere of a rational-critical debate in the world of letters within which the subjectivity originating in the interiority of the conjugal family, by communicating with itself, attained clarity about itself.

7 The Public Sphere in the World of Letters in Relation to the Public Sphere in the Political Realm

The process in which the state-governed public sphere was appropriated by the public of private people making use of their reason and was established as a sphere of criticism of public authority was one of functionally converting the public sphere in the world of letters already equipped with institutions of the public and with forums for discussion. With their help, the experiential complex of audience-oriented privacy made its way also into the political realm's public sphere. The representation of the interests of the privatized domain of a market economy was interpreted with the aid of ideas grown in the soil of the intimate sphere of the conjugal family. The latter and not the public sphere itself (as the Greek model would have it) was humanity's genuine site. With the rise of a sphere of the social, over whose regulation public opinion battled with public power, the theme of the modern (in contrast to the ancient) public sphere shifted from the properly political tasks of a citizenry acting in common (i.e., administration of law as regards internal affairs and military survival as regards external affairs) to the more properly civic tasks of a society engaged in critical public debate (i.e., the protection of a commercial economy). The political task of the bourgeois public sphere was the regulation of civil society (in contradistinction to the *res publica*).[54] With the background experience of a private sphere that had become interiorized human closeness it challenged the established authority of the monarch; in this sense its character was from the beginning both private and polemical at once. The Greek model of the public sphere lacked both characteristics, for the private status of the master of the household, upon which depended his political status as citizen, rested on domination without any illusion of freedom evoked by human intimacy. The conduct of the citizen was agonistic merely in the sportive competition with each other that was a mock war against the external enemy and not in dispute with his own government.

The dimension of the polemic within which the public sphere assumed political importance during the eighteenth century was developed in the course of the two preceding centuries in the context of the controversy in constitutional law over the principle of absolute sovereignty. The apologetic literature defending the secrets of state thematized the means by which the prince could maintain the *jura imperii*, his sovereignty—that is to say, brought up just those *arcana imperii*, that entire catalogue of secret practices first inaugurated by Machiavelli that were to secure domination over the immature people. The principle of publicity was later held up in opposition to the practice of secrets of state.[55] Contemporary opponents, the monarchomachists, asked whether the law was to depend upon the arbitrary will of the princes or whether the latters' commands were to be legitimate only if based on law. Of course at that time it was the assembly of estates whom they had in mind as legislator. The polemics of the monarchomachists still drew life from the tension between the princes and the ruling estates. But they were already aimed against the same absolutist bureaucracy against which, from the end of the seventeenth century, bourgeois polemics were also directed. Indeed, as late as at the time of Montesquieu the battle lines against the common foe were intermingled, often to the point of indistinguishability. The only reliable criterion for distinguishing the more recent from the older polemic was the use of a rigorous concept of law. Law in this sense guaranteed not merely justice in the sense of a duly acquired right, but legality by means of the enactment of general and abstract norms. To be sure, both the Aristotelian-Scholastic and the modern Cartesian philosophical traditions were familiar with the category of the *lex generalis* or *universalis*, but in the domain of social philosophy and politics it was first introduced implicitly by Hobbes and defined explicitly by Montesquieu.[56] "And so, whoever has the legislative or supreme power of any commonwealth, is bound to govern by established standing laws, promulgated and known to the people, and not by extemporary decrees. . . ."[57] Locke ascribed to the law, as opposed to the command or ordinance, "constant and lasting force."[58] In the French literature of the following century this definition was made more precise: "The laws . . . are the necessary relations arising from the nature of things."[59] They were rational rules of a certain universality and permanence. Montesquieu called government by decrees and edicts "a bad sort of legislation."[60] In this way the reversal of the principle of absolute sovereignty formulated with finality in Hobbes's theory of the state is prepared: *veritas non auctoritas facit legem* (truth not authority makes law). In the "law" the quintessence of general, abstract, and permanent norms, inheres a rationality in which what is right converges with what is just; the exercise of power is to be demoted to a mere executor of such norms.

Historically, the polemical claim of this kind of rationality was developed, in conjunction with the critical public debate among private people, against the reliance of princely authority on secrets of state. Just as secrecy was supposed to serve the maintenance of sovereignty based on *voluntas*, so publicity was supposed to serve the promotion of legislation based on *ratio*.

Locke already tied the publicly promulgated law to a common consent; Montesquieu reduced it altogether to *raison humaine*. But it remained for the physiocrats, who will be discussed later,[61] to relate the law explicitly to public opinion as the expression of reason. A political consciousness developed in the public sphere of civil society which, in opposition to absolute sovereignty, articulated the concept of and demand for general and abstract laws and which ultimately came to assert itself (i.e., public opinion) as the only legitimate source of this law. In the course of the eighteenth century public opinion claimed the legislative competence for those norms whose polemical-rationalist conception it had provided to begin with.

The criteria of generality and abstractness characterizing legal norms had to have a peculiar obviousness for privatized individuals who, by communicating with each other in the public sphere of the world of letters, confirmed each other's subjectivity as it emerged from their spheres of intimacy. For as a public they were already under the implicit law of the parity of all cultivated persons, whose abstract universality afforded the sole guarantee that the individuals subsumed under it in an equally abstract fashion, as "common human beings," were set free in their subjectivity precisely by this parity. The clichés of "equality" and "liberty," not yet ossified into revolutionary bourgeois propaganda formulae, were still imbued with life. The bourgeois public's critical public debate took place in principle without regard to all preexisting social and political rank and in accord with universal rules. These rules, because they remained strictly external to the individuals as such, secured space for the development of these individuals' interiority by literary means. These rules, because universally valid, secured a space for the individuated person; because they were objective, they secured a space for what was most subjective; because they were abstract, for what was most concrete. At the same time, the results that under these conditions issued from the public process of critical debate lay claim to being in accord with reason; intrinsic to the idea of a public opinion born of the power of the better argument was the claim to that morally pretentious rationality that strove to discover what was at once just and right. Public opinion was supposed to do justice to "the nature of the case."[62] For this reason the "laws," which it now also wanted to establish for the social sphere, could also lay claim to substantive rationality besides the formal criteria of generality and abstractness. In this sense, the physiocrats declared that *opinion publique* alone had insight into and made visible the *ordre naturel* so that, in the form of general norms, the enlightened monarch could then make the latter the basis of his action; in this way they hoped to bring rule into convergence with reason.

The self-interpretation of the public in the political realm, as reflected in the crucial category of the legal norm, was the accomplishment of a consciousness functionally adapted to the institutions of the public sphere in the world of letters. In general, the two forms of public sphere blended with each other in a peculiar fashion. In both, there formed a public consisting of private persons whose autonomy based on ownership of private property wanted to see itself represented as such in the sphere of the bourgeois family and actualized inside the person as love, freedom, and cultivation—in a word, as humanity.

The sphere of the market we call "private"; the sphere of the family, as the core of the private sphere, we call the "intimate sphere." The latter was believed to be independent of the former, whereas in truth it was profoundly caught up in the requirements of the market. The ambivalence of the family as an agent of society yet simultaneously as the anticipated emancipation from society manifested itself in the situation of the family members: on the one hand, they were held together by patriarchal authority; on the other, they were bound to one another by human closeness. As a privatized individual, the bourgeois was two things in one: owner of goods and persons and one human being among others, i.e., *bourgeois* and *homme*. This ambivalence of the private sphere was also a feature of the public sphere, depending on whether privatized individuals in their capacity as human beings communicated through critical debate in the world of letters, about experiences of their subjectivity or whether private people in their capacity as owners of commodities communicated through rational-critical debate in the political realm, concerning the regulation of their private sphere. The circles of persons who made up the two forms of public were not even completely congruent. Women and dependents were factually and legally excluded from the political public sphere, whereas female readers as well as apprentices and servants often took a more active part in the literary public sphere than the owners of private property and family heads themselves. Yet in the educated classes the one form of public sphere was considered to be identical with the other; in the self-understanding of public opinion the public sphere appeared as one and indivisible. As soon as privatized individuals in their capacity as human beings ceased to communicate merely about their subjectivity but rather in their capacity as property-owners desired to influence public power in their common interest, the humanity of the literary public sphere served to increase the effectiveness of the public sphere in the political realm. *The fully developed bourgeois public sphere was based on the fictitious identity of the two roles assumed by the privatized individuals who came together to form a public: the role of property owners and the role of human beings pure and simple.*

The identification of the public of "property owners" with that of "common human beings" could be accomplished all the more easily, as the social status of the bourgeois private persons in any event usually combined the characteristic attributes of ownership and education. The acceptance of the fiction of the *one* public, however, was facilitated above all by the fact that it actually had positive functions in the context of the political emancipation of civil society from mercantilist rule and from absolutistic regimentation in general. Because it turned the principle of publicity against the established authorities, the objective function of the public sphere in the political realm could initially converge with its self-interpretation derived from the categories of the public sphere in the world of letters; the interest of the owners of private property could converge with that of the freedom of the individual in general. Locke's basic formula of "the preservation of property" quite naturally and in the same breath subsumed life, liberty, and estate under the title of "possessions"; so easy was it at that time to identify political emancipation with "human" emancipation—to use a distinction drawn by the young Marx.

III

Political Functions of the Public Sphere

8 The Model Case of British Development

A public sphere that functioned in the political realm arose first in Great Britain at the turn of the eighteenth century. Forces endeavoring to influence the decisions of state authority appealed to the critical public in order to legitimate demands before this new forum. In connection with this practice, the assembly of estates became transformed into a modern parliament—a process that was, of course, drawn out over the entire century. Why conflicts that were thus fought out by involving the public arose so much earlier in Great Britain than in other countries is a problem not yet resolved. A literary public sphere existed on the Continent too as an authority to which appeal could be made. There, however, it began to become politically virulent only when, under the aegis of mercantilism, the capitalist mode of production had advanced to a stage reached in Great Britain after the Glorious Revolution. For in the second half of the seventeenth century there emerged in Great Britain a large number of new companies engaged in and expanding the manufacture of textiles, the metal industry, and paper production. The traditional opposition between landed and moneyed interests, which in Great Britain (where the younger sons of the gentry quickly rose to become successful merchants, and where often enough the high bourgeoisie purchased landed estates[1]) had not in any event become entrenched as a pronounced conflict between classes, was now overlaid with a new conflict of interests between the restrictive interests of commercial and finance capital on one side and the expansive interests of manufacturing and industrial capital on the other.[2] Awareness of this conflict began at the start of the eighteenth century; only from this time on were "commerce" and "trade" no longer unquestionably synonymous with "manufacture" and "industry." To be sure, this conflict repeated an antagonism already typical of the earlier phases of capitalist development, the conflict between the interests of an older generation already established in the market and those of a younger generation which had as yet to open up markets for new branches of trade and industry. Had this constellation remained confined to the narrow circle of merchant-princes, as was still the case in the age of the Tudors, the situation would have scarcely arisen where both parties appealed to the new authority of the public. In post-revolutionary Great Britain, however, this antagonism, carrying over into the sphere of capital as such, involved broader strata exactly in the measure in which the capitalist mode of production prevailed. Since these very same strata had in the meantime become engaged in rational-critical debate, it was an obvious step for the weaker party to carry the political conflict into the public sphere. Around the turn of the century, party conflict penetrated in this fashion even into the disenfranchised segment of the population.

Three events occurring in 1694 and 1695 mark the beginning of this development. The founding of the Bank of England, unlike that of the stock exchanges in Lyons and Amsterdam, signaled a new stage in the development of capitalism. On the basis of a capitalistically revolutionized mode of production, it promised the consolidation of a system until then held together by commerce.[3] The elimination of the institution of censorship marked a new stage in the development of the public sphere. It made the influx of rational-critical arguments into the press possible and allowed the latter to evolve into an instrument with whose aid political decisions could be brought before the new forum of the public. Finally, the first cabinet government[4] marked a new stage in the development of Parliament. It was a first step along the long path toward the parliamentiarization of state authority that led ultimately to the point at which the public active in the political realm established itself as an organ of the state.

Already in the 1670s the government had found itself compelled to issue proclamations that confronted the dangers bred by the coffee-house discussions. The coffee houses were considered seedbeds of political unrest: "Men have assumed to themselves a liberty, not only in coffee-houses, but in other places and meetings, both public and private, to censure and defame the proceedings of the State, by speaking evil of things they understand not, and endeavouring to create and nourish an universal jealousie and dissatisfaction in the minds of all His Majesties good subjects."[5] Censorship came to an end with the Licensing Act of 1695; the Queen several times admonished the members of Parliament to bring censorship back, but in vain. To be sure, the press continued to be subject to the strict Law of Libel[6] and to the restrictions connected with numerous privileges of Crown and Parliament. The stamp tax,[7] enacted in 1712, resulted in a temporary setback: the journals printed fewer copies and were reduced in volume; some disappeared altogether. Compared to the press in the other European states, however, the British press enjoyed unique liberties.

Harley was the first statesman to understand how to turn the new situation to his advantage. He engaged authors like Defoe (who has been called the first professional journalist), who defended the cause of the Whigs not only in the pamphlets in use up until then but also in the new journals. Indeed, he was the first to make the "party spirit" a "public spirit." Defoe's *Review*, Tutchin's *Observator*, and Swift's *Examiner*, were discussed in clubs and coffee houses, at home and in the streets. Walpole and Bolingbroke themselves addressed the public. Men like Pope, Gay, Arbuthnot, and Swift combined literature and politics in a peculiar fashion comparable to Addison's and Steele's combination of literature and journalism.

In these first years, of course, the leading press was never in the hands of the opposition. The *London Gazette*, for a long time the only official gazette, in the old style of the "political newspaper" discreetly limited to news reports, was supplemented in 1704 by the thrice weekly *Review*; in 1711 the *Ex-*

aminer took the place of the latter. At the end of Queen Anne's rule the Whigs, with the *British Merchant*, entered into competition against the *Mercator*, founded in 1713. Then under George I began the dominance of the Whigs that was to last for decades. But it was not the Whigs who, purchasing the *London Journal* in 1722 (the most important and widely read journal at that time),[8] created political journalism in the grand style; this was the work of the Tories who now constituted themselves as the opposition under Bolingbroke:

The innovation brought about by the opposition was the creation of a popular opinion. Bolingbroke and his friends knew how to form such a public opinion that, aimed at the same objective and furnished with likeminded impulses of will, could be mobilized for political use. It was not demagoguery and sloganeering, uproars and mob scenes that were novel. . . . also, there were still no regular public meetings. . . . Rather, this public opinion was directed by another factor: by the establishment of an independent journalism that knew how to assert itself against the government and that made critical commentary and public opposition against the government part of the normal state of affairs.[9]

In the summer of 1726, inspired by Bolingbroke, there appeared as the "long opposition's" literary prelude three pieces satirizing the times: Swift's *Gulliver*, Pope's *Dunciad*, and Gay's *Fables*. In November of the same year Bolingbroke brought out the first issue of the *Craftsman*, the publicist platform of the opposition until the editor's emigration to France in 1735. With this journal, followed by the *Gentleman's Magazine*, the press was for the first time established as a genuinely critical organ of a public engaged in critical political debate: as the fourth estate.

Thus raised to the status of an institution, the ongoing commentary on and criticism of the Crown's actions and Parliament's decisions transformed a public authority now being called before the forum of the public. This authority thereby became "public" in a double sense. From now on, the degree of the public sphere's development was measured by the state of the confrontation between government and press, as it drew out over the entire century.[10] The *Letters of Junius*, which appeared from 21 November 1768 through 12 May 1772 in the

Public Advertiser (in their way forerunners of the political lead article) marked this state in a highly visible manner. This series of satirical articles have been called "pioneers of the modern press,"[11] because in them the King, the ministers, top military men, and jurists were publicly accused of political machinations, and secret connections of political significance were thereby uncovered in a manner that ever since has been exemplary of a critical press.

Against such criticism Parliament possessed an effective instrument that guaranteed it secrecy of proceedings in a privilege dating from the time of its confrontation with the Crown. To be sure, in 1681 the publication of the "votes," those skimpy reports on certain results of parliamentary deliberations, was authorized;[12] but Parliament insisted stubbornly on the prohibition of the latters' being made publicly accessible. Since Queen Anne's accession to the throne *The Political State of Great Britain* undertook with the utmost caution something in the nature of a report on Parliament, a task also attended to from 1716 on by the *Historical Register*. Naturally, these two journals were partial to the government; the opposition had to remain satisfied with occasional reports on the most important speeches of its representatives in the weekly newspapers or with a collection of these speeches in the form of a brochure. Since the early thirties, in that new climate of political criticism created by the *Craftsman*, the *Gentleman's Magazine*, and soon thereafter its counterpart, the *London Magazine* reported on parliamentary debates. Parliament saw itself repeatedly forced to renew the injunction against publication. Finally in 1738 it tightened up the old decrees to the point that even a publication of its debates between sessions would be deemed a breach of privilege.[13] Only in the year 1771 did Wilkes, as the alderman of London, succeed in nullifying, in fact if not in law, the parliamentary privilege. The sentence of the editor of the *Evening Post* found guilty of breach of privilege was never carried out. The exclusion of the public from the parliamentary deliberations[14] could no longer in any event be maintained at a time in which "Memory" Woodfall was able to make the *Morning Chronicle* into the leading London daily paper because he could reproduce verbatim sixteen columns of parliamentary speeches without taking notes in the gallery of the House of Commons, which was prohibited. A place for journalists in the gallery was officially provided by the Speaker only in the year 1803; for almost a century they had to gain entry illegally. But only in the House of Parliament newly constructed after the fire of 1834 were stands for reporters installed—two years after the first Reform Bill had transformed Parliament, for a long time the target of critical comment by public opinion, into the very organ of this opinion.

This transformation stretched out over almost a century and a half. In its continuity it is uniquely suited to the study of a critically debating public's gradual assumption of the functions of political control. In Great Britain alone at the end of the seventeenth century had a constitution been instituted simultaneously with the termination of the religious civil war. While this development, through the partial actualization of a government based on law (Habeas Corpus Act, Declaration of Rights), did not entirely anticipate the eighteenth- and nineteenth-century bourgeois revolutions on the continent, it made those revolutions superfluous at home. At a stage of capitalist development at which industrial capitalism was just barely emerging (still dominated by the merchant capitalism that was in any case rather more interested in the conservation of the old mode of production), even the leading representatives of the moneyed interests came from the conservative strata of a high bourgeoisie in many ways intimately involved with the nobility. Its members encountered one another in Parliament on the basis of a certain social homogeneity that was aristocratic in character.[15]

In this respect the economically and socially uppermost classes in 1688 had also come to dominate politically. The House of Commons, however, lost its character of an estate assembly not merely because it was composed increasingly of delegates from the corporations, of nominees of the ruling classes. Rather, from the outset those bourgeois strata of the Protestant middle class, involved in business and commerce (whose capitalist interests had been behind their substantial support of the Revolution, without now being represented in Parliament), formed something like a steadily expanding pre-parliamentary forum. Here, as a critical public soon to be aided by appropriate publicist organs, they followed the deliberations and decisions of Parliament, regardless of whether they still had for the most part the vote, as in London and Westminster[16] or whether (as elsewhere) they were part of the disenfranchised mass. Parliament's change in function was not reducible solely to the fact that the sovereign, bound by the Bill of Rights, was demoted to a King in Parliament. In addition, it took the new relationship of Parliament to the public sphere that ultimately led to the full publicity of the parliamentary deliberations to bring about a qualitative difference from the previous system.

Now the King, who could not circumvent Parliament, was also forced to secure for himself a firm following within Parliament. The *origin* of the Whig-Tory opposition in the name of "resistance" here and of "divine right" there, the split of Parliament at the time of the conflict over the Exclusion Bill into "parties" whose antagonism replaced the older one between Parliament and country on one side, Crown and councillors on the other, may be structurally related to the objective interest constellations of the various social groups. The parliamentary *development* of these "factions," however, can only be comprehended in terms of a dynamics internal to Parliament as they evolved during the subsequent century, caught between the public considerations and arguments of a critical public and the corrupting influence of a King forced to resort to rule by indirection. The minority that did not get its way in Parliament could always seek refuge in the public sphere and appeal to the judgment of the public; the majority, held together by bribery,[17] considered itself bound to legitimate the authority at its disposal by reference to reason against the opposition's claims to the contrary. This constellation evolved after that peculiar reversal of battlefronts that for a generation made the party of resistance, the Whigs, the governing party, and conversely compelled the Jacobite legitimists to a practice of resistance on the basis of the revolutionary order. From 1727 on, under the impact of the *Craftsman*, a systematic opposition arose which (for a while even equipped with something like a shadow cabinet) until 1742, via literature and press, informed the public at large about the political controversies in Parliament. The Tories in theory adopted the principles of the Old Whigs; the Modern Whigs in control of the government in practice adopted the principles of the Tories. Until then political opposition at the national level had been possible only as the attempt to push one's interests by resorting to violence in the forms of the Fronde and the Civil War; now, through the critical debate of the public, it took the form of a permanent controversy between the governing party and the opposition. This discussion in principle went beyond the issues of the day to include the "topics of government"; the separation of powers, British liberties, patriotism and corruption, party and faction, the question of the legality of the opposition's new relationship to the government—and even basic questions of political anthropology. Fittingly, the theory of the opposition[18] developed by Bolingbroke himself within the context of his pessimistic anthropology had its origin in the critical debate carried on in the journals of the thirties. Bolingbroke now propounded the relationship of private and public interests as the relationship of court and country, of "in power" and "out of power," of pleasure and happiness, passion and reason. The opposition, as the party of the country, always appeared to be in the right versus the party of the court corrupted by "influence."

From the early part of eighteenth century on, it became usual to distinguish what was then called "the sense of the people" from the official election results. The average results of the county elections were taken to provide an approximate measure of the former. The "sense of the people," "the common voice," "the general cry of the people," and finally "the public spirit" denoted from this time onward an entity to which the opposition could appeal—with whose help, in fact, it more than once forced Walpole and his parliamentary majority to concessions.[19] Such occurrences, of course, must not be construed prematurely as a sign of a kind of rule of public opinion. The true power constellation is more reliably gauged by the ineffectiveness of the numerous mass petitions organized since 1680. To be sure, in 1701 as well as in 1710, the dissolution of Parliament actually followed upon corresponding petitions; but these were basically mere acclamations of which the King made use. This became obvious between 1768 and 1771 when, in connection with the agitation of Wilkes, the demanded dissolution of Parliament did not follow upon the petitions of numerous counties, towns, and villages. Considering that the parliamentary majority was willing to do his bidding anyhow, it was not in the King's interest to expose himself to the risks of a new election. Even the dissolution of Parliament in 1784 (on the occasion of which the King, in a speech before the House of Commons that became famous, stated that he felt obliged "to recur to the sense of the people") was not due chiefly to the pressure of this "opinion of the people."[20]

Nevertheless, besides the new, large daily newspapers like the *Times* (1785), other institutions of the public reflecting critically on political issues arose in these years. In Wilkes's days, public meetings increased in size and frequency. Political associations too were formed in great numbers. The twenty-six county associations, founded in 1779 after the model of the Yorkshire Association, dealt with questions of war expenditures, parliamentary reform, etc. Although as early as the end of the seventeenth century members of Parliament banded together into loosely knit clubs, *Gentleman's Magazine* still found it difficult in 1741 to characterize the elected delegates according to political orientations; they could in no way be categorized as members of a definite party. Only toward the end of the eighteenth century did the parties attain an organizational basis outside of Parliament, "outdoors," that went beyond those petitions, public meetings, and political associations. With the founding of local committees they assumed their first solid organizational form.

In 1792, three years after the outbreak of the French Revolution, the public that was involved, in its function as the carrier of public criticism, in the critical debate of political issues, received indirect sanction through a speech given by Fox in the House of Commons. For the first time public opinion in the strict sense was introduced into Parliament:

It is certainly right and prudent to consult the public opinion. . . . If the public oponion did not happen to square with mine; if, after pointing out to them the danger, they did not see it in the same light with me, or if they conceived that another remedy was preferable to mine, I should consider it as my due to my king, due to my Country, due to my honour to retire, that they might persue the plan which they thought better, by a fit instrument, that is by a man who thought with them . . . but one thing is most clear, that I ought to give the public the means of forming an opinion.[21]

As remarkable as the statement itself was its occasion: Fox was opposing Pitt who in 1791, under the pressure of public opinion, discontinued his war preparations against Russia. But by the turn of the nineteenth century, the public's involvement in the critical debate of political issues had become organized to such an extent that in the role of a permanent critical commentator it had definitively broken the exclusiveness of Parliament and evolved into the officially designated discussion partner of the delegate. Fox's speeches were made with the public in mind; "they," the subjects of public opinion, were no longer treated as people whom, like "strangers," one could exclude from the deliberations. Step by step the absolutism of Parliament had to retreat before their sovereignty. Expressions like "the sense of the people" or even "vulgar" or "common opinion" were no longer used. The term now was "public opinion"; it was formed in public discussion after the public, through education and information, had been put in a position to arrive at a considered opinion. Hence Fox's maxim, "to give the public the means of forming an opinion."

Nevertheless, the discussion about expanding the right to vote was drawn out over four more decades. Finally, two years after the July Revolution, the Reform Bill was passed revising the obsolete apportioning of the electoral districts and according the right to have political input also to the upper middle class out of which the great majority of the critically debating public was recruited. Of the approximately twenty-four million residents at that time, almost a million were now allowed to vote. The conditions for the temporary era of a government by public opinion became complete in 1834 with Peel's Tamworth Manifesto; for the first time a party published its election platform. Public opinion was formed in the conflict of arguments concerning a substantive issue, not uncritically based on common sense in the either naive or plebiscitarily manipulated assent to or vote about persons. Hence it needed a defined issue as its object more than it needed prominent persons. The Conservatives published their program; at the same time, in an election proclamation, the Whigs admonished: "Remember that you are now fighting for things, not men—for the real consequences of your reform."[22]

9 The Continental Variants

In France too arose, although not before roughly the middle of the eighteenth century, a public that critically debated political issues. Before the Revolution, however, it could not effectively institutionalize its critical impulses, as was possible in contemporary England. Not a line could be published without the consent of the censor; a political journalism could not be developed; the periodical press as a whole remained scanty. The official weekly, the *Mercure de France*, although the most widely read journal, in 1763 still had not more than 1600 subscribers of whom a good third lived in Paris and 900 in the provinces; the remaining subscriptions went abroad. Clandestinely, of course, one read the illegally imported journals, especially those from Holland.[23]

Not only was a developed political journalism lacking, but also an estates assembly which under its influence might have gradually been transformed into a representative institution of the people. The Estates General had not been convened since 1614. The existing parliaments—that is, the highest courts, which indeed constituted the only political power not utterly dependent upon the King—did not embody the top layer of the bourgoisie but bourgeoisified intermediate powers, to the extent that they were still able to resist the centralism of absolutist rule. Ultimately, the social basis for such institutions was lacking as well. Admittedly, a bourgeoisie engaged in trade and commerce was not entirely absent; under the Regency the speculators and bankers, trading manufacturers, large merchants and tax farmers already formed an upper bourgeoisie in whose hands the wealth of the nation was gathered. But politically they could not affect the fate of the nation; they were not united, as in England, with the nobility and the higher officialdom (*noblesse de robe*[24]) into a homogeneous top stratum which, supported by a firm prestige, would also have been able to represent politically the interests of the capital-accumulating classes against the King.

The class differences went deep. To be sure, the rich merchants, normally in the third generation, acquired titles of nobility, for the most part those carrying sinecures of high official posts; yet in this fashion they removed themselves from the spheres of production and distribution. Around the middle of the century the Abbé Coyer, in *La Noblesse Commerçante*, drew attention to this problem, triggering a storm of pamphlets. On the other hand, the nobility, which withdrew from trade and commerce as well as from the banking business as pursuits incompatible with its status, became economically dependent on the crown: considered, from the bourgeois standpoint of productive labor, a parasitical stratum paid for its political insignificance with tax privileges and royal patents. The king largely monopolized public authority. Civic equality existed but in its negative form. All except the king (and one official) were equally subjects and equally subjugated to authority—were private. Their sphere, whether bourgeois or not, was the *société civile*—during the eighteenth century a structure not easily analyzed in terms of class theory. In many ways the bourgeoisie was still part of a society organized on the estate principle, as both the feudal role of the bourgeois parliaments and the adaptation of the higher bourgeoisie to the nobility showed; and in many ways the nobility in its *salons* was more receptive to the enlightened mode of thought of bourgeois intellectuals than was the bourgeoisie itself. Nevertheless, bourgeoisie, nobility, and crown were so clearly differentiated from one another in terms of status and function that the "sectors"—the political, the economic, and the one in-between occupied by "society"—could be easily separated.[25]

In the first half of the century, the criticism of the *philosophes* was preoccupied, Montesquieu notwithstanding, with religion, literature, and art; only at the stage of its encyclopedic publication did the moral intent of the *philosophes* develop into a political one, at least indirectly. The Encyclopedia was planned as a publicist undertaking in the grand style.[26] Robespierre could celebrate it later as "the introductory chapter of the Revolution." In the last third of the century, clubs of the sort of the early gentlemen's society that met at the Club d'Entresol,[27] inspired by English ideas, succeeded the *bureaux d'esprit* ruled by women; initiators of public criticism, the *philosophes* changed from belles lettrists into economists. "Economists" was the name for the physiocrats who first met at Quesnay's and later at Mirabeau's and Turgot's; their club lasted for over a decade. They promoted their doctrine in the *Gazette du Commerce* and in the *Journal de l'Agriculture, du Commerce et des Finances*, until finally in 1774 two of their most important proponents, Turgot and Malesherbes, were called into the government—the first exponents, as it were, of public opinion.

As is well known, however, it was Necker who first succeeded in opening a breach in the absolutist system for a public sphere in the political realm: he made public the balance of the state budget. Three months later the King got rid of his minister.[28] Nevertheless, the public's critical debate of political issues had proved its mettle as a check on the government, significantly at the nerve center of bourgeois interests; for the extent of the state debt symbolized the disproportion of economic power and political powerlessness on the one hand and of financial dependence and absolutist rule on the other. Brought into life, with the help of intellectuals who had risen socially, in the womb of a parasitic, economically and politically functionless, yet socially eminent nobility the sphere of a public that eventually also engaged in a critical debate of political issues now definitively became the sphere in which civil society reflected on and expounded its interests. From the time of Necker's *compte rendu*, this public sphere in the political realm could only be suppressed; it could no longer be effectively put out of commission. By way of the *Cahiers de Doléance* the public's considered observations on public affairs were officially permitted. This led, as is well known, to the convening of the Estates General; the tradition of an estates assembly, uninterrupted in Great Britain, was taken up again on a level of social development where it had no alternative but to assume the role of a modern parliament.

The Revolution created in France overnight, although with

less stability, what in Great Britain had taken more than a century of steady evolution: the institutions, which until then had been lacking, for critical public debate of political matters. Club-based parties emerged from which parliamentary factions were recruited; there arose a politically oriented daily press.[29] And already the Estates General successfully asserted the publicity of its deliberations. Beginning in August the daily *Journal des Débattes et des Décrets* appeared, specializing in reports on parliamentary proceedings. At least as important as the factual institutionalization of the public sphere in the political realm was its anchoring in legal statutes. The revolutionary event was immediately interpreted and defined in terms of constitutional law; therein may lie the reason that on the continent the bourgeois public became so precisely aware of its political functions, actual or potential. Here a self-awareness emerged that was terminologically more clearly expressed than in Great Britain at the time. From elements in the codifications of the French revolutionary constitution, the political functions of the public sphere were quickly transformed into slogans that spread all over Europe. It was no accident that the German term for the public sphere, "*Öffentlichkeit*," was formed after the French; in its original version, "*Publizität*," it made the rounds in the satirical poem circulating throughout Germany in the days of the revolution:

The magic word before whose power
Even the people's masters cower,
Flapping their wigs officiously—
Prick up your ears; the word—it is publicity.[30]

The constitution of 1791, which on the whole adopted the *Déclaration des Droits de l'Homme et du Citoyen* of 26 August 1789, supplemented the complex of the "public sphere" in paragraph 11: "The free communication of ideas and opinions is one of the most precious rights of man. Everyone can therefore speak, write, and print freely, with the proviso of responsibility for the misuse of this liberty in the cases determined by law."[31] The constitution of 1793 explicitly included freedom of assembly in the protection of freedom of expression: "The right to communicate one's ideas and opinions, whether through the

press or in any other manner, the right to assemble peaceably
. . . cannot be refused." It then added, as if to offer an excuse
for this precaution, a reference to the *ancien régime*: "The necessity to promulgate these rights arises from the presence or
the fresh memory of despotism."[32] By the time this article was
enacted, of course, it no longer corresponded to the constitutional reality. In August of the preceding year, two days after
the storming of the *Tuileries*, opponents of the revolution were
denounced in an edict of the Paris Commune as *empoisonneurs
de l'opinion publique* (poisoners of public opinion) and their
presses confiscated. On 17 January 1800, two days after the
coup d'etat, Napoleon eliminated the freedom of the press.
Only thirteen papers, listed by name, were excluded from the
prohibition of the political press. From 1811 on he allowed
only three papers besides the official *Moniteur*, and even these
were under strict censorship. The Bourbons, upon their return, introduced themselves with the proclamation that they
would respect the freedom of the press. The *Charte* of June,
1814 (Article 8) also stated: "The French have the right to have
their views published and printed, if they abide by the laws
which are intended to prevent the abuses of this liberty."[33] But
the opposition could express itself only with great caution. Only
the July Revolution, which got its catchword from the opposition paper just founded by Thiers and Mignet, the *National*,[34]
gave back to the press and the parties, and finally to the parliament expanded through electoral reform and deliberating
completely in public, the latitude guaranteed by the revolutionary rights of man.

In Germany something akin to a parliamentary life emerged
only in the train of the July Revolution, and then only for a
brief period, in the capitals of a few southern and southwestern
German territories,[35] where the representative bodies recommended in the Concluding Actions of the Vienna Congress of
1815 ("*Wiener Schlussakte*") had been linked to certain traditions
of the territorial estates but then, of course, almost everywhere
thwarted by the Karlsbad Resolutions.

German conditions differed from the British on account of
the estate barriers, especially those between nobility and bourgeoisie, generally preserved longer by continental absolutism.

The bourgeois, for their part, distanced themselves rigorously from the people. To the latter belonged, besides the rural population (ranging from agricultural laborers through tenants to freeholders) and the lower class proper (day laborers, soldiers, and servants), the shopkeepers, artisans, and workers. *Volk* was coextensive with *peuple*, both categories assumed the same meaning during the eighteenth century; in both countries standing behind a shop counter as well as working at manual labor were the subjectively accepted criteria for exclusion from the genuine bourgeoisie. Those who at one time were the burghers (*Bürger*), townspeople (*Stadtbürger*) par excellence, namely retailers and artisans, were no longer reckoned among the bourgeoisie by those properly "bourgeois." Their criterion was education (*Bildung*); the bourgeois belong to the cultivated (*gebildet*) classes—businessmen and university-trained men (scholars, ministers, officials, physicians, judges, and teachers). However, the German conditions differed from the French because of the nobility's complete dependence on the courts. It was incapable of developing, in communication with bourgeois intellectuals, the economically and politically detached sphere of "society" into that of a culturally dominant and critically involved public.[36]

The public's rational-critical debate of political matters took place predominantly in the private gatherings of the bourgeoisie. During the last decades of the eighteenth century the blossoming journals, including the political ones, were the crystallization points of the "social" life of private people. It was not only that the journals themselves attested to the "addiction" or even the "mania" of the enlightened age for reading;[37] from the seventies on private and commercial reading societies proliferated over all the towns, even the smaller ones, so that a general discussion about the merits and demerits of these establishments could set in. By the end of the century, more than 270 reading societies could be counted in Germany.[38] They were mostly associations with rooms that provide the opportunity both for reading newspapers and journals and, just as importantly, for discussing what had been read. The oldest reading circles had involved nothing more than collective subscriptions that helped to lower the cost of the papers. In contrast, the reading societies no longer arose from such financial motives. These societies, which elected their executive committee according to bylaws, voted on the acceptance of new members by majority and generally dealt with disputes in parliamentary fashion. They excluded women and forbade gambling and exclusively served the need of bourgeois private people to create a forum for a critically debating public: to read periodicals and to discuss them, to exchange personal opinions, and to contribute to the formulation of an opinion that from the nineties on will be called "public." Journals with political content had the largest number of subscribers and were most widely read: Schlözer's *Staatsanzeigen* and Wieland's *Teutscher Merkur*, Archenholz's *Minerva*, the *Hamburger Politische Journal*, and the *Journal von und für Deutschland*.[39] Schlözer's journal, reaching an edition of 4000, enjoyed a Hannoverian reflection of the British freedom of the press; it was considered the "*bête noire* of the high and mighty," as, in the expression of the day, they were afraid of "getting into the Schlözer."[40] Even the brutal reaction of the princes against the first political publicists in southwestern Germany was symptomatic of a certain critical strength of the public sphere. Wekherlin, who in 1778 published the *Felleisen*, and Schubart, who became known in 1774 for his *Deutsche Chronik*, both paid a high price. One died in prison; the other was broken in ten years' confinement in a fortress: brainwashing in the direct mode still existed.[41]

10 Civil Society as the Sphere of Private Autonomy: Private Law and a Liberalized Market

The historical excurses on the rise (in Great Britain and on the Continent) of a functioning public sphere in the political realm remain abstract as long as they are confined to the institutional interrelations of public, press, parties, and the parliament, and to the tension-charged field in which authority and publicity (as the principle of a critical control of the cabinets) confronted each other. They can document *that* the public sphere takes on political functions during the eighteenth century, but the kind of function itself can be grasped only in relation to that specific phase in the developmental history of civil society as a whole in which commodity exchange and social labor became largely emancipated from governmental directives. In the political order in which this process reached its temporary completion, it was not by accident that the public sphere assumed a central place. It became the very organizational principle of the bourgeois constitutional states that feature parliamentary forms of government as, for example, Great Britain after the great Reform Bill of 1832; the same, with certain reservations, also held true for the so-called constitutional monarchies on the model of the Belgian Constitution of 1830.

The public sphere as a functional element in the political realm was given the normative status of an organ for the self-articulation of civil society with a state authority corresponding to its needs. The social precondition for this "developed" bourgeois public sphere was a market that, tending to be liberalized, made affairs in the sphere of social reproduction as much as possible a matter of private people left to themselves and so finally completed the privatization of civil society. Under absolutism, the latter's establishment as a private realm was conceivable at first only in the privative sense that social relationships were stripped of their quasi-public character. The political functions, both judicial and administrative, were consolidated into public authority. The domain separated from this public sphere was by no means already "private" in the sense of a liberation from rule by state authority; it came into existence at all only as a domain subject to mercantilist regulation. On the other hand, the "unifying system" of mercantilism already established the beginnings of a privatization of the process of social reproduction in the positive sense: the latter might gradually evolve autonomously, that is, in accord with the laws intrinsic to the market. For in proportion to the increasing prevalence of the capitalist mode of production, social relationships assumed the form of exchange relationships. With the expansion and liberation of this sphere of the market, commodity owners gained private autonomy; the positive meaning of "private" emerged precisely in reference to the concept of free power of control over property that functioned in capitalist fashion.

The modern history of private law shows how far this process had already advanced in the mercantilist phase. The conception of the legal transaction as involving a contract based on a free declaration of will was modelled on the exchange transaction of freely competing owners of commodities. At the same time, a system of private law that in principle reduced the relationships of private people with one another to private contracts operated with the assumption that the exchange relationships that came about in accordance with the laws of the free market had model character. Of course, parties to a contract were not in every case also exchange partners, but the relationship of the latter, which was central to civil society, supplied the model for all contractual relationships. With the fundamental liberties of the system of private law, the category of a general legal standing—the guarantee of the legal status of the person—was articulated as well; the latter was no longer defined by estate and birth. The *status libertatis*, the *status civitatis*, and the *status familiae* gave way to the one *status naturalis*, now ascribed generally to all legal subjects[42]—thus corresponding to the fundamental parity among owners of commodities in the market and among educated individuals in the public sphere.

With the great codifications of civil law a system of norms was developed securing a private sphere in the strict sense, a sphere in which private people pursued their affairs with one another free from impositions by estate and state, at least in tendency. These codifications guaranteed the institution of private property and, in connection with it, the basic freedoms of contract, of trade, and of inheritance. Admittedly the developmental phases were more clearly demarcated on the continent, precisely because of their codifications, than in Britain, where the same process occurred within the framework of Common Law. Yet the special legal forms and institutions of a society with free traffic in commodities[43] were formed earlier here than in countries with a Roman Law tradition. In Prussia the *Allgemeine Landrecht* was published in 1794; in Austria the *Allgemeine Bürgerliche Gesetzbuch* in 1811; the classic work of bourgeois private law, the *Code Civil* of 1804, came between the two. It was characteristic of all these legal codes that they originated not only in the interest of civil society but also in its specific medium: many times they went through the critical public scrutiny of private people come together as a public. Through prize competitions and through questionnaires, public opinion contributed to legal codification even where parliamentary bodies did not exist or remained ineffective, as in Napoleonic France. As in Berlin and Vienna, so in Paris the proposed legal code was in 1800 submitted for critical assessment to the public and not just to an internal forum of specialists. Indeed, the proposals themselves were not even formulated by the traditional carriers of jurisprudence but by educated and trusted agents of the government who, in a way, were its contacts with a public already a politically active entity; basic ideas were debated in discussion circles such as the Berlin *Mittwochsgesellschaft*, to which Suarez belonged.

The modern history of private law did not start with the eighteenth-century transformation of natural law into positive law. However, the received Roman Law, which was understood as "private" at first only in contrast to canonical law, nevertheless did not begin to develop into the law of emancipated civil society before the dissolution of the traditional legal forms of both the old ruling estates and the town-based occupational status groups (*Berufsstände*). Under absolutism, functioning in any event more as a legal technique than as law, it served the territorial princes as an instrument in the conflict between the authorities bent on centralization and the particularism of the estates. Civil society was to be released from its corporate bonds and subjected to the administrative sovereignty of the prince. In this function too Roman Law did not guarantee an order of "private" law in the strict sense. Even where it was not entirely absorbed by police ordinances, "private law" remained a creature of state authority; these ordinances included in their coverage peripheral problems of the "public welfare"[44] along with commercial, occupational, and labor law. The digests to which the reigning theory of private law was at that time oriented became a fiction when compared with the legally relevant reality:

In labor law, with regard to relationships involving free labor, the digests mention only the rather undifferentiated wage for services rendered by free persons; but the local law concerning domestic servants takes domestic authority and household community as its point of departure; the local law concerning artisans presumes the corporate organization of occupational status groups; the law regulating agricultural labor takes the service obligations of peasants for granted. The digests' regulations concerning debts for the most part presuppose freedom of contract; the local regulations contain a multitude of price controls, taxes, supply and first offer obligations, production restrictions, obligatory contracts. An abstract, universal, and hence apparently free legal order implying an economically free individual stands confronted with an almost suffocating degree of restriction on the law governing contracts, labor, residence, and real estate (that is to say, all social and economic foci of private law) imposed by state, occupational status groups, and corporations.[45]

By the second half of the eighteenth century modern private law had in principle done away with these controls. Nevertheless, it then took yet another hundred years for the development from status to contract to break completely through all the restrictions that at that time hindered the utilization of industrial capital and thus the establishment of the capitalist mode of production; for property to become freely disposable for the exchange transactions of participants in the market; for the specification of its heirs to be left up to the free will of the owner; for the choice and exercise of a trade and the training of workers to become a matter of the entrepreneur's discretion; and for wages to be determined by a free contract between the employer and the employee. In 1757 the justices of the peace in Great Britain lost the task of state-imposed wage regulation, first in the textile industry; by 1813 free wage labor had been introduced in all branches of industry; a year later the Elizabethan law prescribing a seven-year training period for apprentices was abolished. This was complemented by a strict prohibition of unionization. Likewise, from the mid-eighteenth century on, freedom of trade progressed step by step. In France this development started with the outbreak of the Revolution; by 1791 almost all government directives and all estate-related regulations in trade and industry had been eliminated. What in Austria could be accomplished already under Joseph II had to wait in Prussia for the Stein-Hardenberg Reforms following the defeat of 1806. Also, the feudalistic inheritance laws were defended successfully for a long time. In Great Britain the individualistic conception that the passing on of property through inheritance must be detached from the collective economic unit of the household and the family and become a matter of the individual property owner came to prevail only with the Reform Bill of 1843.[46] Before the trade between nations (and in Germany between territories) was freed from customs restrictions, industrial capital battered down all obstacles at home; at the end of this development it was almost exclusively the laws of free competition that governed the market of goods, real estate, labor, and even capital itself.

Even in Great Britain the liberalization of foreign trade could be carried out with consistency only after the repeal of the Corn Laws in 1846. The old contradiction between the defensive interests vested in established market positions, on the one hand, and the expansive interests of capital invested in ever new sectors, on the other, was reproduced at a higher level. This time, however, driven by the tremendous forces of the industrial revolution,[47] it led not merely to a temporary weakening of old monopolies but, in the longer run, to a turnover in the positions of market dominance. The need of the new industries for expanded consumer markets for their goods, for an expanded supply of raw materials for their products, and finally for expanded food imports, which kept the subsistence level of their producers (i.e., the wage laborers) low—this objective interest in a removal of government regulations, privileges, and controls found Great Britain at that time, as the nation dominating both sea and market, in a situation in which it had everything to gain from *laisser faire* and nothing to lose. Great Britain's leading industrial position increased her interest in free trade.[48] Furthermore, after the emancipation of the North American colonies from the mother country it had been possible to put the example to the test. The trade with a free country was proven to be at least as profitable as exchange within one and the same colonial system.[49] In this way free trade,[50] the effectiveness of free competition at home and abroad, determined the entire phase we call liberal. Indeed, we have become accustomed to deriving the essence of all capitalism from the competitive capitalism of this specific form. In contrast to this notion it should be recalled that this phase lasted only for one blissful moment in the long history of capitalist development; for it issued from a unique historical constellation in Great Britain at the close of the eighteenth century. The other countries did not actualize the principles of *laisser faire* in international trade without reserve, even in the middle of the nineteenth century when the liberal era was at its height. Nevertheless, only during this phase was civil society as the private sphere emancipated from the directives of public authority to such an extent[51] that at that time the political public sphere could attain its full development in the bourgeois constitutional state.

11 The Contradictory Institutionalization of the Public Sphere in the Bourgeois Constitutional State

According to civil society's idea of itself, the system of free competition was self-regulating; indeed, only on the presupposition that no extra-economic agency interfered with the transactions in the market did the latter promise to function in a fashion that ensured everyone's welfare and justice in accord with the standard of the individual's capacity to perform. The society solely governed by the laws of the free market presented itself not only as a sphere free from domination but as one free from any kind of coercion; the economic power of each commodity owner was conceived quantitatively to be of an order precluding it from having an influence upon the price mechanism, and thus from ever providing direct power over other owners of commodities. Such a society remained subordinate to the market's nonviolent decisions, being the anonymous and, in a certain way, autonomous outcome of the exchange process.[52] The juridical guarantees of its basic economic constitution also pointed in the direction of a private sphere neutralized as regards power, at least in tendency, and emancipated from domination. The elimination of authoritarian arbitrariness through legal safeguards, that is, binding state functions to general norms, together with the liberties codified in the system of bourgeois civil law, protected the order of the "free market." In terms of their sociological meaning, state interventions without empowerment by law were blameworthy primarily not because they violate principles of justice laid down by natural right but simply because they were unpredictable and thus would preclude exactly the kind and measure of rationality that was in the interest of private persons functioning in a capitalist fashion. Otherwise those "guarantees of calculability," already discovered by Max Weber in regard to industrial capitalism, would be lacking: the calculation of profit opportunities demanded a system in which exchange transactions proceed in accord with calculable expectations.[53] Delimited jurisdictional areas and observance of legal formalism were therefore criteria of the bourgeois constitutional state;[54] a "rational" administration and an "independent" judiciary[55] were its organizational conditions. The law itself, by which the executive and the judiciary had to abide, was to be equally binding for everyone; in principle, no one was to enjoy a dispensation or privilege. In this respect the laws of the state were like those of the market: neither allowed exceptions for citizens and private persons; both were objective, which is to say, not manipulable by the individual; the individual owner of goods had no influence on the market price; and they were not directed at individuals (the free market prohibited collusion).

The laws of the market, of course, prevailed because they were intrinsic; this was precisely why classical economics endowed them with the appearance of an *ordre naturel*. The laws of the state, in contrast, needed to be explicitly enacted. To be sure, the prince could possibly also function as the legislator insofar as he was willing to bind his commands and all state activity to general norms, whereby the latter, in turn, would have to be oriented to the interests of bourgeois commerce. For a state to be constitutional per se did not necessarily require that the public sphere be constitutionalized within the framework of a parliamentary form of government (or at least one in which authority was vested in parliament). The physiocrats indeed had something like this in mind; their so-called legal despotism held out the prospect that precisely under the enlightened monarch public opinion would be sovereign. Even during the liberal phase, however, the interests competing with industrial capital (especially the landed interest, be it that of the manorial lords or that of the great land owners turned bourgeois) were still so strong that they dominated even the British Parliament until 1832 and delayed the repeal of the Corn Laws for another fourteen years.[56] Hence the enlightened monarch of the physiocrats remained a pure fiction; in the conflict of class interests the character of a state as a constitutional state would not guarantee per se legislation geared toward the needs of bourgeois commerce. Only with power to legislate itself did the public, constituted of private people, obtain this certainty. The constitutional state as a bourgeois state established the public sphere in the political realm as an organ of the state so as to ensure institutionally the connection between law and public opinion.

Because of such provenance, however, this state was beset by a peculiar contradiction. The latter was betrayed first of all by an ambivalence in the concept of law:

In the political struggle against a strong royal government, the participation of representatives of the people as the essential characteristic of the law had to be increasingly emphasized and ultimately had to become decisive. If the participation of the people's representatives is politically a preeminent feature of the law, this explains . . . the obverse: whatever comes about with the participation of the people's representatives, is law. The rule of the law then means participation or ultimately rule of the people's representatives.[57]

On the one hand, therefore, the concept of law as an expression of will included as an element the claim, successfully asserted through recourse to violence, to the exercise of domination. On the other hand, however, the concept of law as an expression of reason preserved other, older elements of its origin in public opinion, still traceable in the connection between parliament and public. This is why Carl Schmitt gave first place not to the political definition of law but to the other: "Law is not the will of one or of many people, but something rational-universal; not *voluntas*, but *ratio*."[58] In its intention, the rule of the law aimed at dissolving domination altogether; this was a typically bourgeois idea insofar as not even the political safeguarding of the private sphere emancipating itself from political domination was to assume the form of domination.

The bourgeois idea of the law-based state, namely, the binding of all state activity to a system of norms legitimated by public opinion (a system that had no gaps, if possible), already aimed at abolishing the state as an instrument of domination altogether. Acts of sovereignty were considered apocryphal per se.

Since the critical public debate of private people convincingly claimed to be in the nature of a noncoercive inquiry into what was at the same time correct and right, a legislation that had recourse to public opinion thus could not be explicitly considered as domination. Yet the authority to legislate was so obviously won only in a tough struggle with the old powers that it could not be absolved from having the character of a "coercive power" itself. Locke called it "legislative power," Montesquieu "*pouvoir*"; in both authors' minds only the administration of justice (which merely "applied" the given laws) was without power and hence without a determinate social category as its bearer. Nevertheless, the distinction between legislative and executive power was modelled on the contrast between norm and action, between reason ordering and will acting.[59] Although construed as "power," legislation was supposed to be the result not of a political will, but of rational agreement. Even Rousseau's democratic conversion of the sovereignty of the prince into that of the people did not solve the dilemma. Public opinion was in principle opposed to arbitrariness and subject to the laws immanent in a public composed of critically debating private persons in such a way that the property of being the supreme will, superior to all laws, which is to say sovereignty, could strictly speaking not be attributed to it at all. In accord with its own intention, public opinion wanted to be neither a check on power, nor power itself, nor even the source of all powers. Within its medium, rather, the character of executive power, domination (*Herrschaft*) itself, was supposed to change. The "domination" of the public, according to its own idea, was an order in which domination itself was dissolved; *veritas non auctoritas facit legem.* This inversion of the Hobbesian statement was lost in the attempt to conceive of the function of public opinion both with the help of the concept of sovereignty and in the constitutional law construction of the *pouvoirs.* A public sphere as a functional element in the political realm posed the issue of *pouvoir* as such. *Public debate was supposed to transform* voluntas *into a* ratio *that in the public competition of private arguments came into being as the consensus about what was practically necessary in the interest of all.*

Where the constitutional state did not emerge as a fact out of the older formation of a state structured by estates (as in Great Britain) but was sanctioned (as on the continent) by a piece of legislation on which it was founded, that is, a basic law or constitution, the functions of the public sphere were clearly spelled out in the law.[60] A set of basic rights concerned the sphere of the public engaged in rational-critical debate (freedom of opinion and speech, freedom of press, freedom of assembly and association, etc.) and the political function of private people in this public sphere (right of petition, equality of vote, etc.). A second set of basic rights concerned the individual's status as a free human being, grounded in the intimate sphere of the patriarchal conjugal family (personal freedom, inviolability of the home, etc.). The third set of basic rights concerned the transactions of the private owners of property in the sphere of civil society (equality before the law, protection of private property, etc.). The basic rights guaranteed: the *spheres* of the public realm and of the private (with the intimate sphere at its core); the *institutions* and *instruments* of the public sphere, on the one hand (press, parties), and the foundation of private autonomy (family and property), on the other; finally, the *functions* of the private people, both their political ones as citizens and their economic ones as owners of commodities (and, as "human beings," those of individual communication, e.g., through inviolability of letters).[61]

As a consequence of the constitutional definition of the public realm and its functions,[62] publicness became the organizational principle for the procedures of the organs of the state themselves; in this sense one spoke of their "publicity." The public character of parliamentary deliberations assured public opinion of its influence; it ensured the connection between delegates and voters as parts of one and the same public. At about the same time trial procedures in court were made public too.[63] Even the independent judiciary needed checking by public opinion; indeed, its independence from the executive as well as from private interference seemed to be guaranteed only in the medium of a critical public ready to swing into action. The most effective resistance to the principle of publicity was put up by the state bureaucracy, not primarily, however, because the secrecy of certain actions would be precisely in the public interest but because next to the army the bureaucracy built up under absolutism represented the only means of power in the hands of the princes against the interests of bourgeois society. Nonetheless, even within the framework of enlightened absolutism, an order of the Prussian king to his ministers of state dating from the year 1804 testified in exemplary fashion to the newly spreading insight "that a decent publicity is for both government and subjects the surest guaranty against the negligence and spite of subaltern officials and deserves to be promoted and protected by all means."[64]

Nowhere did the constitutional establishment of a public sphere in the political realm, itself painfully enough won through violence, betray its character as an order of domination more than in the central article stating that all power (*Gewalt*) came from the people. Otherwise the constitutional state predicated on civil rights pretended, on the basis of an effective public sphere, to be an organization of public power ensuring the latter's subordination to the needs of a private sphere itself taken to be neutralized as regards power and emancipated from domination. Thus the constitutional norms implied a model of civil society that by no means corresponded to its reality. The categories drawn from the historical process of capitalism, including its liberal phase, were themselves historical in character. They denoted social tendencies, but tendencies only. Thus, the "private people" on whose autonomy, socially guaranteed by property, the constitutional state counted just as much as on the educational qualifications of the public formed by these people, were in truth a small minority, even if one added the petty to the high bourgeoisie. Incomparably more numerous were the "common people," especially the rural population. And both the princes, supported by army and bureaucracy, and the great landowners, the landed nobility, continued to exercise power in accord with the political laws of precapitalist society.[65] Nevertheless, the new constitutions, written and unwritten, referred to citizens and human beings as such, and indeed necessarily so, as long as "publicity" constituted their organizational principle.

The public sphere of civil society stood or fell with the principle of universal access. A public sphere from which specific groups would be *eo ipso* excluded was less than merely incomplete; it was not a public sphere at all. Accordingly, the public that might be considered the subject of the bourgeois constitutional state viewed its sphere as a public one in this strict sense; in its deliberations it anticipated in principle that all human beings belong to it. The private person too, was simply a human being, that is, a moral person. We have designated the historical and social location in which this self-interpretation developed. The consciousness of this, if you will, formless humanity grew up in the patriarchal conjugal family's intimate sphere that was oriented to a public. In the meantime, the public very much assumed its specific form; it was the bourgeois reading public of the eighteenth century. This public remained rooted in the world of letters even as it assumed political functions; education was the one criterion for admission—property ownership the other. De facto both criteria demarcated largely the same circle of persons; for formal education at that time was more a consequence than a precondition of a social status, which in turn was primarily determined by one's title to property. The educated strata were also the property owning ones. The census, which regulated admission to the public sphere in the political realm, could therefore be identical with the tax list. Indeed, the French Revolution already used the latter as the standard for the distinction between full citizens and those of lesser status.

This restriction of the franchise, however, did not necessarily have to be viewed as a restriction of the public sphere itself as long as it could be interpreted as the mere legal ratification of a status attained economically in the private sphere, which is to say, the status of the private person who both was educated and owned property. The universal accessibility to that sphere whose operation in the political realm was institutionalized by the constitutional state must be decided by the structure of civil society from the outset, and not only ex post facto by the political constitution that it gave itself. The public sphere was safeguarded whenever the economic and social conditions gave everyone an equal chance to meet the criteria for admission: specifically, to earn the qualifications for private autonomy that made for the educated and property owning person. The contemporary science of political economy laid out these conditions; Jeremy Bentham was unthinkable without Adam Smith.[66]

The presuppositions of classical economics are well known. It conceived of a system whose immanent laws afforded the individual a sure foundation for calculating his economic activity rationally according to the standard of profit maximization. Each person made such calculations for himself, without collusion with others; the production of goods was subjectively anarchic, objectively harmonious. The first presupposition was thus economic: the guarantee of free competition. The second one postulated that all commodities were exchanged according to their "value"; the latter, in turn, was to be gauged in terms of the quantity of labor required for its production. In all this the commodities in question included both the goods produced and the labor power producing them. Since this condition was only fulfilled if each supplier produced his commodities himself, and if, conversely, each laborer possessed the means of production himself, the second presupposition amounted to a sociological one: the model of a society of petty commodity producers. It was related to the first insofar as the economic presupposition of the independent formation of prices implied the sociological one of a relatively widely and evenly distributed ownership of means of production. The third presupposition was a theoretical one first introduced by the elder Mill and handed down in a later formulation as Say's Law. According to this law, under conditions of complete mobility of producers, products, and capital, supply and demand would always be in equilibrium. This meant that no production capacities would be idle, that labor reserves would be fully utilized, and that the system would be in principle crisis-free and in equilibrium on a high level that at any given time was commensurate with the state of development of the forces of production.

Under these conditions, but only under these, would each

person have an equal chance, with ability and "luck" (the equivalent for the lack of transparency of the nevertheless strictly determined market dynamics), to attain the status of property owner and thus of "man," that is, the qualifications of a private person admitted to the public sphere—property and education. As was apparent from the polemical function of political economy itself, these conditions were by no means fulfilled even in the first half of the nineteenth century.[67] Nevertheless, the liberal model sufficiently approximated reality so that the interest of the bourgeois class could be identified with the general interest and the third estate could be set up as the nation— during that phase of capitalism, the public sphere as the organizational principle of the bourgeois constitutional state had credibility. If everyone, as it might appear, had the chance to become a "citizen," then only citizens should be allowed into the political public sphere, without this restriction amounting to an abandonment of the principle of publicity. On the contrary, only property owners were in a position to form a public that could legislatively protect the foundations of the existing property order; only they had private interests—each his own—which automatically converged into the common interest in the preservation of a civil society as a private sphere. Only from them, therefore, was an effective representation of the general interest to be expected, since it was not necessary for them in any way to leave their private existence behind to exercise their public role. For the private person, there was no break between *homme* and *citoyen*, as long as the *homme* was simultaneously an owner of private property who as *citoyen* was to protect the stability of the property order as a private one. Class interest was the basis of public opinion. During that phase, however, it must also have been objectively congruent with the general interest, at least to the extent that this opinion could be considered the public one, emerging from the critical debate of the public, and consequently, rational. It would have turned into coercion at that time if the public had been forced to close itself off as the ruling class, if it had been forced to abandon the principle of publicity. Critical debate would have become dogma, the rational insight of an opinion that was no longer public would have become an authoritarian command.

As long as the presuppositions enumerated above could be assumed as given, as long as publicity existed as a sphere and functioned as a principle, what the public itself believed to be and to be doing was ideology and simultaneously more than mere ideology. On the basis of the continuing domination of one class over another, the dominant class nevertheless developed political institutions which credibly embodied as their objective meaning the idea of their own abolition: *veritas non auctoritas facit legem*, the idea of the dissolution of domination into that easygoing constraint that prevailed on no other ground than the compelling insight of a public opinion.

If ideologies are not only manifestations of the socially necessary consciousness in its essential falsity, if there is an aspect to them that can lay a claim to truth inasmuch as it transcends the status quo in utopian fashion, even if only for purposes of justification, then ideology exists at all only from this period on.[68] Its origin would be the identification of "property owner" with "human being as such" in the role accruing to private people as members of the public in the political public sphere of the bourgeois constitutional state, that is, in the identification of the public sphere in the political realm with that in the world of letters; and also in public opinion itself, in which the interest of the class, via critical public debate, could assume the appearance of the general interest, that is, in the identification of domination with its dissolution into pure reason.

However that may be, the developed public sphere of civil society was bound up with a complicated constellation of social preconditions. In any event, before long they all changed profoundly, and with their transformation the contradiction of the public sphere that was institutionalized in the bourgeois constitutional state came to the fore. With the help of its principle, which according to its own idea was opposed to all domination, a political order was founded whose social basis did not make domination superfluous after all.

IV
The Bourgeois Public Sphere:
Idea and Ideology

12 Public Opinion—Opinion Publique—Öffentliche Meinung: On the Prehistory of the Phrase[1]

The self-interpretation of the function of the bourgeois public sphere crystallized in the idea of "public opinion." The prehistory of the latter, up to its articulated meaning in late eighteenth century, was naturally quite long and hitherto known only in its broad outline.[2] Nevertheless, it will serve as an introduction to that idea of the bourgeois public sphere (section 12) which, after having received its classic formulation in the Kantian doctrine of right (section 13), was revealed as problematic by Hegel and Marx (section 14) and which, in the political theory of liberalism around the middle of the nineteenth century, had to admit to the ambivalence of its idea and ideology.

"Opinion" in English and French took over the uncomplicated meaning of the Latin *opinio*: opinion; of the uncertain, not fully demonstrated judgment. Technical philosophical language, from Plato's *doxa* to Hegel's *Meinen*, here corresponded exactly to the term's meaning in everyday language. However, in our context the second meaning of opinion is more important, namely: "reputation"; regard: what one represents in the opinion of others.[3] "Opinion" in the sense of a judgment that lacks certainty, whose truth would still have to be proven, is associated with "opinion" in the sense of a basically suspicious repute among the multitude. Thus, the word carries such a pronounced connotation of collective opinion that all attributes referring to its social character can be dispensed with as pleonastic. Combinations such as: "common opinion," "general opinion," and "vulgar opinion" were still completely lacking in Shakespeare, not to mention "public opinion" or "public spirit."[4] Likewise, in French, mores and customs, current ideas and common conventions in general are simply called *les opinions*.

"Opinion," of course, did not evolve straightforwardly into "public opinion," *opinion publique*, that late eighteenth-century coinage that would refer to the critical reflections of a public competent to form its own judgments. Both of the original meanings—the mere opinion and the reputation that emerged in the mirror of opinions—were antithetical to the kind of rationality claimed by public opinion. Admittedly, however, in English the contrast between opinion and truth, reason, and judgment was not as sharp as the French antithesis, firmly established during the seventeenth century, between *opinion* and *critique*.[5]

Hobbes took a momentous step when he identified "conscience," denoting both consciousness and conscience, with "opinion." As is well known, Hobbes was guided by the experiences of the religious civil war and in *Leviathan* in 1651 projected a state based solely upon the *auctoritas* of the prince, independent of the convictions and views of the subjects. Because the subjects were excluded from the public sphere objectified in the state apparatus, the conflict between their convictions could not be settled politically and, indeed, was completely banned from the sphere of politics. The civil war came to an end under the dictate of a state authority neutralized in religious matters. One's religion was a private matter, a private conviction; it was of no consequence for the state from whose perspective one was worth as much as the other; conscience became opinion.[6] Accordingly, Hobbes defined a "chain of opinions" that extended from faith to judgment. In the sphere of "opinion" he reduced all acts of believing, judging, and opining to the same level. Even "conscience" was "nothing else but man's settled judgment and opinion."[7] As little as Hobbes, by identifying conscience and opinion, intended to add to the latter what he took away from the former—the claim to truth—on the level of intellectual history he nevertheless provided the commentary on a development that, with the privatization of religion and of property and with the emancipation of civil society's private people from the semi-public bonds of the Church and the intermediate powers of the estates, increased the importance of these people's private opinions even more. Hobbes's devaluation of religious conviction actually led to an upward evaluation of all private convictions.[8]

Locke, who three years after the beheading of Charles I and one year after the publication of the *Leviathan* entered Christ Church College in Oxford, could therefore present the "Law of Opinion" as a category of equal rank beside divine and state law; in the later editions of his *Essay Concerning Human Understanding*, he stubbornly defended this position. The Law of Opinion judged virtues and vices; virtue, indeed, was measured precisely in terms of public esteem.[9] As the complete formulation, "Law of Opinion and Reputation," shows, with Locke the original meaning of that which one represented in the opinion of others returned. On the other hand, this opinion was conspicuously cleansed of the unreliability of mere opining, of external and even deceptive mere appearance. As "measure of virtue and vice" the Law of Opinion was also called "Philosophical Law." "Opinion" denoted the informal web of folkways whose indirect social control was more effective than the formal censure under threat of ecclesiastical or governmental sanctions. That law, therefore, was also called "Law of Private Censure." To be sure, in contrast to the collective mores and customs that had emerged naturally, it already possessed that element of awareness that "opinion" now obtained from its origin in privatized religious faith, secularized morality. But nevertheless the expression *"public* opinion" was lacking here, and not without reason. Law of opinion was by no means meant as law of public opinion; for "opinion" neither arose in public discussion—it became binding instead "by a secret and tacit consent"—nor was it applied in some way to the laws of the state, because it was actually grounded in the "consent of private men who have not authority enough to make a law."[10] Finally, unlike public opinion, opinion was not tied to preconditions of education (and of property); for contributing to it, far from requiring participation in a process of critical debate, demanded nothing more than the simple uttering of precisely those "habits" that later on public opinion would critically oppose as prejudices.

Nonetheless, with Locke "opinion," through its identification with "conscience," received a status which freed it from its polemically devalued association with pure prejudice. In French, *opinion* kept this latter connotation. For Locke's contemporary Bayle, the *Régime de la Critique* replaced the Law of Opinion as the "philosophical" law.[11] Bayle separated *critique* from its philological-historical origin and turned it into criticism as such, that is, into the weighing of the *pour et contre* by a *raison* applicable to everything and destructive of *opinion* in any form. Of course, he treated the business of criticism as something strictly private. Although the truth was discovered in public discussion among critical minds, the realm of reason nevertheless remained an inward one, opposed to the public one of the state. Inwardly critical, *raison* remained outwardly subordinate. Just as "conscience" for Hobbes, so *"critique"* for Bayle was a private matter and without consequence for public authority. In the same way he distinguished between *critique* on the one hand, and *satires* and *libelles diffamatoires* on the other. Criticism that became guilty of overstepping the line into the political realm degenerated into pamphleteering. In contrast, in Great Britain during the same period, a press devoted to the debate of political issues developed out of the pamphlet. The Encyclopedists, who certainly invoked Bayle as their predecessor not just because of his encyclopedic enterprise,[12] took over *opinion* in the polemical meaning of a mental condition of uncertainty and vacuousness.[13] Whoever knew how to make use of *raison*, whoever knew how to engage in *critique*, knew how to shake off "le joug de la scolastique, de l'opinion, de l'autorité, en un mot des préjugés et de la barbarie"; the German editor translated somewhat rashly: "das Joch der Scholastik, der öffentlichen Meinung, der Autorität" (the yoke of scholasticism, of *public* opinion, of authority).[14] As a matter of fact, one year earlier an author had for the first time spoken of *opinion publique*, namely Rousseau in his famous *Discourse on the Arts and Sciences*. He used the new combination in the old meaning of *opinion*; the attribute *publique* at best betrayed his switching of sides in the polemic. The critics, on this account, subverted the foundations of faith and destroyed virtue, devoted their talent and their philosophy to the destruction and undermining of all that was sacred to humans. They opposed public opinion: "c'est de l'opinion publique qu'ils sont ennemis" (they are the enemies of public opinion).[15]

In English the development from "opinion" to "public opinion" proceeded via "public spirit." In 1793 Friedrich Georg Forster named as the equivalent of *opinion publique* this older "public spirit" instead of "public opinion," even though at that time the words were synonyms. Steele had already transposed "public spirit" from the lofty and sacrificial attitude of human individuals to that objective entity of the *Zeitgeist*—a general opinion, which from that time on could scarcely be separated from the instrument of this opinion, the press.[16] Bolingbroke took up the word as a basis for connecting the political opposition with the "sense of the people." In the *Craftsman* articles of the year 1730 he called the public spirit of the people, guided and enlightened by the opposition, a "Spirit of Liberty" against the corruption of those in power. "The knowledge of the millions," he claimed, was neither ridiculous nor despicable, since a right sentiment was alive in the mass of the population— "if all men cannot reason, all men can feel."[17] "Public spirit" in this sense still retained traces of the immediacy that characterized "opinion" as used by Locke: the people in their reliable common sense were, so to speak, unerring. The concept nevertheless already exhibited the Enlightenment characteristics of what would soon be called "public opinion"; aided by the political journalism that Bolingbroke himself helped to create, the "sense of the people" formed the oppositional "public spirit." In the mind of this conservative, upon whom was forced the role of the critical *frondeur* and hence of the first opposition member in the sense of modern parliamentary tactics, a piece of anticipated Rousseauism was strangely fused with the principles of public criticism. Both were still united in the "public spirit"; the direct, undistorted sense for what was right and just and the articulation of "opinion" into "judgment" through the public clash of arguments.

Edmund Burke, before the outbreak of the French Revolution (which found its match in him as a critic) finally made the needed distinctions.[18] However, they were not yet drawn in his famous *Speech to the Electors of Bristol*, in which he developed in exemplary fashion the liberal theory of virtual representation. Three years later he wrote to the same electors a letter, *On the Affairs of America*. In the meantime, the secession of the North American colonies from the mother country had taken place, and the *Declaration of Rights* had been published. "I must beg leave to observe that it is not only the invidious branch of taxation that will be resisted, but that no other given part of legislative right can be exercised without regard to the general opinion of those who are to be governed. That general opinion is the vehicle and organ of legislative omnipotence."[19] The definition of public opinion as vehicle and organ of legislative omnipotence (or sovereignty), not very clear from the perspective of constitutional law, nevertheless left no doubt concerning the concept of this "general opinion." The opinion of the public that put its reason to use was no longer just opinion; it did not arise from mere inclination but from private reflection upon public affairs and from their public discussion: "In a free country," wrote Burke a few months later:

every man thinks he has a concern in all public matters; that he has a right to form and a right to deliver an opinion on them. They sift, examine, and discuss them. They are curious, eager, attentive, and jealous; and by making such matters the daily subjects of their thoughts and discoveries, vast numbers contract a very tolerable knowledge of them, and some a very considerable one . . . Whereas in other countries none but men whose office calls them to it having much care or thought about public affairs, and not daring to try the force of their opinions with one another, ability of this sort is extremely rare in any station of life. In free countries, there is often found more real public wisdom and sagacity in shops and manufactories than in the cabinets of princes in countries where none dares to have an opinion until he comes into them. Your whole importance, therefore, depends upon a constant, discreet use of your own reason.[20]

Soon thereafter Burke's "general opinion," parallel with "public spirit," received the name "public opinion": the *Oxford Dictionary* dates the first documentation to 1781.

In France the corresponding word occurred already around the middle of the century; but at that time its meaning still barely differed from *opinion*. *Opinion publique* was the term for the opinion of the people supported by tradition and *bon sens*—whether Rousseau, as a critic of culture, appealed to its naturalness, or the Encyclopedists tried to dissolve it through a critique of ideology. Only when the physiocrats ascribed it to the *publique éclairé* itself did *opinion publique* receive the strict meaning of an opinion purified through critical discussion in the public sphere to constitute a true opinion. In *opinion publique* the contradiction between *opinion* and *critique* vanished. It is well known that the physiocrats, exponents of a public that now also debated about political matters, were the first to assert that civil society followed laws of its own versus the interventions of the state; yet in relation to the absolutist regime they acted as apologists. As Marx said, their doctrine amounted to a bourgeois reproduction of the feudal system.[21] In the transition from mercantilism to liberalism they continued to affirm the basis of feudal domination, that is, agriculture as the single productive labor. Yet the latter was already apprehended from the perspective of capitalist production. The function of the monarch was to watch over the *ordre naturel*; he received his insight into the laws of the natural order through the *public éclairé*. Louis Sebastien Mercier, who seems to have been the first to extract from such connections the rigorous concept of *opinion publique* and to have thought through its social function,[22] also distinguished painstakingly between the governors and the scholars.[23] The latter determined the public opinion, the former converted into practice whatever conclusions were drawn from the critical reflection of the public guided by experts: "The good books are dependent on the enlightened people in all classes of the nation; they are an ornament to truth. They are the ones that already govern Europe; they enlighten the government about its duties, its shortcoming, its true interest, about the public opinion to which it must listen and conform: these good books are patient masters, waiting for the moment when the state administrators wake up and when their passions die down."[24] *L'opinion publique* was the enlightened outcome of common and public reflection on the foundations of social order. It encapsulated the latter's natural laws: it did not rule, but the enlightened ruler would have to follow its insight.

With this doctrine of the dual authority of public opinion and of the Prince, of *ratio* and *voluntas*, the physiocrats, remaining within the confines of the existing regime, interpreted the place of a public that critically scrutinized political matters. Whereas their British contemporaries understood the public spirit as an authority that could compel lawmakers to legitimize themselves, in France the continuing isolation of society from the state manifested itself in the fact that, in the minds of these intellectuals, the critical function of *opinion publique* remained strictly separated from the legislative function. Nevertheless, the specific idea of a public sphere as an element in the political realm was already part of this early concept of public opinion. Le Harpe was once able to say of Turgot: "He is the first among us to transform the acts of sovereign authority into works of reason and persuasiveness."[25] This already signified a rationalization of sovereignty. But no more than the other physiocrats did Turgot connect this idea with the democratic guarantee that the private people, who in the form of public opinion produced the apposite insights, were now also in a position to endow these with legislative authority. Although the maxim of absolutism, *auctoritas facit legem*, was no longer in force, its opposite had not yet been achieved. In spite of everything, the rationality of public opinion was in the end still deprived of its constitutive function. Rousseau, in contrast, who with all desirable clarity provided the foundation for the public's democratic self-determination, linked the *volonté générale* to an *opinion publique* coinciding with unreflected *opinion*—that is, opinion that was publicly known.

Rousseau also wanted to reconstitute the "social condition" as an *ordre naturel*, although the latter did not appear to him immanent in the laws of civil society but entirely transcendent of hitherto existing society. For inequality and lack of freedom followed from the corruption of that state of nature in which human beings actualized nothing but their common human nature, while the break between nature and society tore each individual asunder into *homme* and *citoyen*. The primordial process of alienation from oneself was charged to the progress of civilization. The ingenious artifice of the *contrat social* was supposed to heal this rift: everybody submitted to the community his person and property along with all rights so as to have from then on a share in the rights and duties of all through the mediation of the general will.[26] The social contract demanded self-surrender without reservation; the *homme* was absorbed by the *citoyen*. Rousseau projected the unbourgeois idea of an intrusively political society in which the autonomous private sphere, that is, civil society emancipated from the state, had no place. The same held true of the basis of such a society: property was private and public at once, in the same fashion in which each citizen only in his capacity as participant in the general will was subject to himself.[27] Consequently, the general will did not emerge from the competition of private interests; such a *volonté de tous* would correspond to the liberal model presupposing the private autonomy eliminated in the model of the *contrat social*. Instead the *volonté générale*, the guarantee of a reconstituted state of nature under the conditions of the social state as a kind of saving instinct of humanity, projected from the former into the latter. Thus Rousseau, in a turn against Montesquieu, saw the spirit of the constitution neither engraved on marble nor cast in bronze, but anchored in the hearts of the citizens, in *opinion*: "I am speaking of mores, customs, and especially of opinion."[28]

Locke's "Law of Opinion" became sovereign by way of Rousseau's *Contrat Social*. Under the rubric of a different *opinion publique* unpublic opinion was elevated to the status of sole legislator, and this involved the elimination of the public's rational-critical debate in the public sphere. The legislative procedure envisaged by Rousseau left no doubt in this regard.[29] *Bon sens* (common sense, *gesunder Menschenverstand*) was all that was needed to perceive the common welfare. The simple people, indeed simpletons, would be merely irritated by the political maneuvers of public discussion; long debates would bring particular interests to the fore. Rousseau contrasted the dangerous appeals of silver-tongued orators with the harmony of assemblies. The *volonté générale* was more a consensus of hearts than of arguments.[30] That society was governed best in which the laws (*lois*) corresponded to the already established mores (*opinions*). The simplicity of mores was a protection against "thorny discussions" (*discussions épineuses*),[31] whereas luxury corrupted healthy simplicity, subjugated one group to another and all of them to public opinion (*et tous à l'opinion*).[32] In this passage, the competing usage of the term came to the fore again: *L'opinion* was the opinion of the *public éclairé*, articulated through the press and *salon* discussions. Against its corrupting influence Rousseau, entirely in the style of his prize-winning essay of 1750, posited emphatically the *opinion* of simple morals and of the good soul.

In spite of its quasi-naturalness, the latter *opinion* needed guidance in its dual function. For one thing, as the direct expression of convention it had the task of social control; yet it was under the surveillance of a censor who acted less as the judge of the people's opinion than as its spokesman: "Public opinion is the sort of law whose censor is the minister."[33] This was the only chapter in the *Contrat Social* in which "*opinion publique*" was mentioned. The commentary on it in fact reveals plainly an almost verbatim agreement with Locke's "Law of Opinion": "Whoever judges mores judges honor; and whoever judges honor derives his law from opinion."[34] Yet in contrast to Locke this opinion had the additional task of legislation. Here it was also in need of direction. Just as *opinion* in its function of social control required articulation by the *censeur*, so *opinion* in its legislative function required the *législateur*. Vis-à-vis an *opinion* indeed sovereign but also in danger of being narrow-minded, the latter found himself in a precarious situation. Since he could rely neither on force nor on public discussion (*ni la force ni la résolution*), he had to take refuge in the authority of an indirect influence, "which can compel without violence and persuade without convincing."[35] Rousseau's democracy of unpublic opinion ultimately postulated the manipulative exercise of power. The general will was always right, the notorious passage stated, but the judgment that guided it was not always enlightened. It was therefore necessary to present matters as they were, sometimes as they were to appear.[36] But why did Rousseau not call the sovereign opinion of the people simply *opinion*? Why did he identify it with *opinion publique*? The explanation is simple. A direct democracy required that the sovereign be actually present. The *volonté générale* as the *corpus mysticum* was bound up with the *corpus physicum* of the people as a consensual assembly.[37] The idea of a plebiscite in permanence presented itself to Rousseau in the image of the Greek *polis*. There the people were assembled in the square without interruption; thus, in Rousseau's view, the *place publique* became the foundation of the constitution. *Opinion publique* derived its attribute from it, that is, from the citizens assembled for acclamation and not from the rational-critical public debate of a *public éclairé*.

The physiocrats spoke out in favor of an absolutism complemented by a public sphere that was a place of critical activity; Rousseau wanted democracy without public debate. Both sides lay claim to the same title: *opinion publique*. Hence, the meaning of the latter became particularly polarized in prerevolutionary France. However, the Revolution itself combined the two sundered functions of public opinion, the critical and the legislative.[38] The Constitution of 1791 joined the principle of popular sovereignty with that of the parliamentary constitutional state, which provided a constitutional guarantee for a public sphere as an element in the political realm. The French concept of public opinion was radicalized compared to the British notion. The delegate Bergasse, in a discussion in the National Assembly about the constitutional significance of *opinion publique*, expressed it in the following formula: "You know that it is only through public opinion that you can acquire any power to promote the good; you know that it is only through public opinion that the cause of the people—for so long given up as hopeless—has prevailed; you know that before public opinion all authorities become silent, all prejudices disappear, all particular interests are effaced."[39] During the same period in Great Britain Jeremy Bentham wrote an essay on the needs of the *constituante*[40] which explicated for the first time in monographical form the connection between public opinion and the principle of publicity.

On the one hand "the greater the number of temptations to which the exercise of political power was exposed," the more it needed a permanent control by public opinion; the public character of the parliamentary deliberations ensured a "superintendence of the public," whose critical capacity was treated as an established fact. Its totality (i.e., the public, *le corps publique*) composed a tribunal worth more than all other tribunals taken together. One might pretend to disregard its decrees or might represent them as fluctuating and contradictory opinions that neutralized and destroyed one another; but everyone felt that though this tribunal might err, it was incorruptible, it continually tended to become enlightened, it comprised all the wisdom and all the justice of a nation, it always decided the destiny of public men (*hommes publiques*), and punishments imposed by it were inescapable.[41] Besides, the assembly became capable of profiting from the insights of the public: "Under the guidance of publicity (*sous le régime de la publicité*), nothing is more easy."[42] Yet, of course, public opinion in its turn needed the publicity of parliamentary deliberations to keep itself informed: "Among a people who have been long accustomed to public assemblies, the general feeling (*esprit général*) will be raised to a higher tone—sound opinion will be more common—hurtful prejudices, publicly combated, not by rhetoricians but by statesmen, will have less dominion. . . . A habit of reasoning and discussion will penetrate all classes of society."[43] Bentham conceived of the parliament's public deliberations as nothing but a part of the public deliberations of the public in general. Only publicity inside and outside the parliament could secure the continuity of critical political debate and its function, to transform domination, as Burke expressed it, from a matter of will into a matter of reason. The appointment of delegates was not to be the consequence of a resolve, but was itself to be the intelligent decision of an issue: "In an assembly elected by the people, and renewed from time to time, publicity is absolutely necessary to enable the electors to act from knowledge."[44] Chiefly since the accession of George III the living force of public opinion had prevailed against the dead statutes—"since public opinion, more enlightened, has had a greater ascendancy (*depuis l'opinion publique plus éclairée a pris plus d'ascendent*)

. . . "; in the text of the German translation, the term used still was "opinion of the people" (*Volks-Meinung*).[45] What was best in Britain was brought about through a constant violation of the laws: hence Bentham speaks of the "regime of publicity" as "very imperfect as yet, and newly tolerated" (*le régime de la publicité, très imparfait encore et nouvellement toléré*).

Guizot, younger by about a generation, who from 1820 on held lectures on the origin and history of the constitutional state predicated on civil rights, provided the classic formulation of the "rule of public opinion":

It is, moreover, the character of that system, which nowhere admits the legitimacy of absolute power, to compel the whole body of citizens incessantly, and on every occasion, to seek after reason, justice, and truth, which should ever regulate actual power. The representative system does this, (1) by discussion, which compels existing powers to seek after truth in common; (2) by publicity, which places these powers when occupied in this search, under the eyes of the citizens; and (3) by the liberty of the press, which stimulates the citizens themselves to seek after truth, and to tell it to power.[46]

In the early nineties, Friedrich Georg Forster seems to have given currency to *opinion publique* as "*öffentliche Meinung*" initially in the Western part of Germany; his *Parisische Umrisse*, letters written to his wife toward the close of the year 1793, in any case contain the earliest evidence of this new entity in German literature.[47] Forster's important distinction between public opinion (*öffentliche Meinung*) and common spirit (*Gemeingeist*) shows that the concept of a public sphere as an element in the political realm was completely formed in Britain and France before it was imported into Germany: "Although we have 7,000 authors there nevertheless is no common spirit (*Gemeingeist*) in Germany, just as there is no German public opinion (*öffentliche Meinung*). Even these words are so new to me, and so strange, that everyone asks for explanations and definitions, whereas no Englishman misunderstands the other when there is mention of public spirit, no Frenchman when there is mention of *opinion publique*."[48] Just how right Forster was about the need for a commentary concerning these borrowed words was confirmed by Wieland,[49] who at that time was better known to the wider public as a publicist than as a future "classic." Half a century after Forster's remarks this *öffentliche Meinung* was the subject of one of his *Gespräche unter vier Augen* (Private Conversations).[50] Wieland's definitions added nothing new. *Öffentliche Meinung* made a breakthrough "where imaginary notions and prejudices concerning our immediate good or bad fortune . . . finally give way to the superior power of truth";[51] it ultimately amounted to the same thing as "the most incisive investigation of an issue, after the most exact weighing of all the reasons pro and con"; even in Germany it should soon "have the force of a law."[52] Public opinion originated from those who were informed and spread "chiefly among those classes that, if they are active in large number, are the ones that matter."[53] Of course, the "lowest classes of the people," the *sansculottes*, did not belong to them, because, under the pressure of need and drudgery, they had neither the leisure nor the opportunity "to be concerned with things that do not have an immediate bearing on their physical needs."[54]

To be sure, Rousseauan elements clearly entered into Wieland's reflections as well, elements that at a later time, during the Wars of Liberation, were picked up by political Romanticism in order to identify public opinion with the mute *Volksgeist*.[55] In Wieland's own work, however, a concept of public opinion dominated whose aim, in the somewhat pedantic tradition of the German Enlightenment, was above all to call priestly deception and cabinet secrecy before the forum of critical public debate.[56]

13 Publicity as the Bridging Principle between Politics and Morality (Kant)

Even before "public opinion" became established as a standard phrase in the German-speaking areas, the idea of the bourgeois public sphere attained its theoretically fully developed form with Kant's elaboration of the principle of publicity in his philosophy of right and philosophy of history.

The critical process that private people engaged in rational-critical public debate brought to bear on absolutist rule, interpreted itself as unpolitical: public opinion aimed at rationalizing politics in the name of morality. In the eighteenth century the Aristotelian tradition of a philosophy of politics was reduced in a telling manner to moral philosophy, whereby the "moral" (in any event thought as one with "nature" and "reason") also encompassed the emerging sphere of the "social," its connotations overlapping with those of the word "social" given such peculiar emphasis at the time. It was no coincidence that the author of the *Wealth of Nations* held a Chair of Moral Philosophy. The following statement had its place in this context: "Thus, true politics can never take a step without rendering homage to morality. Though politics by itself is a difficult art, its union with morality is no art at all, for this union cuts the knot which politics could not untie when they were in conflict."[57] Kant wrote this sentence in Appendix I to his essay *Perpetual Peace*. There he repeated two postulates derived in his doctrine of law: the civil constitution of every state should be republican, and the mutual relationships among states should be pacifist, within the framework of a cosmopolitan federation. All the legal obligations that protected the citizens' freedom internally and cosmopolitan peace externally converged in the idea of a perfectly just order. Compulsion could then no longer occur in the form of personal rule or of violent self-assertion but only in such a fashion "that reason alone has force." The juridical relationships, their authority grown absolute, originated in practical reason and were conceived as the possibility of a mutual constraint that, on the basis of general laws, harmonized with the freedom of every single person— the most extreme counterposition to the principle *auctoritas non veritas facit legem*.

At one time Hobbes could sanction the absolute power of the princes with this formula because the establishment of peace, that is, the end of religious civil war, was obviously only to be attained at the price of monopolizing public power in the hands of the monarch and of neutralizing civil society, along with its conflicts of conscience, as a private sphere. In the face of decisions inspired by a wisdom become manifest existentially, so-to-speak, in the person of the sovereign, any reasoning according to rules of morality was demoted to the status of politically inconsequential ethical preference. When it was rehabilitated by Kant two centuries later in the form of the law of practical reason, when even political legislation was asserted to be morally subordinated to its control, those private people had in the meantime formed themselves into a public and had endowed the sphere of its critical use of reason, that is, the public sphere, with the political functions of articulating the state with society. Hence, Kant's publicity held good as the one principle that could guarantee the convergence of politics and morality.[58] He conceived of "the public sphere" at once as the principle of the legal order and as the method of enlightenment.

"Tutelage," as the opening sentence of the famous essay went, "is man's inability to make use of his understanding without direction from another. Self-incurred is this tutelage when its cause lies not in lack of reason but in lack of resolution and courage. . . ."[59] Liberation from self-incurred tutelage meant enlightenment. With regard to the individual, this denoted a subjective maxim, namely: to think for oneself. With regard to humanity as a whole, it denoted an objective tendency, progress toward a perfectly just order. In both cases enlightenment had to be mediated by the public sphere: "For any single individual to work himself out of the life under tutelage which has become almost his nature is very difficult. . . . But that the *public* should enlighten itself is more possible; indeed, if only freedom is granted, enlightenment is almost sure to follow."[60] In regard to enlightenment, therefore, thinking for oneself seemed to coincide with thinking aloud[61] and the use of reason with its public use: "Certainly one may say, 'Freedom to speak or write can be taken from us by a superior power, but never the freedom to think!' But how much, and how correctly, would we think if we did not think as it were in common with others, with whom we mutually communicate!"[62]

Like the Encyclopedists Kant viewed enlightenment, the public use of reason, at first as a matter for scholars, especially those concerned with the principles of pure reason—the philosophers. At issue were (just as in the disputations of the Scholastics and in the famous debates of the Reformers) the doctrines and opinions "that the faculties, as theorists, have to settle with one another . . . ; the people are resigned to understanding nothing about this. . . ."[63] The conflict of the faculties proceeded in the form of a critical debate between the lower and the higher ones. The latter—theology, jurisprudence, and medicine—were based in one way or another on authority. They were also subject to control by the state, since they trained "businessmen of learning": ministers, judges, and doctors. They merely applied science (i.e., know how to make things work, *savoir faire*). In contrast, the lower faculties had to do with knowledge based on pure reason. Their representatives, the philosophers, let themselves be directed by reason alone, independent of the interest of the government. Their spirit "has the public presentation of truth as its function."[64] In such a conflict of the faculties, reason had to be "authorized to speak out publicly. For without a faculty of this kind, the truth would not come to light. . . ."[65] And this would indeed occur, as Kant added, to the government's own detriment.

However, although its center was the academy, the public sphere within which the philosophers pursued their critical craft was not merely academic. Just as the discussion of the philosophers took place in full view of the government, to instruct it and give it things to consider, so too did it occur before the public of the "people," to encourage it in the use of its own reason. The position of this public was ambiguous. Being, on the one hand, under tutelage and still in need of enlightenment, it yet constituted itself, on the other hand, as a public already claiming the maturity of people capable of enlightenment. For in the end anyone who understood how to use his reason in public qualified for it, and by no means only philosophers. The conflict of the faculties was only the center of the fire from which the flames of enlightenment spread, and where it found ever new nourishment. The public sphere was realized not in the republic of scholars alone but in the public use of reason by all who were adept at it. Of course, they had to emerge from the confines of their private spheres as if they were scholars:

By the public use of one's reason, I understand the use which a person makes of it as a scholar before the reading public. Private use I call that which one may make of it in a particular civil post or office which is entrusted to him. . . . Here argument is certainly not allowed—one must obey. But so far as a part of the mechanism regards himself at the same time as a member of the whole community or of a society of world citizens, and thus in the role of a scholar who addresses the public (in the proper sense of the word) through his writings, he certainly can argue. . . .[66]

From this followed the postulate of publicity as a principle: "The public use of one's reason must always be free, and it alone can bring about enlightenment among men. The private use of reason, on the other hand, may often be very narrowly restricted without particularly hindering the progress of enlightenment."[67] Each person was called to be a "publicist," a scholar "whose writings speak to his public, the world."[68]

The "world" in which the public was constituted designated the realm of the public sphere. Kant spoke of knowledge of the world (*Weltkenntnis*); he referred to the man of the world (*Mann von Welt*). This sense of cosmopolitanism (*Weltläufigkeit*) was articulated, in the concept of world citizenship and ultimately in the concept of world progress (*Weltbeste*), as the idea of a world emerging perhaps most clearly in the "cosmical concept" (*Weltbegriff*) of science—for in all its purity world was constituted in the communication of rational beings. Whereas the scholastic concept of science referred only to "disciplines designed in view of certain optionally chosen ends," the cosmical concept of science was one "which relates to that in which everyone necessarily has an interest."[69] This was not world in the transcendental sense, as the quintessential concept of all phenomena, as the totality of their synthesis and to that extent identical with "nature." Rather, "world" here pointed to humanity as species, but in that guise in which its unity presented itself in appearance: the world of a critically debating reading public that at the time was just evolving within the broader bourgeois strata. It was the world of the men of letters but also that of the *salons* in which "mixed companies" engaged in critical discussions; here, in the bourgeois homes, the public sphere was established. "If we attend to the course of conversation in mixed companies consisting not merely of scholars and subtle reasoners but also of business people or women, we notice that besides storytelling and jesting they have another entertainment, namely, arguing."[70]

The public of "human beings" engaged in rational-critical

debate was constituted into one of "citizens" wherever there was communication concerning the affairs of the "commonwealth." Under the "republican constitution" this public sphere in the political realm became the organizational principle of the liberal constitutional state. Within its framework, civil society was established as the sphere of private autonomy (everyone was to be permitted to pursue his "happiness" in any way he thought useful). The citizen's liberties were safeguarded by general laws; corresponding to the freedom of the "human being" was the equality of citizens before the law (the elimination of all "rights by birth"). Legislation itself was traced back to the "popular will that has its source in reason"; for laws empirically had their origin in the "public agreement" of the public engaged in critical debate. This was why Kant also called them "public" laws in contradistinction to the "private" ones that, like custom and mores, tacitly claimed to be obligatory.[71] "But a public law which defines for everyone that which is permitted and prohibited by right, is the act of a public will, from which all right proceeds and which must not therefore itself be able to do an injustice to anyone. And this requires no less than the will of the entire people (since all men decide for all men and each decides for himself)."[72] This line of argument entirely followed Rousseau's with the decisive exception of one point: the principle of popular sovereignty[73] could be realized only under the precondition of a public use of reason. "In every commonwealth, there must . . . be a *spirit of freedom*, for in all matters concerning universal human duties, each individual requires to be convinced by reason that the coercion which prevails is lawful, otherwise he would be in contradiction with himself." The restriction of the public sphere, Kant argued with a view to the then hotly disputed lodges of the Freemasons, was "the effective cause of all *secret societies*. For it was a natural vocation of man to communicate with his fellows, especially in matters affecting mankind as a whole."[74] The famous statement about the freedom of the pen being "the only safeguard of the rights of the people" was made in this connection.

Already in the *Critique of Pure Reason* Kant had ascribed the function of a pragmatic test of truth to the public consensus arrived at by those engaged in rational-critical debate with one another: "The touchstone whereby we decide whether our holding a thing to be true is conviction or mere persuasion is therefore external, namely the possibility of communicating it and of finding it to be valid for all human reason."[75] This agreement of all empirical consciousnesses, brought about in the public sphere, corresponded to the intelligible unity of transcendental consciousness. Later on, in the philosophy of right, this "agreement of all judgments with each other, notwithstanding the differing characters of individuals," vouched for by publicity (which in Kant only lacked the name of "public opinion"), obtained a constitutive significance beyond its pragmatic value. Political actions, that is, those referring to the rights of others, were themselves declared to be in agreement with law and morality only as far as their maxims were capable of, or indeed in need of, publicity.[76] Before the public it had to be possible to trace all political actions back to the foundation of the laws, which in turn had been validated before public opinion as being universal and rational laws. In the framework of a comprehensively norm-governed state of affairs (uniting civil constitution and eternal peace to form a "perfectly just order") domination as a law of nature was replaced by the rule of legal norms—politics could in principle be transformed into morality.

But how could the congruence of politics with morality be ensured as long as this juridical condition (*Rechtszustand*) had not yet come into existence? To bring it about, the will of all individuals (that is, the distributive sameness of all wills) to live within the framework of a constitution that had the force of law according to the principles of freedom was by no means sufficient; rather, a collective oneness of the combined will would be required. Everyone would have to will this state of affairs in unison. Consequently, Kant did not believe that he should expect any other beginning of a juridical condition (*rechtlicher Zustand*) than one achieved by political force. The indirect assumption of power by private individuals assembled to constitute a public, however, was not seen as itself political;[77] the moral self-interpretation of the bourgeois public sphere imposed even on the very efforts to give it a political function to begin with an abstinence from the methods of precisely that political coercion from which publicity promised liberation. Kant resolved this dilemma through a philosophy of history according to which, even without the active efforts of inwardly free individuals, outwardly free conditions would come about under which politics could be permanently merged in morality. Kant's construction of a progress of the human race and its social condition is familiar. This progress was postulated to result from nothing but the constraints of nature, without having to take into account the efforts that the laws of freedom obligated men to undertake themselves. Naturally, this progress did not consist in an ever growing quantity of morality but exclusively in an increase of the products of legality.[78]

If nature employed the "antagonism within society," that is, both the struggles within and the wars between nations, as the means of bringing about the development of all the innate endowments of humanity in a "civil society which can administer justice universally," then this "perfectly just civil constitution" could itself necessarily be no more than a "pathologically enforced social union" representing a "moral whole" in appearance only.[79] Therewith a problem found its practical resolution, which Kant poses theoretically in the following form: "Given a multitude of rational beings requiring universal laws for their preservation, but each of whom is secretly inclined to exempt himself from them, to establish a constitution in such a way that, although their *private* intentions conflict, they check each other, with the result that their *public* conduct is the same as if they had no such intentions."[80] This was a variation of Mandeville's formula, "private vices, public benefits."

And it was precisely on the basis of this principle that Kant developed the specific sociological conditions for a public sphere as an element in the political realm. These depended altogether on social relationships among freely competing commodity owners, falling within the sphere that was the preserve of their private autonomy.

Only *property-owning private people* were admitted to a public engaged in critical political debate, for their autonomy was rooted in the sphere of commodity exchange and hence was joined to the interest in its preservation as a private sphere:

The only qualification required by a citizen (apart, of course, from being an adult male) is that he must be his *own master* (*sui iuris*), and must have some *property* (which can include any skill, trade, fine art, or science) to support himself. In cases where he must earn his living from others, he must earn it only by *selling* that which is his, and not by allowing others to make use of him; for he must in the true sense of the word *serve* no one but the commonwealth. In this respect, artisans (*Kunstverwandte*) and large or small landowners are all equal. . . .[81]

Kant, who noticed how unsatisfactory this distinction was— ". . . I do admit that it is somewhat difficult to define the qualifications which entitle anyone to claim the status of being his own master"—still accomplished a very apt differentiation from what later was to be called free wage labor.[82] While the wage laborers were forced to exchange their labor power as their sole commodity, the property-owning private people related to each other as owners of commodities through an exchange of goods. Only the latter were their own masters; only they should be enfranchised to vote—admitted to the public use of reason in the exemplary sense.

This restriction, in turn, was compatible with the principle of publicity only if, in virtue of the effective mechanism of free competition, equal chances for the acquisition of property existed within the private sphere.[83] Thus free commodity exchange may indeed

over a series of generations create considerable inequalities in wealth among the members of the commonwealth (the employee and the employer, the landowner and the agricultural servants, etc.). But he may not prevent his subordinates from raising themselves to his own level if they are able and entitled to do so by their talent, industry and good fortune. If this were not so, he would be allowed to practice coercion without himself being subject to coercive counter-measures. . . . He [any man] can be considered happy in any condition so long as he is aware that, if he does not reach the same level as others, the fault lies either with himself (i.e., lack of ability or serious endeavour) or with circumstances for which he cannot blame others, and not with the irresistible will of any outside party. For as far as right is concerned, his fellow-subjects have no advantage over him.[84]

Consequently the propertyless were excluded from the public of private people engaged in critical political debate without thereby violating the principle of publicity. In this sense they were not citizens at all, but persons who with talent, industry, and luck some day might be able to attain that status; until then they merely had the same claim to protection under the law as the others, without being allowed to participate in legislation themselves.

Kant shared the confidence of the liberals that with the privatization of civil society such social preconditions as the natural basis of the juridical condition (*Rechtszustand*) and a public capable of functioning politically would come about by themselves and indeed might already be near actualization; because a social constitution of this kind, as *ordre naturel*, seemed to loom so clearly on the horizon, it was not difficult for Kant to suppose, within the framework of his philosophy of history, that precisely *the* juridical condition would emerge out of natural necessity that allowed him to turn politics into a question of morality. The fiction of a justice immanent in free commerce was what rendered plausible the conflation of *bourgeois* and *homme*, of self-interested, property-owning private people and autonomous individuals per se. The specific relationship between private and public sphere, from which arose the duplication of the selfish *bourgeois* in the guise of the unselfish *homme*, of the empirical subject in that of the intelligible one, was what made it possible to consider the *citoyen*, the citizen eligible to vote, under the twofold aspect of legality and morality. In his "pathologically enforced" conduct he could at the same time appear as a morally free person as long as the concordance of the political public sphere with its self-interpretation (derived from the literary public sphere) was ensured by the intent of nature, that is to say, on the basis of a society of freely competing property-owning private people emancipated from domination and insulated from intrusions of power. This had to occur in such a way that these interested private people, assembled to constitute a public, in their capacity as citizens, behaved outwardly as if they were inwardly free persons. Under the social conditions that translated private vices into public virtues, a state of cosmopolitan citizenship and hence the subsumption of politics under morality was empirically conceivable. As *res publica phaenomenon* it could actualize the *res publica noumenon*. It could, in the same world of experience, unite two heterogeneous legislations without one being likely to encroach upon the other: the legislations of private people propelled by their drives as owners of commodities and simultaneously that of spiritually free human beings. Indeed, for the world in general as for the social realm the relationship of the phenomenal to the noumenal assumed the following form (according to the resolution of the third antinomy of pure reason): with regard to its intelligible cause every effect was to be thought of as free yet, at the same time, as necessary with regard to its empirical occurrence; it was to be thought of, that is, as a link in the continuous causal connectedness of all events in the empirical world.[85]

Of course, in his political philosophy Kant could not consistently maintain this distinction, which from a systematic point of view was central, for he could not seriously make laws of practical reason dependent on empirical conditions. However, in so far as the natural basis of the juridical condition as such was problematic, the establishment of such a situation—which to this point had been treated as *precondition* for a moral politics—was itself to be made the content and task of politics. A new function would thereby also accrue to the public sphere which was to keep politics in harmony with the laws of morality—a function which it would ultimately be impossible to accommodate within the Kantian system.

Whoever those political agents might be—the prince, a party, an appointed leader, or the individual citizen—if they could not be guided by existing laws but intended to bring about a juridical condition (*rechtlicher Zustand*) to begin with, it did not suffice for them to be satisfied with a merely negative agreement with whatever might be the arbitrary will (*Willkür*) of all others. Rather, they had to try to exercise a positive influence upon it. This might and as a rule did happen through force. Influence upon the arbitrary will of others, however, if it proceeded morally, demanded to be oriented toward the universal end of the public, toward the need for the welfare of civil society a a whole. Within the domain of this sort of politics the moral intent of an action consequently was to be checked as to its possible success in the empirical world. Political virtue was not to be indifferent to happiness. All political maxims, to be in accord with law and politics combined, therefore required publicity; this was so because "they must accord with the public's universal end, happiness." It was the proper task of politics "to make the public satisfied with its condition."[86] Earlier on in the same essay, however, Kant had put it this way: "[P]olitical maxims must not be derived from the welfare or happiness which a single state expects from obedience to them, and thus not from the end which one of them proposes for itself . . . , as the supreme . . . principle of political wisdom, but rather from the pure concept of the duty of right, . . . regardless of what the physical consequences may be."[87]

Given the presupposition of his philosophy of history, that is, of an already existing natural basis for a juridical condition, Kant could (and indeed had to) separate the welfare of the state from the welfare of its citizens and morality from legality. But he did not consistently rely on this presupposition: the ambivalence in his philosophy of history shows this. Besides the many statements that were in harmony with his system by exempting morality from progress, limiting the latter to an increase in the products of legality, one also finds the contradictory admission "that, since the human race is constantly progressing in cultural matters (in keeping with its natural purpose), it is also engaged in progressive improvement in relation to the moral end of its existence."[88] And in the same context Kant wrote: "Besides, various evidence suggests that in our age, as compared with all previous ages, the human race has made considerable moral progress."[89] If a juridical condition itself needed first to be brought about politically, and indeed by means of a politics kept in agreement with morality, progress in legality was directly dependent upon a progress in morality, and the *res publica phaenomenon* became a product of the *res publica noumenon* itself: ". . . gradually develop all talents, and taste is refined; through continued enlightenment the beginnings are laid for a way of thought which can in time convert the coarse, natural disposition for moral discrimination into definite practical principles, and thereby *change* a society of men driven together by their natural feelings *into a moral whole*.[90]

The relationship of *res publica phaenomenon* and *res publica noumenon* was no longer compatible with the theoretically established relationship of essence and appearance: "The Idea," wrote Kant in the dispute between the philosophical faculty and the faculty of law,

of a constitution in harmony with the natural right of man, one namely in which the citizens obedient to the law, besides being united, ought also to be legislative, lies at the basis of all political forms; and the body politic which, conceived in conformity to it by virtue of pure concepts of reason, signifies a *Platonic Ideal* (*res publica noumenon*), is not an empty chimera, but rather the eternal norm for all civil organization in general, and averts all war.[91]

At this point one must remember the Kantian use of "ideal," which referred to an idea in *individuo*, namely an individual thing that through the idea alone was determinable or even determined.[92] It was, Kant wrote, even further removed from reality than the idea; to either, only a regulative function could be ascribed. Just as the idea supplied the rule, so the ideal served as the archetype for the determination of the copy, always only a "standard for our actions" and entirely different from the idea to which, as to an idea of the divine intellect, Plato erroneously imputed constitutive significance. It is all the more astounding that in the context of the passage discussed here the *res publica noumenon* was called precisely a *Platonic* ideal. This was no mere verbal lapse, for in the subsequent passage we read: "A civil society organized conformably to this ideal is the representation of it in agreement with the laws of freedom by means of an example in our experience (*res publica phaenomenon*) and can only be painfully acquired after multifarious hostilities and wars; but its constitution, once won on a large scale, is qualified as the best among all. . . ." Similar in meaning, the preceding sentence had already closed in the indicative: "and averts all war." Yet when he defined the ideal as such, Kant stated:

But to attempt to realize the ideal in an example, ... as, for instance, . . . the wise man in a romance, is impracticable. There is indeed something absurd, and far from edifying, in such an attempt, inasmuch as the natural limitations, which are constantly doing violence to the completeness of the idea, make the illusion that is aimed at altogether impossible, and so cast suspicion on the good itself—the good that has its source in the idea—by giving it the air of being a mere fiction.[93]

In Kant's political philosophy *two* versions can be clearly distinguished. The official one relied on the construction of a cosmopolitan order emerging from natural necessity alone; on the basis of this presupposition the theory of right could then derive the political actions in the mode of moral action. In a state of affairs that already had the attributes of a juridical condition (that is, by that kind of external condition under which human beings could really get their right), moral politics amounted to nothing more than legal conduct out of duty under positive laws. The rule of law was guaranteed by publicity, namely, by a public sphere whose ability to function was posited by implication together with the posited natural basis of the juridical condition.

The other version of the philosophy of history, the unofficial one, proceeded from the notion that politics had first to push for the actualization of a juridical condition. It employed, therefore, the construct of a cosmopolitan order that issued from *both* natural necessity *and* moral politics. Politics could not be conceived of exclusively as moral, that is, as action in conformity with one's duty under existing positive laws; rather, making them positive, which was the proper goal of its action, needed to take into account a will collectively in agreement on the univeral end of the public, namely: its welfare. This again was supposed to be guaranteed through publicity. But in this case the public sphere was supposed to link politics and morality in a specific sense: it was the place where an intelligible unity of the empirical ends of everyone was to be brought about, where legality was to issue from morality.

For this purpose, the philosophy of history took on the task of giving guidance to the public, for in this philosophy (as the propaedeutic of a cosmopolitan condition) the laws of reason were congruent with the requirements of welfare. It was itself to become public opinion. In this fashion we come upon the remarkable self-implication of the philosophy of history; it took into account the effect of a theory of history on the course of this history itself: "A philosophical attempt to work out a universal history according to a natural plan directed to achieving the civic union of the human race must be regarded as possible and, indeed, as contributing to this end of nature."[94] With enlightenment progressing, "a certain commitment of heart which the enlightened man cannot fail to make to the good he clearly understands, must step by step ascend the throne. . . ."[95] Thus, by virtue of the fact that its insights entered into the public's processes of critical reflection, the philosophy of history itself was to become a part of the enlightenment diagnosed as history's course. Consequently, in the context of his "prophetic history of humanity," Kant devoted a special paragraph to the difficulties "of the maxims applying to world progress (*Weltbeste*) with regard to their publicity."[96] For the public instruction of the nation persons were to be appointed who freely taught what was right, precisely the philosophers who under the name of enlighteners had been decried as persons dangerous to the state. World progress, however, was in need of their unhindered activity in public—"thus the prohibition of publicity impedes the progress of a people toward improvement."[97]

The system-exploding consequences of a philosophy of history that implied its own political intent and effect come to the fore precisely in connection with the category of publicity. It laid claim to such publicity, for reason in its historical process of becoming actual required a union of empirical consciousnesses as a corollary to the intelligible unity of consciousness as such. Publicity was to be the vehicle through which the latter was linked to the former; its universality was that of an empirical consciousness in general, and Hegel's philosophy of right would bestow its name: public opinion.

The public sphere fit easily into the categories of the Kantian system only as long as the division between the empirical and the intelligible subject, between the phenomenal and the noumenal realm in general (initially also upheld in the political philosophy), could count on the social conditions of the liberal model of the public sphere, on the classic relationship of *bourgeois-homme-citoyen*, which is to say on civil society as the *ordre naturel* converting private vices into public virtues. A series of fictions in which the self-understanding of the bourgeois consciousness as "public opinion" was articulated extended right into the Kantian system, and therefore it was possible to derive from it in turn the idea of the bourgeois public sphere precisely in its connection with the presupposition of a natural basis of the juridical condition. It was no accident that the concept of public sphere, as soon as this connection became questionable, turned against the foundations of the system itself. Already Hegel explicitly doubted that civil society could ever function as this kind of natural order. Although it was the natural basis of the juridical condition, the privatized sphere of commodity exchange and of social labor threatened to break apart on account of its immanent conflicts. Under such conditions, however, even the public sphere no longer sufficed as a principle for the linking of politics and morality—in Hegel's concept of opinion the idea of the public of civil society was already denounced as ideology.

14 On the Dialectic of the Public Sphere (Hegel and Marx)

In the public of private people engaged in rational-critical debate, there came about what in Kant was called "public agreement" (*das öffentliche Zusammenstimmen*) and in Hegel "public opinion." It brought into existence "an empirical universal, of which the thoughts and opinions of the Many are particulars."[98] At first sight, Hegel's definitions of this entity seem to differ from Kant's only by nuances: "The formal subjective freedom of individuals consists in their having and expressing their own private judgments, opinions, and recommendations on affairs of state. This freedom is collectively manifested as what is called 'public opinion'...."[99] In a comment on this paragraph, he defined the function of the public sphere in accord with the eighteenth-century model: the subjection of domination to reason. "What is to be authoritative nowadays derives its authority, not at all from force, only to a small extent from habit and custom, really from insight and argument;" and a little later: "The principle of the modern world requires that what anyone is to recognize shall reveal itself to him as something entitled to recognition."[100] And just as Kant made the public nature of critical debate the touchstone of truth that put everything proclaimed as true to the test of whether its validity could be upheld before any rational human being, so Hegel too expected much from public opinion: ". . . that a man's castle-building at his fireside with his wife and his friends is one thing, while what happens in a great assembly, where one shrewd idea devours another, is something quite different."[101] On the other hand, public opinion was also beset by the contingency of merely formal universality whose substance lay in something external to it: it was knowledge merely as appearance. To the degree that the public use of reason was an affair of the scholars—Kant's *Streit der Fakultäten* (Conflict of the Faculties)—knowledge went beyond its mere appearance; hence for Hegel science fell outside the domain of public opinion: "The sciences, however, are not to be found anywhere in the field of opinions and subjective views, provided, of course that they be sciences in other respects. Their exposition is not a matter of clever turns of phrase, allusiveness, half-utterances and semi-reticences, but consists in the unambiguous, determinate, and open expression of their meaning and purport. It follows that they do not fall under the category of public opinion."[102]

This demotion of public opinion was a necessary consequence of Hegel's concept of civil society. Admittedly, at one point he praised its laws, referring to the political economy of Smith, Say, and Ricardo as the manifestation of rationality; but his insight into the at once anarchic and antagonistic character of this system of needs decisively destroyed the liberal pretenses upon which the self-interpretation of public opinion as nothing but plain reason rested. For Hegel discovered the profound split in civil society which "is so far from anulling this natural inequality that it . . . raises it to an inequality of skill and resources, and even to one of moral and intellectual attainment."[103] For

the amassing of wealth is intensified by generalizing (a) the linkage of men by their needs, and (b) the methods of preparing and distributing the means to satisfy these needs. This is one side of the picture. The other side is the subdivision and restriction of particular jobs. This results in the dependence and distress of the class tied to work of that sort. . . . It hence becomes apparent that despite an excess of wealth civil society is not rich enough, i.e., its own resources are insufficient to check excessive poverty and the creation of a penurious rabble.[104]

Admittedly, the proletariat was defined merely negatively in relation to the strata of bourgeois society, namely: as a category of poverty relief. But the sketched theory of underconsumption (including the consequences of an anticipated imperialism, cf. *Philosophy of Right*, Section 246) diagnosed a conflict of interests that discredited the common and allegedly universal interest of property-owning private people engaged in political debate by demonstrating its plainly particularist nature. The public opinion of the private people assembled to form a public no longer retained a basis of unity and truth; it degenerated to the level of a subjective opining of the many.

The ambivalent status of public opinion followed necessarily from the "disorganization of civil society." For how could one imagine a state that, in Hegel's expression, was "confused" with civil society, that is, "whose specific end is laid down as the security and protection of property and personal freedom?"[105] To be sure, the bourgeois constitutional state with whose aid private people were supposed to transform domination into reason according to the guiding light of their public opinion did exhibit a tendency to become, as it were, absorbed into civil society and "confused" with it. However, wherever those whose status was that of private people as such rose "to the level of participating in matters of state,"[106] the disorganization of civil society necessarily infiltrated the state. If the antagonistic system of needs was torn asunder by particularist interests, a public sphere of private people as an element in the political realm would lead to "an unorganized opinion and volition . . . and into a powerful *bloc* in opposition to the organized state."[107] In order to prevent this, precautionary measures by both police and corporate bonds had to be used to counteract such threatening disorganization. The interest in freedom of trade and commerce, "the more blindly it sinks into self-seeking aims, the more it requires such control to bring it back to the universal.

Control is also necessary to diminish the danger of upheavals arising from clashing interests and to abbreviate the period in which their tensions should be eased through the working of a necessity of which they themselves know nothing."[108] With this concept of a society that was corporatively reintegrated Hegel has definitely left liberalism behind. Accordingly, the concept of the public sphere complementing a private sphere restricted to this extent could no longer be the liberal, either.

Public opinion had the form of common sense. It was dispersed through a people in the form of prejudices, but even in this turbidity it reflected "the genuine needs and correct tendencies of common life. . . ."[109] It attained consciousness of itself—in the assembly of estates, where the occupational status organizations of civil society participated in legislation. "The publicity of Estates Assemblies,"[110] however, did not for this reason serve to link parliamentary discussions with the critical political debate of a public that criticized and checked government power. It was rather the principle of integrating the citizens into the state from above; for

the opening of this opportunity to know has a more universal aspect, because by this means public opinion first reaches thoughts that are true and attains insight into the situation and concept of the state and its affairs, and so first acquires ability to estimate these more rationally. By this means also, it becomes acquainted with and learns to respect the work, abilities, virtues, and dexterity of ministers and officials. While such publicity provides these abilities with a potent means of development and a theater of higher distinction, it is at the same time another antidote to the self-conceit of individuals singly and *en masse*, and another means—indeed one of the chief means— of their education.[111]

The public sphere thus demoted to a "means of education" counted no longer as a principle of enlightenment and as a sphere in which reason realized itself. The public sphere served only to integrate subjective opinions into the objectivity assumed by the spirit in the form of the state. Hegel held fast to the idea of the realization of reason in a "perfectly just order" in which justice and happiness coincided. Critical political debate by the public—public opinion—however, was disqualified as a warrant of this agreement; the state as the actuality of the ethical idea assumed its guarantee per se, through its mere existence:

Public opinion therefore deserves to be as much respected as despised—despised for its concrete expression and for the concrete consciousness it expresses, respected for its essential basis, a basis which only glimmers more or less dimly in that concrete expression. But, in itself it has no criterion of discrimination, nor has it the ability to extract the substantive element it contains and raise it to precise knowledge. Thus to be independent of public opinion is the first formal condition of achieving anything great or rational whether in life or in science.[112]

Opinion publique was relegated to the sphere of *opinion*; hence the reason that was realized in the existing state in its turn retained the very element of impenetrability characterizing personal domination that in Kant's view was to be penetrated and dissolved in the medium of publicity. Hegel summarized his analysis of public opinion in the statement: "Subjectivity is manifested in its most external form as the undermining of the established life of the state by opinion and ratiocination when they endeavour to assert the authority of their own fortuitous character and so bring about their own destruction. But its true actuality is attained in the opposite of this, i.e., in the subjectivity identical with the substantive will of the state, the subjectivity of which constitutes the concept of the power of the crown. . . ."[113] Within the state, subjective freedom attained to its right, as if by a play on words, in the subject of the monarch. The latter, of course, did not at all execute the right of the public in which alone, according to Kant, the unification of the ends of all was possible. The power of the crown instead had its foundation directly in that ethical world out of which the subjects first had to labor to raise themselves to attain the right to their subjectivity. For the monarch came to know "that a people does not allow itself to be deceived about its substantive basis, the essence and specific character of its mind. On the other hand, it is self-deceived about the manner of its knowledge of these things and about its corresponding judgment of its actions, experiences, etc."[114] Domination found its limit solely in a nation's mind that was one with the quasi-natural (*naturwüchsig*) order of substantive morality; the realm of enlightenment, in contrast, in which the mind of the nation was aware of itself as public opinion, had no power to obligate. In general, Hegel rejected the problem of the congruence of politics and morality as a false question. Against the idea of making domination rational via the public sphere, Hegel posited a world-historical existentialism of national minds:

At one time the opposition between morals and politics, and the demand that the latter should conform to the former, were much canvassed. On this point only a general remark is required here. The welfare of a state has claims to recognition totally different from those of the welfare of the individual. The ethical substance, the state, has its determinate being, i.e., its right, directly embodied in something existent, something not abstract but concrete, and the principle of its conduct and behavior can only be this concrete existent and not one of the many universal thoughts supposed to be moral commands. When politics is alleged to clash with morals and so to be always wrong, the doctrine propounded rests on superficial ideas about morality, the nature of the state, and the state's relation to the moral point of view.[115]

Hegel took the teeth out of the idea of the public sphere of civil society; for anarchic and antagonistic civil society did not constitute the sphere, emancipated from domination and insulated from the interference of power, in which autonomous private people related to one another. Thus it did not provide the basis on which a public of private people could translate political into rational authority. Even civil society could not dispense with domination; indeed, to the extent to which it naturally tended toward disorganization, it had a special need for integration by political force. Hegel's construction of a state organized on the basis of estates reacted to contradictions which he certainly had already noticed in the reality of the constitutional state predicated on civil rights in its British and French versions; only he had not wanted to accept this reality as constituting that of advanced civil society.[116]

The young Marx saw through this. He knew that the "political" estates of prerevolutionary society had dissolved into merely "social" classes in civil society. To ascribe to them nevertheless the political function of linking state and society amounted to the impotent attempt of turning back the clock, an attempt "within the political sphere itself to plunge man back into the limitations of his private sphere."[117] The resuscitation of an estate-based constitution such as the Prussian one glorified by Hegel attempted to rescind, by means of a "reminiscence," the factually completed separation of state and society. Marx realized that a "republic," precisely the form of the constitutional state predicated on civil rights, had to emerge wherever "the private spheres have achieved an independent existence."[118] Up until that point, society

had a *directly political* character; that is, the elements of civil life such as property, the family, and types of occupation had been raised, in the form of lordship, caste, and guilds, to elements of political life. They determined, in this form, the relation of the individual to the *state as a whole*; that is, his *political* situation, or in other words, his separation and exclusion from the other elements of society. . . . The political revolution . . . which made . . . the political state a matter of *general* concern, i.e., a real state, necessarily shattered everything— estates, corporations, guilds, privileges. . . . The political revolution therefore *abolished* the *political character of civil society.* It dissolved civil society into its basic elements, on the one hand *individuals,* and on the other hand the *material and cultural elements* which formed the life experience and the civil situation of these individuals. It set free the political spirit which had, so to speak, been dissolved, fragmented and lost in the various culs-de-sac of feudal society; it reassembled these scattered fragments, liberated the political spirit from its connection with civil life and made of it the community sphere, the *general* concern of the people, in principle independent from these particular elements of civil life.[119]

As the last statement reveals, Marx treated the political public sphere ironically—the "independence in principle" of a public opinion of property-owning private people engaged in rational-critical debate who viewed themselves as nothing but autonomous human beings. But in order to grasp the ideological aspect of this, he took the idea of the bourgeois public sphere as seriously as was required by the self-image of the politically advanced conditions in Great Britain and France. Marx criticized the constitution based on neo-estates as propounded in the Hegelian philosophy of state, using the criterion of the bourgeois constitutional state only to unmask the "republic" before its own idea as the existing contradiction and, holding fast to the idea of the bourgeois public sphere, to confront it as in a mirror with the social conditions for the possibility of its utterly unbourgeois realization.

Marx denounced public opinion as false consciousness: it hid before itself its own true character as a mask of bourgeois class interests. His critique of political economy was indeed aimed at the presuppositions upon which the self-interpretation of the public sphere in the political realm rested. According to this critique the capitalist system, if left to itself, could not without crises reproduce itself as a "natural order." Furthermore, the process of capital valorization was based on the appropriation of the surplus value from the surplus labor of those commodity owners who possessed their own labor power as their sole commodity—instead of a middle class society of small commodity producers. Consequently a class society came into being in which the chances of upward social mobility from wage earner to owner became smaller and smaller. Finally, in the course of the accumulation of capital, the markets became deformed into oligopolies, so that one could no longer count on an independent formation of prices—the emancipation of civil society from authoritarian state regulation did not lead to the insulation of the transactions between private people from the intrusion of power. Instead, new relationships of power, especially between owners and wage earners, were created within the forms of civil freedom of contract.

This critique demolished all fictions to which the idea of the public sphere of civil society appealed. In the first place, the social preconditions for the equality of opportunity were obviously lacking, namely: that any person with skill and "luck" could attain the status of property owner and thus the qualifications of a private person granted access to the public sphere, property and education. The public sphere with which Marx saw himself confronted contradicted its own principle of universal accessibility—the public could no longer claim to be identical with the nation, civil society with all of society. Similarly, the equation of "property owners" with "human beings" was untenable; for their interest in maintaining the sphere of commodity exchange and of social labor as a private sphere was demoted, by virtue of being opposed to the class of wage earners, to the status of a particular interest that could only prevail by the exercise of power over others. From this viewpoint, control over private property could not without further circumstance be transposed into the freedom of autonomous human beings. Private civil autonomy led "every man to see in other men, not the *realization*, but rather the *limitation* of his own liberty";[120] and the rights that guaranteed this "egoism" were "rights of man" in the sense of the abstract human being who in the pursuit of his private interests never left behind the unfreedom of the property owner, of an agent in the process of capital valorization, who hence never developed into that "actual and authentic" human being in whose capacity the *bourgeois* wanted to assume the functions of a *citoyen*. To the separation of state and society corresponded "the division of man into the *public person* and the *private person*."[121] But as *bourgeois* the private person was so far from being an *homme* in general that, to actually be able to engage in his interests as a citizen, he had to "abandon his civil reality, abstract from it and withdraw from the whole organization into his individuality."[122] The view on which the private people, assembled to form a public, reached agreement through discourse and counter-discourse must not therefore be confused with what was right and just: even the third and central identification of public opinion with reason became untenable. As long as power relationships were not effectively neutralized in the reproduction of social life and as long as civil society itself still rested on force, no juridical condition which replaced political authority with rational authority could be erected on its basis. Consequently, the dissolution of feudal relations of domination in the medium of the public engaged in rational-critical debate did not amount to the purported dissolution of political domination in general but only to its perpetuation in different guise. The bourgeois constitutional state, along with the public sphere as the central principle of its organization, was mere ideology. The separation of the private from the public realm obstructed at this stage of capitalism what the idea of the bourgeois public sphere promised.

The struggle for the realization of the bourgeois constitutional state was objectified in the conflict over electoral reforms, which at the start of the thirties had resulted in a certain extension of equal voting rights in Great Britain and France. But Marx characteristically saw here already a process that pushed beyond the constitutionalization of the bourgeois public sphere: "Hence if civil society forces its way into the *legislature en masse,* or even *in toto,* the real civil society wishes to substitute itself for the fictitious civil society of the legislature, then all that is nothing but the striving of civil society to create a *political* existence for itself."[123] Before 1848 the young Marx gave a radical-democratic interpretation to the tendency toward the expansion of the franchise; he anticipated a shift in the function of the bourgeois public sphere which, after the June uprising of the Paris workers, he would diagnose far more clearly:

The parliamentary regime lives by discussion; how shall it forbid discussion? Every interest, every social institution, is here transformed into general ideas, debated as ideas; how shall any interest, any institution, sustain itself above thought and impose itself as an article of faith? The struggle of the orators on the platform evokes the struggle of the scribblers of the press; the debating club in the parliament is necessarily supplemented by debating clubs in the salons and the pothouses; the representatives, who constantly appeal to public opinion, give public opinion the right to speak its real mind in petitions. The parliamentary regime leaves everything to the decision of majorities; how shall the great majorities outside parliament not want to decide? When you play the fiddle at the top of the state, what else is to be expected but that those down below dance?[124]

Ten years earlier Marx had his eye on the perspective of this development: to the extent that non-bourgeois strata penetrated the public sphere in the political realm and took possession of its institutions, participated in press, parties, and parliament, the weapons of publicity forged by the bourgeoisie were pointed against it itself. Marx's idea was that along this path society itself would take on a political form; inside the established public sphere electoral reforms already seemed to indicate the tendency toward its dissolution: "By really establishing its *political* existence as its authentic existence, civil society ensures that its civil existence, in so far as it is distinct from its political existence, is *inessential.* And with the demise of the one, the other, its opposite, collapses also. Therefore, *electoral reform* in the *abstract political state* is equivalent to a demand for its *dissolution* and this in turn implies the *dissolution of civil society.*"[125]

The bourgeois public sphere arose historically in conjunction with a society separated from the state. The "social" could be constituted as its own sphere to the degree that on the one hand the reproduction of life took on private forms, while on the other hand the private realm as a whole assumed public relevance. The general rules that governed interaction among private people now became a public concern. In the conflict over this concern, in which the private people soon enough became engaged with the public authority, the bourgeois public sphere attained its political function. The private people, gathered to constitute a public, turned the political sanctioning of society as a private sphere into a public topic. Yet by about the middle of the nineteenth century it was possible to foresee how, as a consequence of its inherent dialectic, this public sphere would come under the control of groups that, because they lacked control over property and therefore a basis of private autonomy, could have no interest in maintaining society as a private sphere. When *they*, as an enlarged public, came to the fore as the subject of the public sphere in place of the bourgeoisie, the structure of this sphere would have to be transformed from the ground up. As soon as the mass of non-owners made the general rules governing transactions in society into a topic of *their* critical public debate, the reproduction of social life as such (and no longer just its form of private appropriation) became a universal concern. The democratically revolutionized public sphere "that wishes to substitute" the real civil society for "the fictitous civil society of the legislature" thus became in principle a sphere of public deliberation and resolution concerning the direction and administration of every process necessary for the reproduction of society. The enigma of a "political society" that Marx posited with his critique of the Hegelian doctrine of state found its resolution a few years later in the phrase of a socialization of the means of production.

Under such conditions, then, the public sphere was also presumed to be able to realize in earnest what it had promised from the start—the subjection of political domination, as a domination of human beings over human beings, to reason. "When, in the course of development, class distinctions have disappeared, and all production has been concentrated in the hands of a vast association of the whole nation, the public power will lose its political character. Political power, properly so called, is merely the organized power of one class for oppressing another."[126] Marx had closed his essay on Proudhon's *Poverty of Philosophy* with the statement that "it is only in an order of things in which there are no more classes and class antagonisms that *social evolutions* will cease to be *political revolutions.*"[127] With the dissolution of "political" power into "public" power, the liberal idea of a political public sphere found its socialist formulation. As is well known, Engels, inspired by a phrase of Saint-Simon's, interpreted it in such a way that the administration of things and direction of production processes would take the place of the rule over men.[128] Not authority as such but certainly political authority would disappear; the remaining and in part newly forming public functions changed their political character into an administrative one. However, this was only possible for "the associated producers, rationally regulating their interchange with nature, . . . instead of being ruled by it as by . . . blind forces. . . ."[129]

From the dialectic immanent in the bourgeois public sphere Marx derived the socialist consequences of a counter-model in which the classical relationship between the public sphere and the private was peculiarly reversed. In this counter-model, criticism and control by the public were extended to that portion of the private sphere of civil society which had been granted to private persons by virtue of their power of control over the means of production—to the domain of socially necessary labor. According to this new model, autonomy was no longer based on private property; it could in principle no longer be grounded in the private sphere but had to have its foundation in the public sphere itself. Private autonomy was a derivative of the original autonomy which alone constituted the public of a society's citizens in the exercise of the functions of the socialistically expanded public sphere. Private persons came to be the private persons of a public rather than a public of private persons. The identity of *bourgeois* and *homme*, of property-owning private persons and human beings, was replaced by that of *citoyen* and *homme*; the freedom of the private person was a function of the role of human beings as citizens of society. No longer was the role of the citizen of a state the function of a human being's freedom as property-owning private person, for the public sphere no longer linked a society of property-owning private persons with the state. Rather, the autonomous public, through the planned shaping of a state that became absorbed into society, secured for itself (as composed of private persons) a sphere of personal freedom, leisure, and freedom of movement. In this sphere, the informal and personal interaction of human beings with one another would have been emancipated for the first time from the constraints of social labor (ever a "realm of necessity") and become really "private." Examples of the new form of derivative private autonomy owed to the primary publicity of a public of citizens of society were found in an intimate sphere set free from economic functions. As Engels, antedating the *Communist Manifesto*, said in his *Principles of Communism*, with the elimination of private property the old basis and previous function of the family, including the dependence of the wife on the husband and of the children on the parents were also removed. This would make "the relations between the sexes a purely private affair, which concerns only the two persons involved; a relationship which is in no way the concern of society."[130] In the *Rheinische Zeitung* Marx had already expressed himself in the same vein: "If marriage were not the basis of the family, it would not be subject to legislation, just as friendship is not."[131] Both Marx and Engels considered a relationship to be actualized as "private" only when it was no longer saddled with any legal regulations.

15 The Ambivalent View of the Public Sphere in the Theory of Liberalism (John Stuart Mill and Alexis de Tocqueville)

The dialectic of the bourgeois public sphere was not completed as anticipated in the early socialist expectations. The extension of equal political rights to all social classes proved to be possible within the framework of this class society itself. The "widened" public sphere did not in principle lead to the elimination of that basis upon which the public of property-owning private people had at first tried to achieve something akin to a rule of public opinion. On the other hand, the critique of the idea of the bourgeois public sphere as an ideology was so obviously correct that under the altered social preconditions of "public opinion" around the middle of the century, when economic liberalism was just reaching its peak, its social-philosophical representatives were forced almost to deny the principle of the public sphere of civil society even as they celebrated it. This ambivalent conception of the public sphere in the theory of liberalism did not, to be sure, admit to itself the structural conflict of the society whose very product it was. The liberalist apologetic, however, was superior to the socialist critique in another respect: it called into question the fundamental pre-suppositions common to both the classic model of the bourgeois public sphere and its dialectically projected counter-model.

Eighteenth-century bourgeois consciousness had conceived the idea of making political domination rational within the framework of a philosophy of history. From this perspective even the social preconditions of a public sphere as an element in the political realm could be viewed as a kind of "natural order," for there was to be a natural basis for the public sphere that would in principle guarantee an autonomous and basically harmonious course of social reproduction. Correspondingly, on the one hand public opinion would be set free from structural contradictions; on the other hand in the degree that it acknowledged the laws of motion immanent in society and took them into account, it would be able to decide in accord with binding criteria which regulations were practically necessary in the general interest. Presupposing such circumstances, it would not be necessary to form a general will with regard to detailed dispositions; it would only be necessary to establish the truth in principle. The model of a public sphere in the political realm that claimed the convergence of public opinion with reason supposed it to be objectively possible (through reliance on an order of nature or, what amounted to the same, an organization of society strictly oriented to the general interest) to keep conflicts of interest and bureaucratic decisions to a minimum and, in so far as these could not be completely avoided, to subject them to reliable criteria of public evaluation. Thus, while the socialists demonstrated that the basis of the bourgeois public sphere did not satisfy these preconditions and had to be set up differently in order to meet them, the liberals took the manifestation of the same contradiction as an occasion for casting into doubt the very presuppositions of a natural basis upon which the idea of a political public sphere rested—and to argue all the more determinedly in favor of conserving a relativized form of the *bourgeois* public sphere. With liberalism, therefore, the bourgeois self-interpretation of the public sphere abandoned the form of a philosophy of history in favor of a common sense meliorism[132]—it became "realistic."

Even the outward appearance of the public sphere, from which its idea up to this time might still have drawn a certain plausibility, was thoroughly altered by the Chartist movement in Britain and the February Revolt on the Continent. Until then, although it had in fact been more or less solidly integrated into the hierarchically ordered, locally rooted representation of the social ranks, the public could nevertheless be interpreted as composed of free individuals. Social intercourse occurred in the medium of "society" (adopted from the nobility and at the same time given a bourgeois modulation) in accord with firm rules of equality and frankness, under a code of self-protection and courteousness. The mutual willingness to accept the given roles and simultaneously to suspend their reality was based on the justifiable trust that within the public—presupposing its shared class interest—friend-or-foe relations were in fact impossible. And a certain rationality admittedly expressed itself in the reasonable forms of public discussion as well as in the convergence of opinions regarding the standards of criticism and the goal of polemics. Once the public sphere of civil society had developed, however, thoughtful contemporaries could not help but notice how this veil was rent. The public was expanded, informally at first, by the proliferation of press and propaganda; along with its social exclusiveness it also lost the coherence afforded by the institutions of sociability and a relatively high level of education. Conflicts hitherto pushed aside into the private sphere now emerged in public. Group needs that could not expect to be satisfied by a self-regulating market tended to favor regulation by the state. The public sphere, which now had to deal with these demands, became an arena of competing interests fought out in the coarser forms of violent conflict. Laws passed under the "pressure of the street" could hardly be understood any longer as embodying the reasonable consensus of publicly debating private persons. They corresponded more or less overtly to the compromise between competing private interests.

In this situation Mill observed how manual workers, women, and (in the United States) blacks pressed for the general franchise. He explicitly approved of all movements rebelling against the aristocracy of money, gender, and color, against the minority democracy of the propertied (*Warenbesitzer*), and against the plutocracy of the *grande bourgeoisie*.[133] Tocqueville, as an opposition delegate in the National Assembly and a few days before the February Revolt that he predicted with precision, implored the government to expand, little by little, the franchise to the whole people:

There has, perhaps, at no time and in no country ever been a parliament (excepting only the Assemblée Constituante of 1789) that contained more diverse and brilliant talents than ours today. Nevertheless, the large part of the nation pays scant attention to what happens, and barely listens to what is being said, on the official stage of its affairs; the actors themselves who appear on it, more preoccupied with what they hide than with what they show, do not seem to take their role all too seriously. In reality, public life makes its appearance in places where it should not, and it has stopped to exist where alone, according to the laws, one should find it. What is the cause?—The cause is that the laws have narrowly restricted the exercise of all political rights to a single class. . . .[134]

The competitive order no longer lent sufficient credibility to its promise that, along with the alleged equality of opportunity to accumulate private property, it also maintained open access to the public sphere in the political realm. The principle of the latter, rather, demanded the direct admittance of the laboring classes, of the uneducated masses without property—precisely through the extension of equal political rights. Electoral reform was the topic of the nineteenth century: no longer the principle of publicity as such, as had been true in the eighteenth century, but of the enlargement of the public. The self-thematization of public opinion subsided to the same extent that with the secrecy of cabinet government it lost its firmly circumscribed polemical goal and itself became diffuse, as it were. The unity of public opinion and its unambiguousness were no longer guaranteed by the common foe. Liberals like Mill and Tocqueville, therefore, who favored the process for the sake of the same principle also devalued its consequences. This was because the unreconciled interests which, with the broadening of the public, flooded the public sphere were represented in a divided public opinion and turned public opinion (in the form of the currently dominant opinion) into a coercive force, whereas it had once been supposed to dissolve any kind of coercion into the compulsion of reason. Thus Mill even deplored the "yoke of public opinion" or "moral means of coercion in the form of public opinion." His great plea *On Liberty* was already aimed against the power of the public that until then had been deemed the guarantee of reason against force in general. There was manifest "in the world at large an increasing inclination to expand unduly the powers of society over the individual, by the force of public opinion." The reign of public opinion appeared as the reign of the many and the mediocre:

In politics it is almost a triviality to say that public opinion now rules the world. The only power deserving the name is that of masses, and of governments while they make themselves the organ of the tendencies and instincts of masses. . . . And what is a still greater novelty, the masses do not now take their opinions from dignitaries in Church or State, from ostensible leaders, or from books. Their thinking is done for them by men much like themselves, addressing them or speaking in their name, on the spur of the moment, through the newspapers.[135]

Tocqueville too treated public opinion more as a compulsion toward conformity than as a critical force:

The nearer men are to a common level of uniformity, the less are they inclined to believe blindly in any man or in any class. But they are readier to trust the mass, and public opinion becomes more and more mistress of the world. . . . So in democracies public opinion has a strange power. . . . It uses no persuasion to forward its beliefs, but by some mighty pressure of the mind of all upon the intelligence of each it imposes its ideas and makes them penetrate men's very souls. The majority in the United States takes over the business of supplying the individual with a quantity of ready-made opinions and so relieves him of the necessity of forming his own. So there are many theories of philosophy, morality, and politics which everyone adopts unexamined on the faith of public opinion.[136]

Like Mill, Tocqueville also believed the time had come to treat public opinion as a force that at best could serve to curb powers but that above all was itself to be subjected to effective limitation: "When a man or a party suffers an injustice in the United States, to whom can he turn? To public opinion? That is what forms the majority. To the legislative body? It represents the majority and obeys it blindly. To the executive power? It is appointed by the majority. . . . To the police? They are nothing but the majority under arms. A jury? The jury is the majority. . . .[137]

This is the same question that for Mill placed the old problem of freedom of thought and speech in a perspective differing from the one that ever since Milton's famous discourse *Areopagitica* had been dominant in the struggle of the public with authorities. Wherever the apparently no less arbitrary power of the public itself had taken the place of princely power, the accusation of intolerance was now leveled against the public opinion that had become prevalent. The demand for tolerance was addressed to it and not to the censors who had once suppressed it. The right to the free expression of opinion was no longer called on to protect the public's rational-critical debate against the reach of the police but to protect the nonconformists from the grip of the public itself. "In this age, the mere example of nonconformity . . . is itself a service. Precisely . . ., it is desirable, in order to break through that tyranny, that people should be eccentric."[138] For the opinions conflicting in the public sphere Mill developed a concept of toleration on the analogy of religious conflicts. The public engaged in critical debate was entirely prevented from attaining a rational opinion because "only through diversity of opinion is there, in the existing state of human intellect, a chance of fair play to all sides of the truth."[139] This resignation before the inability to resolve rationally the competition of interests in the public sphere was disguised as perspectivist epistemology: because the particular interests were no longer measured against the general, the opinions into which they were ideologically transposed possessed an irreducible kernel of faith. Mill demanded not criticism but tolerance, because the dogmatic residues could indeed be suppressed but not reduced to the common denominator of reason. The unity of reason and of public opinion lacked the objective guarantee of a concordance of interests existing in society, the rational demonstrability of a universal interest as such.

Bentham still could refer to the majority as the criterion for knowing whether a decision had been made in the general interest. On the basis of his experience with the Chartist movement Mill, in contrast, pointed to the fact that the majority of the expanded public consists no longer of property-owning private persons, but of proletarians

all standing in the same social position and having, in the main, the same pursuits; namely, unskilled manual labourers. And we mean no disparagement to them: whatever we say to their disadvantage, we say equally of a numerical majority of shopkeepers or of squires. Where there is identity of position and pursuits, there also will be identity of partialities, passions, and prejudices; and to give to any one set of partialities, passions, and prejudices, absolute power, without counterbalance from partialities, passions, and prejudices of a different sort, is the way to render the correction of any of those imperfections hopeless. . . .

Public opinion became one power among other powers. Hence Mill could not believe

that Bentham made the most useful employment which might have been made of his great powers, when, not content with enthroning the majority as sovereign, by means of universal suffrage, without king or house of lords, he exhausted all the resources of ingenuity in devising means for riveting the yoke of public opinion closer and closer round the necks of all public functionaries. . . . Surely, when any power has been made the strongest power, enough has been done for it: care is thenceforth wanted rather to prevent that strongest power from swallowing up all others.[140]

The political public sphere no longer stood for the idea of a dissolution of power; instead, it was to serve its division; public opinion became a mere limit on power. Mill's admission betrayed the origin of this reinterpretation. *Thenceforth* care had to be taken that the power of public opinion not swallow up all power in general. The liberalist interpretation of the bourgeois constitutional state was reactionary: it reacted to the power of the idea of a critically debating public's self-determination, initially included in its institutions, as soon as this public was subverted by the propertyless and uneducated masses. Far from having united from the beginning so-called democratic with originally liberal elements (i.e., heterogeneous motives),[141] the bourgeois constitutional state was interpreted under this dualist aspect for the first time by liberalism. Mill turned against the idea of a public sphere in accord with which it would be desirable "that the multitude bring all political questions before their own tribunal and decide according to their own judgment, because under such conditions the philosophers are required to enlighten the crowd and to bring it to the point of learning to appreciate their more profound conception of things."[142] Instead, he advocated "that political questions be decided not by a direct or indirect appeal to the insight or the will of an uninformed multitude, but only by appeal to views, formed after due consideration, of a relatively small number of persons specially educated for this task."[143] Tocqueville shared Mill's conception of "Representative Government": public opinion determined by the passions of the masses was in need of purification by means of the authoritative insights of materially independent citizens. Although the press was an important instrument of enlightenment, it did not suffice for this. Political representation admittedly rested upon a social hierarchy; Tocqueville recalled the *pouvoirs intermédiaires*, the corporative powers of the pre-bourgeois society structured into estates, the families and individuals distinguished by birth, education, and wealth, especially landed estates and the privileges connected with them, "who seemed destined to command."[144] He remained aware that a new artistocracy could not simply be created overnight from the soil of bourgeois society, "but I think that associations of plain citizens can compose very rich, influential, and powerful bodies, in other words, aristocratic bodies. . . . An association, be it political, industrial, commercial, or even literary or scientific, is an educated and powerful body of citizens which cannot be twisted to any man's will or quietly trodden down. . . ."[145] Educated and powerful citizens were supposed to form an elite public (in view of the lack of an aristocracy by birth) whose critical debate determined public opinion.

Against a public opinion that, as it seemed, had been perverted from an instrument of liberation into an agent of repression, liberalism, faithful to its own *ratio*, could only summon public opinion once again. Yet what was needed now was a restricted arrangement to secure for a public opinion finding itself in the minority an influence against the prevailing opinions that *per se* it was incapable of developing. In order to save the principle of publicity even against the tyranny of an unenlightened public opinion itself, it was to be augmented with elements of representative publicity (*repräsentative Öffentlichkeit*) to such an extent that an esoteric public of representatives could emerge. In relation to the latter, the public that was only permitted to have itself represented would have to be satisfied that "their judgment must in general be exercised rather upon the characters and talents of the person whom they appoint to decide these questions for them, than upon the questions themselves."[146] Mill wrote this sentence only four years after an election proclamation in which the Whigs reminded their electorate of the rigorous intent behind a political public sphere: remember that you are now fighting for things, not men. Only too easily did the pro and con of argument become supplanted by the mechanism of personalization; only too easily did objective conditions appear in biographical disguise. Mill made his peace with the social psychology of the mass public and called for a public sphere literally declassed and structured into layers of representation.

Tocqueville, by provenance more akin to the *fronde* that opposed the monarchical absolutism of the eighteenth century than to nineteenth-century liberals, and for this very reason again almost made to order for liberalism, bewailed the loss of the ancient *pouvoirs intermédiaires* and demanded the creation of new intermediate powers for the sake of integrating public opinion effectively into the division and interlocking of powers. This, of course, was why Mill bestowed on him the name of the "Montesquieu of our age." The no longer liberal bourgeoisie, converting to liberalism, had recourse to the safeguards of pre-bourgeois structures, those defensive rights of estate liberties which differed essentially from the liberties of the bourgeois rights of man.[147] Yet Tocqueville went beyond Mill inasmuch as his analysis of the public sphere referred not only to the "tyranny of public opinion" but also to a complementary phenomenon, namely, the despotism of an increasingly bureaucratized state. With the perspective of the estates' opposition against the *ancien régime* ingrained in him Tocqueville observed with great concern the tendency toward what he called the "centralization of government power." In fact, the strong power of the state for which mercantilism had striven in vain was generated by the liberal nineteenth century; only at this time was a modern central administration—the Civil Service—created in Great Britain. Tocqueville, using the example of the United States, demonstrated how the citizen slipped into a state of tutelage:

Over this kind of men stands an immense, protective power which is alone responsible for securing their enjoyment and watching over their fate. That power is absolute, thoughtful of detail, orderly, provident and gentle. It would resemble parental authority if, fatherlike, it tried to prepare its charges for a man's life, but on the contrary, it only tries to keep them in perpetual childhood. It likes to see the citizens enjoy themselves, provided that they think of nothing but enjoyment. It gladly works for their happiness but wants to be the sole agent and judge thereof. It provides for their security, foresees and supplies their necessities, facilitates their pleasures, manages their principal concerns, directs their industry, makes rules for their testaments, and divides their inheritances. Why should it not entirely relieve them from the trouble of thinking and all the cares of living?[148]

Socialism too appeared to Tocqueville to be only an extension of these tendencies which would ultimately liquidate the tax-supported state in favor of a state economy and would establish the horrors of a totally administered world. Thus in 1848, as minister in the revolutionary cabinet, he opposed the demand to include the right to work in the constitution by arguing that thereby the state would necessarily become the only industrialist: "Once things have reached that point, then taxation is no longer the means for running the machinery of government, but the key means for supporting industries. Thus, accumulating all particular capitals in its hands, the state finally becomes the sole owner of everything. But that is communism."[149]

During the same period, the theory of revolution formulated in the *Communist Manifesto* was itself still gauged to the limited state power of liberalism. Only a few years later, in the 1852 essay on the *coup* of Napoleon III,[150] did Marx have second thoughts regarding a phenomenon to which he gave the same name as had Tocqueville before him: "centralization of government power." In the address to the General Council at the Paris Commune, he showed himself to be already so worried by the sheer weight of state power—"with its ubiquitous organs of standing army, police, bureaucracy, clergy, and judicature—organs wrought after the plan of a systematic and hierarchic division of labor"[151]—that he considered socialism, i.e., the transformation of political into public authority, possible only if the working class did "not simply lay hold of the ready-made state machinery. . . ."[152] Instead, the bureaucratic-military machinery had to be smashed—a sentence which Marx wrote to Kugelmann in 1871 and to whose exegesis Lenin, as we know, devoted his most important book before seeing himself forced by economic and technical circumstances to replace the "smashed" Tsarist state apparatus with the incomparably more powerful one of the Central Committee. In "The Critique of the Gotha Program" Marx once again summarized the socialist idea of a political public sphere in the suggestive metaphor of the withering away of the state. The realization of this sphere had to be preceded by the "smashing of the bureaucratic machinery of the state." The liberalist warning against the centralization of government authority reminded the socialists of the problematic presupposition that their own idea of the public sphere shared with that of the bourgeoisie: a "natural order" of social reproduction. Underlying the proposal for the constitution of the Commune, the anticipation of the replacement of bourgeois parliamentarianism by a system of worker councils, was the conviction that, stripped of its political character, public authority, the administration of things and the direction of production processes, could be regulated by the laws (discovered once and for all) of political economy without extended controversies. Implicitly, socialistically emancipated public opinion was still viewed by Marx as it had once been viewed by the physiocrats: as an insight into the *ordre naturel.*

In the hundred years following the heyday of liberalism, during which capitalism gradually became "organized," the original relationship of public and private sphere in fact dissolved; the contours of the bourgeois public sphere eroded. But neither the liberal nor the socialist model were adequate for the diagnosis of a public sphere that remained peculiarly suspended between the two constellations abstractly represented in the models. Two tendencies dialectically related to each other indicated a breakdown of the public sphere. While it penetrated more *spheres* of society, it simultaneously lost its political *function*, namely: that of subjecting the affairs that it had made public to the control of a critical public. M. L. Goldschmidt recorded the same "two disturbing tendencies . . .: first, a tendency toward too much publicity with a consequent disregard of the individual's right of privacy; and second, a tendency toward too little publicity, with a consequent increase of secrecy in areas hitherto considered public."[153] The *principle* of the public sphere, that is, critical publicity, seemed to lose its strength in the measure that it expanded as a *sphere* and even undermined the private realm.

V

The Social-Structural Transformation of the Public Sphere

16 The Tendency toward a Mutual Infiltration of Public and Private Spheres

The bourgeois public sphere evolved in the tension-charged field between state and society. But it did so in such a way that it remained itself a part of the private realm. The fundamental separation of those two spheres, upon which it rested, initially referred merely to the disengagement of elements of social reproduction and political power, which in the forms of domination typical of the High Middle Ages were welded together. With the growth of a market economy arose the sphere of the "social," which broke the fetters of domination based on landed estate and necessitated forms of administration invested with state authority (*obrigkeitlich*). In the measure to which it was linked to market exchange, production was disengaged from its connection with functions of public authority; conversely, political administration was released from production tasks. Public power, concentrated in national and territorial states, rose above a privatized society, however much the latter's affairs might be initially directed by interventions of state authority (*Obrigkeit*). This private sphere evolved into a sphere of private autonomy only to the degree to which it became emancipated from mercantilist regulation. For this reason even the reversal of this tendency, that is, the increasing state interventionism very noticeable from the last quarter of the nineteenth century onward, did not per se lead to an interlocking of the public sphere with the private realm. Without touching the ongoing separation of state and society, an interventionist policy (which has been characterized as "neomercantilist") could restrict the autonomy of private people without yet affecting the private character of their commerce with each other as such. That society was essentially a private sphere became questionable only when the powers of "society" themselves assumed functions of public authority. A policy of "neomercantilism" then went hand in hand with a kind of "refeudalization" of society.

The new interventionism of the waning nineteenth century was embraced by a state that in virtue of the constitutionalization (albeit quite limited in Germany) of a political public sphere tended to adopt the interests of civil society as its own. As a result, the interventions by public power in the affairs of private people transmitted impulses that indirectly grew out of the latters' own sphere. Interventionism had its origin in the transfer onto a political level of such conflicts of interest as could no longer be settled within the private sphere alone. Consequently, in the long run state intervention in the sphere of society found its counterpart in the transfer of public functions to private corporate bodies. Likewise, the opposite process of a substitution of state authority by the power of society was connected to the extension of public authority over sectors of the private realm. Only this dialectic of a progressive "societalization" of the state simultaneously with an increasing "state-ification" of society gradually destroyed the basis of the bourgeois public sphere—the separation of state and society. Between the two and out of the two, as it were, a repoliticized social sphere emerged to which the distinction between "public" and "private" could not be usefully applied. It also led to the disintegration of that specific portion of the private realm within which private people, assembled to constitute a public and to regulate those aspects of their commerce with each other that were of general concern, namely, the public sphere in its liberal form. The downfall of the public sphere, demonstrated by its changing political functions (Chapter VI), had its source in the structural transformation of the relationship between the public sphere and the private realm in general (Chapter V).

From the time of the great depression that began in 1873, the liberal era was coming to a close, accompanied by a visible shift in trade policy. Gradually all the capitalistically advanced countries abandoned the sacred principles of free trade (which had anyway found unambiguous support only in Great Britain, which dominated the world market) in favor of a new protectionism. Similarly, in the domestic markets and especially in the core industries the trend toward oligopolistic mergers became more pronounced. The movement on the capital market went in the same direction. In Germany the *Aktiengesellschaft* proved to be an effective vehicle of concentration, as did the trust company in the United States. Soon this development triggered antitrust legislation in the United States and anticartel legislation in Germany. Characteristically, these two relatively young industrial nations surpassed in this respect both France and especially Great Britain, where capitalism had a longer and more continuous tradition, or at least one more deeply rooted in the so-called manufacturing period. In a recently united Germany, in contrast, industrial capitalism developed "spontaneously" only with the beginning of the imperialist period and was immediately forced to secure for itself politically privileged spheres for foreign trade and the export of capital.[1] In view of the change in state functions, especially the *increase* in functions of the state machinery demanded by capitalism in this phase, it had become impossible for Germany to catch up with the Western European-North American development of the parliamentary constitutional state.[2]

In the last third of the past century the restriction of competition in the commodity market came to prevail on an international scale, be it through the concentration of capital and the merger of larger companies enjoying oligopolistic positions or through a dividing up of the market by way of price and production agreements. The interplay between expansive and restrictive tendencies, which already during the developmental period of commercial and finance capital had ensured that there would never be a real chance for a liberalization of the market, also determined the movements of industrial capital and, contrary to the optical distortion of classical economics, made the liberal era a mere episode. From the perspective of the overall development of capitalism the period between 1775 and 1875 appeared to be no more than a "vast secular boom."[3] What Say in his famous Law ascribed to laisser-faire capitalism as such, that is, an automatic tendency toward the equilibration of production and consumption on the level of the economy as a whole, was actually a function not of the system as such, but of concrete historical circumstances.[4] These changed during the same century, not unaffected by the antagonism inherent in the capitalist mode of production itself. Besides, Say's Law came to grief in the additional respect that after a crisis the system's equilibrium was by no means automatically reestablished on the highest level attainable on the basis of the available productive forces.

In the course of this development, society was forced to relinquish even the flimsiest pretense of being a sphere in which the influence of power was suspended. The liberal model (in truth one of an economy based on petty commodity exchange) had envisaged only horizontal exchange relationships among individual commodity owners. Under conditions of free competition and independent prices, then, no one was expected to be able to gain so much power as to attain a position that gave him complete control over someone else. Contrary to these expectations, however, under conditions of imperfect competition and dependent prices social power became concentrated in private hands.[5] Within the web of vertical relationships between collective units, conditions emerged that were partly characterized by one-sided dependency and partly by mutual pressure. Processes of concentration and crisis pulled the veil of an exchange of equivalents off the antagonistic structure of society. The more society became transparent as a mere nexus of coercive constraints, the more urgent became the need for a strong state. Against the liberal self-interpretation of the state's role as no more than that of a "nightwatchman,"[6] Franz Neumann correctly objected that its role had always been as strong as the interests of the bourgeoisie required it to be in a given political and social situation.[7]

Nevertheless, as long as the state was liberal, one of these interests was that on the whole the spheres of commodity exchange and of social labor remain realms of private autonomy (unless one were to see, following Achinger,[8] the first beginnings of intervention in the private sphere as early as the introduction of compulsory education and military service). The "centralization of government power" that became a problem simultaneously for both Marx and Tocqueville strictly speaking did not yet touch upon the relationship between public and private realms constitutive of the bourgeois constitutional state. Even the interest that large industry took in an expansion of the military apparatus for the sake of the conquest and protection of privileged markets abroad at first only strengthened one of the already existing functions of public authority. Only when *new* functions accrued to the state did the "barrier" between it and society begin to lose its firmness.

The concentration of power in the private sphere of commodity exchange on the one hand, and in the public sphere with its institutionalized promise of universal accessibility (established as an organ of the state) on the other, strengthened the propensity of the economically weaker parties to use political means against those who were stronger by reason of their position in the market. In Great Britain there were electoral reforms in 1867 and 1883; in France, Napoleon III had introduced universal suffrage; Bismarck kept its plebiscitary-conservative consequences in mind when he included the universal franchise first in the constitution of the North German Federation, then in that of the newly founded German Empire. On the basis of this formally conceded possibility of a voice in political affairs, both the pauperized strata and the classes threatened by them tried to gain an influence that was to compensate politically for the violation of equality of opportunity in the economic realm (if, indeed, it had ever existed at all). The attempt to relieve the public sphere of the intrusion of private interests failed as soon as the conditions under which the privatization of interests was to be accomplished were themselves drawn into the conflict of organized interests. The labor unions constituted an organized counterweight not only in the labor market; by means of the socialist parties they strove to influence legislation itself. The entrepreneurs and generally all forces "friendly to the state" (*staatserhaltend*, as they have been called ever since) responded by immediately exchanging their private societal power for political power. Bismarck's Socialist Law was a prime example, but the Social Security Insurance which he established at the same time demonstrated to which extent state intervention into the private sphere had to yield to pressure from below. The interferences of the state in the private sphere since the end of the last century showed that the masses, now entitled to political participation, succeeded in translating economic antagonisms into political conflicts. In part these interferences favored the interests of the economically weaker strata, in part they served to reject them. In any given case it was not always easy to establish clearly which side's collective private interests were favored more. In general terms, at any rate, state interventions, even where they prevailed in opposition to "ruling" interests, were guided by the interest of maintaining the equilibrium of the system which could no longer be secured by way of the free market. Strachey drew from this the conclusion that was only *prima facie* paradoxical, "that it has been, precisely, the struggle of the democratic forces *against* capitalism which has saved the system. It has done so not only by making tolerable the conditions of life of the wage earners, but also by keeping open that indispensable market for the final product which the self-destructive drive of capitalism to a more and more inequitable distribution of the national income would otherwise have closed."[9]

This mechanism, which Galbraith analyzed also from the perspective of countervailing powers,[10] explained the connection between tendencies toward a concentration of capital[11] and a growing state interventionism. The size alone of the state budgets sufficiently indicated the increase in state activity.[12] Nevertheless, this quantitative criterion must be supplemented; only a qualitative analysis of the public interventions in the private sphere provides clear evidence that the state expanded its activity not merely within the limits of its old functions but added to them a series of altogether new ones. Besides the traditional functions of maintaining order (which the state already fulfilled in the liberal era, domestically by means of the

police and the judicial system and a very cautiously handled
tax policy, and internationally based on military forces), it began to assume formative functions as well.[13] The distinction
between the two became easier, of course, the more the field
of state-provided social services became differentiated in the
course of the twentieth century. We have already mentioned
the task of providing protection, compensation, and subsidies
to the economically weaker social groups, to workers and to
employees, tenants, consumers, etc. (all the measures aimed at
a redistribution of income, for instance, fall under this heading). Of a different order was the task of preventing or at least
alleviating long-term changes in the social structure or of systematically supporting and even guiding them (such as the set
of policies designed to strengthen the middle classes). The
momentous task of influencing private and of regulating public
investments was already an element belonging to the larger
function of controlling and balancing the economic process in
its entirety. The processes of concentration had not only led to
the emergence of a policy concerned with business cycles; with
the trend toward large units, these processes also created certain preconditions which made large-scale policies of this sort
possible to begin with, for in the same degree the economy was
rendered accessible to the econometric methods of modelling
the total national economy, as introduced in Great Britain, the
United States, and Canada shortly before the outbreak of the
Second World War.[14]

Finally, over and above its normal administrative concerns
the state also took over the provision of services that hitherto
had been left to private hands, whether it entrusted private
persons with public tasks, coordinated private economic activities within the frame of an overall plan,[15] or became active
itself as a producer and distributor. The sector of public services was necessarily extended "because with mounting economic growth factors became effective that alter the
relationship of private to social costs."[16] In proportion to the
increasing buying power of the broad masses, the public costs
of private production were complemented by the public costs
of private consumption.[17]

The formula of "collective provision for the necessities of

life" obscures the multiplicity of functions newly accrued to the state making social welfare its concern;[18] it also hides the complexly interwoven, collectively organized private interests at the basis of this development. Through law and regulation the state intervened deeply in the sphere of commodity exchange and social labor because the competing interests of the societal forces translated themselves into a political dynamism and, mediated by state interventionism, reacted back on their own sphere. Considered as a whole the "democratic influence" on the economic order could not be denied. Through public interventions into the private realm countering the tendency toward the concentration of capital and oligopolistic organization, the unpropertied masses had been able to make sure that their share of the national income had not decreased over the long run. By the middle of the present century, however, it did not seem to have increased essentially.[19]

As interventionism had its source in such interconnections, the social areas protected by interventionism should be strictly distinguished from a private sphere that was merely state-regulated. The private institutions themselves assumed to a considerable extent a semipublic character; one may even speak of the quasi-political character of private economic units.[20] From the midst of the publicly relevant sphere of civil society was formed a repoliticized social sphere in which state and societal institutions fused into a single functional complex that could no longer be differentiated according to criteria of public and private. On the legal level this new interdependence of hitherto separate spheres found its expression in the breakdown of the boundaries of the classical system of private law.

In an industrial society constituted as a social-welfare state, relationships and conditions multiplied which could not be adequately ordered through institutions of either purely private or purely public law. Instead they required the introduction of norms of so-called social legislation.

The socialist critique of the merely formal character of bourgeois law has constantly stressed that the autonomy guaranteed by private law could be enjoyed by all persons subject to it only to the extent that equal economic opportunities permitted the realization of legally equal chances for shaping one's life.[21]

Especially the separation of the producer from the means of production—the class relationship fully evolved in the industrial capitalism of the nineteenth century—transformed the formally equal legal relationship between capitalists and wage earners into a relationship of factual subordination; its conceptualization in terms of private law shrouded a quasi-public authority. Karl Renner[22] analyzed the central institution of private law (ownership of the means of production, along with its corresponding guarantees; freedom of contract, of trade, and of inheritance) from this vantage point; he showed that in accordance with its actual functioning it should be a component of public law, that private law secures for the capitalist the exercise of a "delegated public power of command." Since the end of the First World War at the latest, however, legal development too up to a certain point has taken cognizance of societal development, and this produced a complicated set of mixed types initially subsumed under the heading of a "publification of private law."[23] Later on one became accustomed to considering the same process from the reciprocal perspective of a privatization of public law: "elements of public law and elements of private law become mutually interwoven to the point of unrecognizability and inextricability."[24]

Property rights became restricted not only by the already mentioned interventionist economic policy but also by legal guarantees intended to restore materially the formal equality of the partners contracting within typical social situations. Collective contracts, which took the place of individual ones (in exemplary fashion in labor law), protected the weaker partner. Protective clauses in the interest of the tenant turned the lease into a relationship restricting the landlord almost as if it involved the use of public space. And just like workers and tenants, consumers enjoyed special guarantees. Similar developments were visible in the legislations governing industrial relations, housing projects, and domestic regulations. Considerations of public safety constrained the owners of businesses, land, building, etc., at times to such an extent that one could speak of a "super-ownership on the part of the public."[25] Liberal constitutional jurists bewailed this trend toward the "undermining" of property rights with the argument that nowadays property was formally left in the hands of the property owners while they were nevertheless expropriated, without compensation or the benefit of legal protection in terms of regulated expropriation procedures: "thus forms of socialization arise by way of confiscatory legislation, forms that even doctrinaire Marxism had not foreseen."[26]

Simultaneously with the central institution of private law, that is, property, the guarantees closely connected with it were naturally affected as well, especially freedom of contract. The classical contractual relationship presumed complete independence in the determination of the conditions of the contract. In the meantime it had been subjected to considerable restrictions. To the degree that legal relationships tended to converge on socially similar types, the contracts themselves also tended to be schematized. Normally the mounting standardization of contractual relationships curtailed the freedom of the economically weaker partner, whereas the already mentioned instrument of collective contracts was intended to bring about equality in market position. Wage agreements between employers' associations and labor unions lost their character as matters of private law in the strict sense; they took on a practically public character because the agreed upon series of regulations functioned as a surrogate law: "The function of employers' associations and unions, when they come to terms on a comprehensive labor agreement, is less akin to the exercise of private autonomy than to legislation in virtue of delegation."[27] Even from a juridical standpoint original private autonomy had become degraded into something derivative to such an extent that it was often no longer considered necessary for the validity of contracts. The legal effect of factual contractual relationships became equivalent to classical legal relationships.[28]

Finally, the system of private law became infracted by the increasing number of contracts between the public authority and private persons.[29] The state entered into pacts with private persons on the basis of *do ut des*; here too the inequality between the partners and the dependence of one upon the other dissolved the foundation of the strict contractual relationship. Gauged in terms of the classical model these pacts were nothing more than pseudo-contracts. When, in the exercise of their social welfare functions, authorities today extensively replace legal regulation by the instrument of the contract, such contracts have a quasi-public character irrespective of their form as agreements under private law; for "our legal system" actually rests "upon the idea that contracts under private law stand on a level below the law, not on the same level with it; and our public law leaves room for contracts only for relationships on the same level. . . ."[30]

With the state's "flight" out of public law, with the transfer of tasks of public administration to enterprises, institutions, corporations, and semiofficial agencies under private law, the flipside of the "publification" of private law also became apparent: the privatization of public law. Especially when public administration itself used the instruments offered by private law in its performance of distributing, providing, and supporting tasks, the classical criteria of public law became obsolete.[31] For neither did its organization under public law hinder, say, some service-providing township from contracting with its "customers" under private law; nor was the far-reaching normative regulation of such a legal relationship incompatible with its nature as an act under private law. Neither a monopoly position and absence of contractual freedom nor the involvement of a public administrative agency in the creation of a legal relationship required that such a relationship come under public law. The public element of public interest fused with the private element of contractual formulations under private law to the extent that along with the concentration of capital and interventionism a new sphere emerged from the reciprocal permeation of the state by society and of society by the state. This sphere could be meaningfully conceived neither as purely private nor as genuinely public, nor could it be unequivocally located in a realm to which *either* private *or* public law pertains.[32]

17 The Polarization of the Social Sphere and the Intimate Sphere

To the degree that state and society permeated each other, the institution of the conjugal family became dissociated from its connection with processes of social reproduction. The intimate sphere, once the very center of the private sphere, moved to its periphery to the extent that the private sphere itself became deprivatized. The bourgeoisie of the liberal era spent their private lives prototypically in occupation and family; the realm of commodity exchange and of social labor belonged to the private sphere as much as the "household" relieved of any directly economic functions. These two realms, at that time structured in concordance, now began to develop into different directions: "And indeed one can say that the family became ever more private and the world of work and organization ever more 'public.'"[33]

The phrase, "world of work and organization" betrayed already something of the tendency toward the objectification of a realm that once was a domain of private control—whether one's own, as in the case of the property owner, or that of another, as in the case of the wage laborer. The development of the large industrial enterprise depended directly on the state of capital concentration, that of the large bureaucracy depended on it indirectly. In both, forms of social labor evolved which specifically deviated from the type of work in a private occupation. From the perspective of a sociology of work, the formal categorization of a business enterprise as belonging to the private realm and of a bureaucracy as belonging to the public realm lost its differentiating power. In whatever way a large enterprise might still be under the control of individual owners, large shareholders, or administrative executives, with regard to private power of control it nevertheless had to become objectified to such an extent that the "world of work" was established as a sphere in its own right between the private and public realms—in the consciousness of the employees and workers and also of those whose powers were more extensive. Of course this development was also based on the material deprivatization of a formally preserved autonomy on the part of owners of the means of production. This has been repeatedly analyzed (under the heading of the separation of ownership and control) with respect to large stock companies, because here the restriction upon the direct exercise of property rights in favor of top management and a few large shareholders became particularly evident. Through self-financing such enterprises often became independent of the capital market; in the same degree they expanded their independence from the mass of the shareholders.[34] Whatever the economic effect, the sociological outcome represented in an exemplary way a development that removed from the large enterprise in general, regardless of its particular form, the character of a sphere of private individual autonomy typical of both business and the workshops of the self-employed in the liberal era. This was recognized early on by Rathenau and summed up in the formula that large enterprises developed into "social institutions" (*Anstalten*). Legal institutionalism seized upon this suggestion and elaborated it into a theory of its own.[35] Although similar doctrines presented by James Burnham and Peter F. Drucker in relation to the American situation became postwar best sellers, they scarcely bore fewer ideological traits. Nevertheless, they did have a certain descriptive value: their diagnosis of the "disappearance of the private" in the sphere of social labor hit the mark.

Initially large enterprises assumed certain status guarantees for their employees and workers, either by putting them in charge of parcelled-out areas of jurisdiction, by granting social securities and services, or by their efforts—however problematic in each case—toward integrating the employed at the work place. But more extreme than these objective changes were the subjective ones. The summary statistical category of "functionaries" (*Diensttuende*) by its very name betrayed a new attitude toward work. The distinction, at one time sharply demarcated (also on the subjective level) by private property, between those who could work in their own private sphere and those who had to do so in that of others was erased in favor of the status of "function performance" (*Dienstverhältnis*). In comparison to the "civil service functionary" (*öffentlicher Dienst*) this status did not involve the rights (and duties) of the civil servant, to be sure, but it assumed the characteristics of a depersonalized work relationship linking the employee to an institution rather than to other persons. With large enterprises, the dominant organizational type of social labor became a social structure neutral to the separation of private and public spheres:

The industrial firms build apartments or even help the employee to become a home owner; they organize concerts and theater performances, offer continuing education classes; they provide for the elderly, widows and orphans. In other words, a series of functions originally fulfilled by institutions that were public not only in the legal but also in the sociological sense, are taken over by organizations whose activity is non-public. . . . The *oikos* of a big firm at times permeates the entire life of a town and brings forth that sort of phenomenon that is correctly labelled "industrial feudalism". . . . *Mutatis mutandis*, the same holds true for the great administrative bureaucracies of the metropoles which lose their public character (in the sociological sense) to the same extent that they are transformed into big enterprises.[36]

American authors could therefore investigate the social psychology of the so-called organization man irrespective of whether they happened to be dealing with a private firm, a semipublic corporation, or a public bureaucracy—"organization" simply referred to any large enterprise.

In comparison with the typical private enterprises of the nineteenth century the occupational sphere gained independence as a quasi-public realm in relation to a private sphere reduced to the family. Today time not spent on the job represents precisely the preserve of the private, while the "job" begins with the step into occupational activity. This process presented itself, however, as a deprivatization of the occupational sphere only in the historical perspective of the property-owning private person. Conversely, it appeared as a privatization to the workers and employees and did so to the extent that they were no longer subject exclusively and without regulation to a patriarchal regiment but instead to a psychological arrangement promoting the human relations on the job that create a pseudo-private well-being.[37]

In the same measure that the occupational sphere became independent, the family withdrew back upon itself. What has characterized the structural transformation of the family since the liberal era is less the loss of productive functions in favor of consumptive ones than its progressive disengagement from the functional complex of social labor in general. For even the patriarchal conjugal family of the bourgeois type had long ceased to be a community of production; nevertheless, it was

based essentially upon family property that functioned capitalistically. Its maintenance, increase, and passing on was the
task of the private person as both the owner of commodities
and head of the family. The exchange relationships of bourgeois society deeply influenced the personal relations between
the members of the bourgeois family. With the loss of its basis
and the replacement of family property by individual incomes
the family lost, beyond its functions *in* production (which it
had already shed to a great extent), those *for* production. The
reduction (typical in our day) of family property to the incomes
of its individual wage and salary earners additionally deprived
the family of the possibility of self-support in cases of emergency and of self-provision for old age.

The classical risks, especially of unemployment, accident,
illness, age, and death are nowadays largely covered by welfare
state guarantees incorporating basic support measures, normally in the form of income supplements.[38] These aids are not
addressed to the family, nor is the family itself expected to
provide subsidiary support to any considerable extent. Against
the so-called basic needs, which the bourgeois family once had
to bear as a private risk, the individual family member today
is publicly protected.[39] In fact, not only was the catalogue of
"typical risks" expanded beyond the classical emergency situations to include assistance of all sorts (i.e., such services as
finding shelter and employment, occupational and educational
counselling, health maintenance, etc.); compensations were
more and more supplemented by preventive measures
whereby "prevention as a matter of social policy is de facto
identical with intrusion into new, hitherto private spheres."[40]
The social-political compensation for the largely eroded basis
of family property stretched beyond material income supplements to functional aids for managing life. For along with its
functions in capital formation the family increasingly lost also
the functions of upbringing and education, protection, care,
and guidance—indeed, of the transmission of elementary tradition and frameworks of orientation. In general it lost its
power to shape conduct in areas considered the innermost
provinces of privacy by the bourgeois family. Thus, in a certain
fashion even the family, this private vestige, was deprivatized

by the public guarantees of its status. On the other hand, the family now evolved even more into a consumer of income and leisure time, into the recipient of publicly guaranteed compensations and support services. Private autonomy was maintained not so much in functions of control as in functions of consumption; today it consists less in commodity owners' power to dispose than in the capacity to enjoy on the part of persons entitled to all sorts of services. As a result there arose the illusion of an intensified privacy in an interior domain whose scope had shrunk to comprise the conjugal family only insofar as it constituted a community of consumers. Once again both aspects asserted their right. A series of functions under private control was replaced by status guarantees; within the narrower framework of these rights and obligations bestowed by the social-welfare state, however, this primary loss in private power of control had the secondary effect of reducing a burden, since the consumption of income, support, and leisure opportunities could be indulged in all the more "privately." In the tendency, observed by Schelsky, toward polarization of large firms enriched by "public" substance, on the one hand, and groups that withdrew into an interior realm of constricted super-private existence, on the other, and hence toward "an increasing split between private and public life,"[41] a complicated developmental history found expression.

Parallel to its release from economic tasks the family lost power as an agent of personal internalization. The trend, diagnosed by Schelsky, toward the elimination from intrafamilial relationships of all aspects not directly relevant to task performance corresponded to a development in the course of which the family was decreasingly relied upon as the primary agency of society. The frequently invoked dismantling of paternal authority, that is, the tendency toward the leveling of the intrafamilial authority structure that can be observed in all advanced industrial nations,[42] was also part of this configuration. To a greater extent individual family members are now socialized by extrafamilial authorities, by society directly.[43] Recall here only those explicitly pedagogical functions that the bourgeois family had to hand over formally to the schools and informally to anonymous forces outside the home.[44] The family, increas-

ingly disengaged from its direct connections with the reproduction of society, thus retained only the illusion of an inner
space of intensified privacy. In truth it lost its protective functions along with its economic tasks. The economic demands
placed upon the patriarchal conjugal family from without corresponded to the institutional strength to shape a domain devoted to the development of the inner life. In our day this
domain, abandoned under the direct onslaught of extrafamilial
authorities upon the individual, has started to dissolve into a
sphere of pseudo-privacy.

This surreptitious hollowing out of the family's intimate
sphere received its architectural expression in the layout of
homes and cities. The closedness of the private home, clearly
indicated to the outside by front yard and fence and made
possible on the inside by the individualized and manifold structuring of rooms, is no longer the norm today, just as, conversely, its openness to the social intercourse of a public sphere
was endangered by the disappearance of the *salon* and of rooms
for the reception of visitors in general. The loss of the private
sphere and of ensured access to the public sphere is characteristic of today's urban mode of dwelling and living, whether
technological and economic developments have quietly
adapted the old forms of urban dwelling to new functions or
new suburban settlement forms have been developed on the
basis of these experiences.

William H. Whyte furnished the American model of such a
suburban world. Under pressure to conform arising from interaction with neighbors—prefigured architecturally in the lay-
ing out of common courtyards for several houses—there
evolved in the socially homogeneous milieu of the prototypical
suburb "a lay version of Army post life."[45] The intimate sphere
dissolved before the gaze of the "group": "Just as doors inside
houses . . . are disappearing, so are the barriers against neighbors. The picture in the picture window . . . is what is going
on *inside*—or, what is going on inside other people's picture
windows."[46] Thin walls guaranteed, if need be, a freedom of
movement protected from sight but not from hearing; they
too assumed functions of social communications difficult to
distinguish from social control. Privacy was not the given me-

dium of home life, but rather one that had first to be brought about: "To gain privacy, one has to *do* something. One court resident, for example, moves his chair to the front rather than the court side of his apartment to show he doesn't want to be disturbed."[47] In proportion as private life became public, the public sphere itself assumed forms of private closeness—in the "neighborhood" the pre-bourgeois extended family arose in a new guise. Here again private and public sphere could not be clearly distinguished. The public's rational-critical debate also became a victim of this "refeudalization." Discussion as a form of sociability gave way to the fetishism of community involvement as such: "Not in solitary and selfish contemplation . . . does one fulfill oneself" in the circles of the bourgeois public—private reading has always been the precondition for rational-critical debate—"but in doing things with other people . . . even watching television together . . . helps make one more of a real person."[48]

Yet the tendency toward the destruction of the relationship between public and private spheres is to be observed not only where modern urban development favored this trend; it was the same elsewhere, where the existing architecture was, as it were, drowned by it. Bahrdt has shown this in the arrangement of "blocks," which in former days, with their fronts toward the street and their backward-facing separate gardens and yards, made possible both a practical internal division of the dwelling and a meaningful ordering of the city as a whole. Today this arrangement has been overtaken, to mention just one factor, by changes in the function of streets and squares due to the technical requirements of traffic flow. The resulting configuration does not afford a spatially protected private sphere, nor does it create free space for public contacts and communications that could bring private people together to form a public. Bahrdt summarizes his findings as follows:

'The process of urbanization can be described as a progressive polarization of social life under the aspects of "public" and "private." In this regard we must note that there always exists a reciprocal relationship between the two. Without a protective and supportive private sphere the individual is sucked into the public realm which, however, becomes denatured by this very process. If the element of distance that is constitutive of the public sphere is eliminated, if its members are in too close touch, the public sphere is transformed into a mass ... at the moment the social problem of the modern city consists not so much in that life in it has become all too urbanized, but rather in that it has again lost essential features of urban life. The reciprocity of the public and the private spheres is disturbed. It is not disturbed because the city dweller is mass man per se and hence no longer has any sensibility for the cultivation of the private sphere; but because he no longer succeeds in getting an overview of the ever more complicated life of the city as a whole in such a fashion that it is really public for him. The more the city as a whole is transformed into a barely penetrable jungle, the more he withdraws into his sphere of privacy which in turn is extended ever further; but at length he comes to realize nevertheless that not the least reason why the urban public sphere disintegrates is that public space has been turned into an ill-ordered arena for tyrannical vehicle traffic'.[49]

The shrinking of the private sphere into the inner areas of a conjugal family largely relieved of function and weakened in authority—the quiet bliss of homeyness—provided only the illusion of a perfectly private personal sphere; for to the extent that private people withdrew from their socially controlled roles as property owners into the purely "personal" ones of their noncommittal use of leisure time, they came directly under the influence of semipublic authorities, without the protection of an institutionally protected domestic domain. Leisure behavior supplies the key to the floodlit privacy of the new sphere, to the externalization of what is declared to be the inner life. What today, as the domain of leisure, is set off from an occupational sphere that has become autonomous, has the tendency to take the place of that kind of public sphere in the world of letters that at one time was the point of reference for a subjectivity shaped in the bourgeois family's intimate sphere.[50]

18 From a Culture-Debating (kulturräsonierend) to a Culture-Consuming Public

The social psychology of the type of privacy that evolved during the eighteenth century out of the experiential context of the conjugal family's audience-oriented intimate sphere provides a key both to the development of a literary public sphere and to certain conditions of its collapse. The public sphere in the world of letters was replaced by the pseudo-public or sham-private world of culture consumption. At that time, when private people were conscious of their double role as *bourgeois* and *homme* and simultaneously asserted the essential identity of property owner with "human being," they owed this self-image to the fact that a public sphere evolved from the very heart of the private sphere itself. Although, in regard to its function, it was only preliminary to a public sphere in the political realm, nevertheless this public sphere in the world of letters itself already had the kind of "political" character by virtue of which it was removed from the sphere of social reproduction.

Bourgeois culture was not mere ideology. The rational-critical debate of private people in the *salons*, clubs, and reading societies was not directly subject to the cycle of production and consumption, that is, to the dictates of life's necessities. Even in its merely literary form (of self-elucidation of the novel experiences of subjectivity) it possessed instead a "political" character in the Greek sense of being emancipated from the constraints of survival requirements. It was for these reasons alone the idea that later degenerated into mere ideology (namely: humanity) could develop at all. The identification of the property owner with the natural person, with the human being as such, presupposed a separation inside the private realm between, on the one hand, affairs that private people pursued individually each in the interests of the reproduction of his own life and, on the other hand, the sort of interaction that united private people into a public. But as soon as and to the degree that the public sphere in the world of letters spread into the realm of consumption, this threshold became levelled. So-called leisure behavior, once it had become part of the cycle of production and consumption, was already apolitical, if for no other reason than its incapacity to constitute a world emancipated from the immediate constraints of survival needs. When leisure was nothing but a complement to time spent on the job,[51] it could be no more than a different arena for the pursuit of private business affairs that were not transformed into a public communication between private people. To be sure, the individuated satisfaction of needs might be achieved in a public fashion, namely, in the company of many others; but a public sphere itself did not emerge from such a situation. When the laws of the market governing the sphere of commodity exchange and of social labor also pervaded the sphere reserved for private people as a public, rational-critical debate had a tendency to be replaced by consumption, and the web of public communication unraveled into acts of individuated reception, however uniform in mode.

Through this development the privacy that had its referent in the public as audience was turned into a travesty. The literary patterns that once had been stamped out of its material circulate today as the explicit production secrets of a patented culture industry whose products, spread publicly by the mass media, for their part bring forth in their consumers' consciousness the illusion of bourgeois privacy to begin with. This social-psychological transmutation of the original relation between the intimate domain and the literary public sphere was linked sociologically to the structural transformation of the family itself.

On the one hand, private people were able to free themselves from the ideological fusion of their double role as *bourgeois* and *homme*; but this uncoupling of the intimate sphere from the basis of property functioning as capital—which seemed to make possible the actualization of its idea within a public sphere of emancipated private people—also brought about new relationships of dependence. The autonomy of private people now no longer grounded in the genuine control over private property would be realizable as an autonomy derived from public status guarantees of privacy only as long as the "human beings" (no longer in their capacity as *bourgeois*, as before, but) in their capacity as *citoyens* themselves attained control over these conditions of their private existence by means of a public sphere that operated in the political realm. Under the given circumstances, this was not to be expected. But if citizens in their familial existence could not draw autonomy from their control over private property, and *also* could not do so from participation in the political public sphere, two things were no longer given. On the one hand, there was no longer institutional support for an individuation of the person on the model of the "Protestant Ethic"; nor, on the other hand, were there social conditions within sight that could replace the classical path of internalization via the educational route of a "political ethics" and in this fashion supply a new foundation for the process of individuation.[52] The bourgeois ideal type assumed that out of the audience-oriented subjectivity's well-founded interior domain a public sphere would evolve in the world of letters. Today, instead of this, the latter has turned into a conduit for social forces channeled into the conjugal family's inner space by way of a public sphere that the mass media have transmogrified into a sphere of culture consumption. The deprivatized province of interiority was hollowed out by the mass media; a pseudo-public sphere of a no longer literary public was patched together to create a sort of superfamilial zone of familiarity.

Since the middle of the nineteenth century, the institutions that until then had ensured the coherence of the public as a critically debating entity have been weakened. The family lost the function of a "circle of literary propaganda"; already the *Gartenlaube* was the idyllically transfigured form in which the middle-class, small-town family absorbed and on the whole merely imitated the thriving educational tradition of the literary high bourgeois family of the preceding generations. The almanacs of the Muses and poetry journals, whose tradition in Germany started in 1770 with those of Leipzig and Göttingen and continued into the following century with those of Schiller, Chamisso, and Schwab, were displaced around 1850 by a type of literary family periodical that—through successful publishing ventures such as *Westermanns Monatshefte* and the *Gartenlaube*—commercially stabilized a reading culture that had already almost become an ideology. But even these still presupposed the family as a sounding board for literature. By now this supposition no longer holds good. The programmatic literary periodicals which since the end of the nineteenth century have functioned as the polemical platforms for an avant-garde that changes with the fashions have never had, nor even sought, links with the stratum of a culturally interested bourgeoisie. Literary family periodicals became themselves obsolete with the structural transformation of the bourgeois family.

Today their place is taken by the popular advertiser-financed illustrated magazines distributed by subscriber services—themselves witness to a culture that no longer trusts the power of the printed word, their official goal of raising the level of book sales notwithstanding.

When the family lost its link with the world of letters, the bourgeois *salon* that had complemented and partly also replaced the reading societies of the eighteenth century also went out of fashion. In this development "the disappearance of alcohol often played the opposite role to the introduction of coffee in seventeenth-century Europe which stimulated sociability. Gentlemen's societies and associations died out, drinking groups were dissolved, and clubs went into eclipse; the notion of social obligations that had played such a great role became hollow."[53] In the course of our century, the bourgeois forms of sociability have found substitutes that have one tendency in common despite their regional and national diversity: abstinence from literary and political debate. On the new model the convivial discussion among individuals gave way to more or less noncommittal group activities. These too assumed fixed forms of informal sociability, yet they lacked that specific institutional power that had once ensured the interconnectedness of sociable contacts as the substratum of public communication—no public was formed around "group activities." The characteristic relationship of a privacy oriented toward an audience was also no longer present when people went to the movies together, listened to the radio, or watched TV. The communication of the public that debated critically about culture remained dependent on reading pursued in the closed-off privacy of the home. The leisure activities of the culture-consuming public, on the contrary, themselves take place within a social climate, and they do not require any further discussions.[54] The private form of appropriation removed the ground for a communication about what has been appropriated. The dialectical relationship between the two was smoothly resolved within the social framework of group activity.[55]

On the other hand, there was also a continuation of the tendency toward rational public debate. So-called debates were formally organized and at the same time compartmentalized as an element of adult education. Religious academies, political forums, and literary organizations owe their existence to the critical review of a culture worthy of discussion and in need of commentary;[56] radio stations, publishers, and associations have turned the staging of panel discussions into a flourishing secondary business. Thus, discussion seems to be carefully cultivated and there seems to be no barrier to its proliferation. But surreptitiously it has changed in a specific way: it assumes the form of a consumer item. To be sure, at one time the commercialization of cultural goods had been the *precondition* for rational-critical debate; but it was itself in principle excluded from the exchange relationships of the market and remained the center of exactly that sphere in which property-owning private people would meet as "human beings" and only as such. Put bluntly: you had to pay for books, theater, concert, and museum, but not for the conversation about what you had read, heard, and seen and what you might completely absorb only through this conversation. Today the conversation itself is administered. Professional dialogues from the podium, panel discussions, and round table shows—the rational debate of private people becomes one of the production numbers of the stars in radio and television, a salable package ready for the box office; it assumes commodity form even at "conferences" where anyone can "participate." Discussion, now a "business," becomes formalized; the presentation of positions and counterpositions is bound to certain prearranged rules of the game; consensus about the subject matter is made largely superfluous by that concerning form. What can be posed as a problem is defined as a question of etiquette; conflicts, once fought out in public polemics, are demoted to the level of personal incompatibilities. Critical debate arranged in this manner certainly fulfills important social-psychological functions, especially that of a tranquilizing substitute for action; however, it increasingly loses its publicist function.[57] The market for cultural goods in the expanded form of the leisure market takes over new functions. To be sure, at one time the unaccustomed commodity form remained so little external to the works of literature and art, of philosophy and science, that only via the market could they constitute themselves as the autonomous products of a culture that, so it seemed, had become independent from praxis. For the public for which they became accessible related to them as objects of judgment and of taste, of free choice and preference. The critical and aesthetic relevances which took themselves to be independent of sheer consumption arose precisely through the medium of the market. For exactly the same reason, however, the function of the market was confined to the distribution of the cultural goods and to their removal from the exclusive use of wealthy patrons and noble connoisseurs. Exchange value still failed to influence the quality of the goods themselves: something of the incompatibility between these kinds of products and the commodity form has been attached to the trade with cultural goods down to our own day. It is not by chance, however, that this consciousness that once characterized the art business as a whole continues to be maintained only in specific preserves; for the laws of the market have already penetrated into the substance of the works themselves and have become inherent in them as formative laws. No longer limited to the distribution and selection, the presentation and furnishing of the works, the perspectives of sales strategy have come to guide their very production in the wide fields of a culture of consumers. Indeed, mass culture has earned its rather dubious name precisely by achieving increased sales by adapting to the need for relaxation and entertainment on the part of consumer strata with relatively little education, rather than through the guidance of an enlarged public toward the appreciation of a culture undamaged in its substance.

It was in this old-fashioned manner that at the close of the eighteenth century the public of the educated strata expanded to include strata of the self-employed petty bourgeoisie. At that time retailers, who as shopkeepers were usually excluded from bourgeois clubs, in many places established their own associations; still more widespread were the trade societies[58] which took the form of reading societies. In many cases they were branches of the bourgeois reading societies: their direction and also the selection of the reading materials were left to dignitaries who, so very much in the fashion of the enlightenment, wanted to improve the education of the so-called lower classes.

Anyone who owned an encyclopedia was educated; this standard was subsequently taken over also by grocers and craftsmen. The "people" were brought up to the level of culture; culture was not lowered to that of the masses.

Correspondingly, the different functions of the market had to be rigorously distinguished: whether it created an initial access to cultural goods for a public and then, in keeping with the cheapening of the cost of the products, *economically eased* the access for an ever larger public; or whether it adapted the content of the cultural goods to its own needs in such a way that it also *facilitated* access for broad strata *psychologically*. Meyersohn speaks in this context of the reduction of the "entrance requirements into leisure."[59] To the degree that culture became a commodity not only in form but also in content, it was emptied of elements whose appreciation required a certain amount of training—whereby the "accomplished" appropriation once again heightened the appreciative ability itself. It was not merely standardization as such that established an inverse relationship between the commercialization of cultural goods and their complexity, but that special preparation of products that made them consumption-ready, which is to say, guaranteed an enjoyment without being tied to stringent presuppositions. Of course, such enjoyment is also entirely inconsequential. Serious involvement with culture produces facility, while the consumption of mass culture leaves no lasting trace; it affords a kind of experience which is not cumulative[60] but regressive.[61]

The two functions of the market for cultural goods—the easing of access in a purely economic or in a psychological fashion—did not go hand in hand. This is demonstrated in our own day in the sector most essential to critical literary debate, the book market, which is dominated by two complementary phenomena. Through paperback series printed in large editions[62] a relatively small stratum of readers educated or ready to be educated (overwhelmingly pupils and students) have high quality literature made available to them which in their standard hardbound version would be unaffordable. Although attractive design and well organized distribution has given to this species of book (as to no other) the appearance of a commodity prepared for easy use and quick deterioration, in this case the market preserves the emancipatory function of an exclusively economic easing of access. The content of the paperbacks remains undisturbed by the laws of mass production to which they owe wide distribution. That is to say, with the paperbacks there appears the permanent in the guise of the transitory—a paradox pointed out by Wolfgang Kayser[63]— in contrast to the Readers' Circle (*Lesering*) books, which present the transitory in the guise of the permanent: half-calf and gilt-stamped.

The book clubs first formed in the Anglo-Saxon countries after the First World War and which today already control the largest share of the market[64] also reduce the publisher's risk and cheapen the price per copy. Sales strategies and distribution, however, which circumvent the retail trade and diminish the consumer's selection opportunity to the same degree to which they intensify the direct contact of the editors with the needs of mass taste, ease the access to literature not merely economically for consumers from overwhelmingly lower social strata. Instead they lower the "entrance requirements" psychologically in such a way that the literature itself has to be tailored to the convenience and ease of a reception of fewer requisites and weaker consequences. With this example, moreover, it becomes clear how the social-psychological criterion of a culture of consumers, namely, noncumulative experience, goes together with the sociological criterion of a destruction of the public sphere. Book clubs remove the great mass of fiction not only from availability in the retail trade selection but also from criticism. The clubs' illustrated magazines, an internal advertising vehicle, as the single link between publishers and readers short-circuit the communication network. Book clubs administer their clientele directly as part of the business—outside the public sphere in the world of letters. Conversely, the weakening of the role of criticism itself may be connected with this, a criticism in which at one time, when reviewers of the caliber of Schiller and Schlegel did not regard themselves as too good for voluminous incidental activity of this sort, the lay judgment of the private people with an interest in literature had been institutionalized.

The full extent of the tendency toward the collapse of a

literary public sphere, however, becomes evident in its entirety only when the broadening of the reading public to include almost all strata of the population is compared with the actual prevalence of book reading. In West Germany more than a third of all potential readers read no books at all and more than two-fifths buy no books;[65] the relevant figures for the Anglo-Saxon countries and France are comparable. The replacement of a reading public that debated critically about matters of culture by the mass public of culture consumers is therefore only inadequately reflected in the breadth of the market for books. This process avails itself of transforming devices other than the bourgeois means of education par excellence—the book.[66]

The first newspaper with a mass edition of over 50,000 copies was, significantly, the organ of the Chartist movement—Cobbett's *Political Register*, published beginning in 1816. The same economic situation that pressured the masses into participating in the public sphere in the political realm denied them the level of education that would have enabled them to participate in the mode and on the level of bourgeois readers of journals. Soon, therefore, a penny press, which in the early thirties reached runs of 100,000 and 200,000 copies, and (by the middle of the century) the more widely distributed weekend press supplied the "psychological facilitation" that has characterized the commercial printed mass media ever since. Parallel developments occurred with Emile Girardin after the July Revolution in Paris and Benjamin Day's *New York Sun* in the United States. It would be another fifty years before Pulitzer bought the *New York World* and, at the same time as *Lloyd's Weekly Newspaper* in London, really penetrated the broad masses with the aid of the methods of "yellow journalism" and in editions that quickly approached one million. The sensationalist press of the eighties was dubbed yellow journalism because of the yellow color of the comics (whose representative figure was the "Yellow Kid"). The techniques of the cartoon, news picture, and human-interest story grew out of the repertory of the weekly press, which even earlier had presented its news and fictional stories in a way that was as optically effective as it was undemanding on the literary level.[67] Toward the end of the

century the "American" form of mass press also became dominant on the continent; here too the weekend press and illustrated magazines were the pacesetters for boulevard papers
proper.

The mass press was based on the commercialization of the
participation in the public sphere on the part of broad strata
designed predominantly to give the masses in general access
to the public sphere. This expanded public sphere, however,
lost its political character to the extent that the means of "psychological facilitation" could become an end in itself for a
commercially fostered consumer attitude. In the case of the
early penny press it could already be observed how it paid for
the maximization of its sales with the depoliticization of its
content—by eliminating political news and political editorials
on such moral topics as intemperance and gambling.[68]

The journalistic principles of the illustrated newspaper had
an honorable tradition. In relation to the expansion of the
news-reading public, therefore, the press that submitted political issues to critical discussion in the long run lost its influence.
Instead, the culture-consuming public whose inheritance
derived from the public sphere in the world of letters more
than from that in the political realm attained a remarkable
dominance.[69]

Admittedly, this consumption of culture was to a high degree
detached from literary vehicles. Nonverbal communications or
those that, if they had not been translated into picture and
sound altogether, were facilitated by optical and acoustic support, replaced to a greater or lesser extent the classical forms
of literary production. These trends can also be observed in
the daily press which is still closest to them. By means of
variegated type and layout and ample illustration reading is
made easy at the same time that its field of spontaneity in
general is restricted by serving up the material as a ready-made
convenience, patterned and predigested. Editorial opinions re-
cede behind information from press agencies and reports from
correspondents; critical debate disappears behind the veil of
internal decisions concerning the selection and presentation of
the material. In addition the share of political or politically
relevant news changes. Public affairs, social problems, eco-

nomic matters, education, and health—according to a categorization suggested by American authors,[70] precisely the
"delayed reward news"—are not only pushed into the background by "immediate reward news" (comics, corruption, accidents, disasters, sports, recreation, social events, and human
interest) but, as the characteristic label already indicates, are
also actually read less and more rarely. In the end the news
generally assumes some sort of guise and is made to resemble
a narrative from its format down to stylistic detail (news stories); the rigorous distinction between fact and fiction is ever
more frequently abandoned.[71] News and reports and even editorial opinions are dressed up with all the accoutrements of
entertainment literature, whereas on the other hand the bel-
letrist contributions aim for the strictly "realistic" reduplication
of reality "as it is" on the level of cliches and thus, in turn,
erase the line between fiction and report.[72]

What in this way only intimates itself in the daily press has
progressed further in the newer media. The integration of the
once separate domains of journalism and literature, that is to
say, of information and rational-critical argument on the one
side and of *belles lettres* on the other, brings about a peculiar
shifting of reality—even a conflation of different levels of reality. Under the common denominator of so-called human interest emerges the *mixtum compositum* of a pleasant and at the
same time convenient subject for entertainment that, instead
of doing justice to reality, has a tendency to present a substitute
more palatable for consumption and more likely to give rise to
an impersonal indulgence in stimulating relaxation than to a
public use of reason. Radio, film, and television by degrees
reduce to a minimum the distance that a reader is forced to
maintain toward the printed letter—a distance that required
the privacy of the appropriation as much as it made possible
the publicity of a rational-critical exchange about what had
been read. With the arrival of the new media the form of
communication as such has changed; they have had an impact,
therefore, more penetrating (in the strict sense of the word)
than was ever possible for the press.[73] Under the pressure of
the "Don't talk back!" the conduct of the public assumes a
different form. In comparison with printed communications

the programs sent by the new media curtail the reactions of their recipients in a peculiar way. They draw the eyes and ears of the public under their spell but at the same time, by taking away its distance, place it under "tutelage," which is to say they deprive it of the opportunity to say something and to disagree.[74] The critical discussion of a reading public tends to give way to "exchanges about tastes and preferences"[75] between consumers—even the talk about what is consumed, "the examination of tastes," becomes a part of consumption itself.

The world fashioned by the mass media is a public sphere in appearance only. By the same token the integrity of the private sphere which they promise to their consumers is also an illusion. In the course of the eighteenth century, the bourgeois reading public was able to cultivate in the intimate exchange of letters (as well as in the reading of the literature of psychological novels and novellas engendered by it) a subjectivity capable of relating to literature and oriented toward a public sphere. In this form private people interpreted their new form of existence which was indeed based on the liberal relationship between public and private spheres. The experience of privacy made possible literary experimentation with the psychology of the humanity common to all, with the abstract individuality of the natural person. Inasmuch as the mass media today strip away the literary husks from that kind of bourgeois self-interpretation and utilize them as marketable forms for the public services provided in a culture of consumers, the original meaning is reversed. On the one hand, the socialized patterns of eighteenth-century literature that are used to serve up twentieth-century affairs for human interest and the biographical note[76] transfer the illusion of an untouched private sphere and intact private autonomy to conditions which have long since removed the basis for both. On the other hand, they are also imposed on political matters of fact to such an extent that the public sphere itself becomes privatized in the consciousness of the consuming public; indeed, the public sphere becomes the sphere for the publicizing of private biographies, so that the accidental fate of the so-called man in the street or that of systematically managed stars attain publicity, while publicly relevant developments and decisions are garbed in private dress and through personalization distorted to the point of unrecognizability. The sentimentality toward persons and corresponding cynicism toward institutions which with social psychological inevitability result naturally curtail the subjective capacity for rational criticism of public authority, even where it might objectively still be possible.

Even in the strata which once counted as "cultured," the formerly protective space of the family's inner sanctum has been pried open to such an extent that the private activities of reading novels and writing letters as preconditions for participation in the public sphere of the world of letters are suspended. Concerning the conduct of the bourgeois reading public it may be considered an established fact that the frequency of book reading in the expanded public of the mass media has been decreasing rapidly. The custom of exchanging personal letters appears to have disappeared to at least the same extent. It is replaced in many ways by the participation in the letter exchanges carried on by the editors of newspaper and periodicals and by radio and television stations with their readership. In general, the mass media recommend themselves as addressees of personal needs and difficulties, as authorities for advice on the problems of life. They offer abundant opportunity for identification—for a kind of regeneration of the private realm out of the readily available pool of public support and counseling services.[77] The original relationship of the domain of interiority to the public sphere in the world of letters is reversed. An inner life oriented toward a public audience tends to give way to reifications related to the inner life. The problems of private existence are to a certain degree absorbed by the public sphere; although they are not resolved under the supervision of the publicist agencies, they are certainly dragged into the open by them. On the other hand, the consciousness of privacy is heightened precisely by such publication; by means of it the sphere generated by the mass media has taken on the traits of a secondary realm of intimacy.[78]

What corresponds sociologically to this social-psychological diagnosis is not, as a widespread prejudice would have it, a public overwhelmed and shredded only at the periphery by semiliterate masses of consumers while at its center (especially

in the higher ranks of the new middle class) still continuing to
a degree in the tradition of those eighteenth- and early nineteenth-century private people who carried on a rational-critical
literary debate. For if this were so, one would expect that the
institutions and modes of behavior of the new culture of consumers would proliferate more and further among the lower
social strata than among the higher ones. Present conditions
do not support such an assumption. Instead, regular reading
of weekend magazines, illustrated periodicals, and boulevard
sheets, regular reception of radio and television, and regular
visits to the movies are still more prevalent among relatively
higher status groups and among city dwellers than in lower
status groups and the rural population. Almost without exception this kind of culture consumption increases directly with
status, as measured by criteria of occupation, income, and formal schooling, as well as with the degree of urbanization, ranging from village through small town to medium and large
cities.[79] On the one hand, the lines along which the public has
expanded cannot simply be projected backward, with regard
to its social composition today, as if ever new strata had been
integrated at the margin into the circle of the urban-bourgeois
reading public of that "educated class." On the other hand,
the data also contradict the opposite version, that the public of
the mass media has exploded and pushed aside the old public
"from below" (i.e., out of the working class) or "from outside"
(i.e., from the rural population). The facts of social history
suggest instead that one may extrapolate to a certain extent
from the case of an expansion of the public with the introduction of television in the United States (which could be verified
by the controlled observations of empirical social research) to
the processes of expansion and simultaneous transformation
at earlier stages as well (i.e., from a public that made culture
an object of critical debate into one that consumes it). In the
United States it has been established that among the groups
first to purchase television sets, buyers prevailed whose education did not match their income levels.[80] If a generalization
be permitted, the consumer strata first penetrated by the new
form of mass culture belonged neither to the established stratum of educated persons nor to the lower social strata but often

to upwardly mobile groups whose status was still in need of cultural legitimation.[81] Introduced by this trigger group the new medium then spread within the higher social stratum, gradually taking over the lower status groups last.

Interrelations of this sort may also explain how a stratum of "intellectuals" split off from the highly educated bourgeois strata; their ideologically conserved self-interpretation notwithstanding, the latter have fully maintained their (now, of course, less glorious) leadership role even among the new public of culture consumers. Of Richardson's *Pamela* it could be said that it was read by the entire public, that is, by "everyone" who read at all. Roughly with the advent of naturalism this intimate relationship between artists and men of letters and their public dissipated a bit; at the same time, the public that had been "left behind" lost its critical power over the producers. From this point on modern art lived under a shroud of propaganda. The recognition in print of an artist and work was only fortuitously related to their recognition by the public at large. Only then did there arise a stratum of "intellectuals" that explains to itself its progressive isolation from, at first, the public of the educated bourgeoisie as an—illusory—emancipation from social locations altogether and interprets itself as "free-floating intellectuals." Hauser dates its origin from about the middle of the nineteenth century:

It was only after its victory over the Revolution and the defeat of Chartism that the bourgeoisie felt so safely entrenched that it no longer felt any qualms and twinges of conscience and imagined that it was no longer in any need of criticism. But the cultural elite, and especially its literarily productive section, thereby lost the feeling of having a mission to fulfill in society. It saw itself cut off from the social class of which it had hitherto been the mouthpiece and it felt completely isolated between the uneducated classes and the bourgeoisie. It was this feeling that first gave rise to the replacement of the earlier cultural stratum with its roots in the middle class by the social group that we call the "intelligentsia."[82]

A century later, to be sure, this stratum of intellectuals has become completely integrated socially.[83] A group of well paid cultural functionaries has risen from lumpenproletarian bohemia to the respectability of the managerial and bureaucratic elite. What has remained is the avant-garde as an institution. Corresponding to it is a continuing alienation between, on the one hand, the productive and critical minorities of specialists and specializing amateurs—who keep up with the processes of high-grade abstraction in art, literature and philosophy, with the way of becoming dated that is specific to the ambit of modernity,[84] and, of course, with mere changes in scene and trendy humbug—and, on the other hand, the great public of the mass media.

This phenomenon once more sums up the disintegration of the public sphere in the world of letters. The sounding board of an educated stratum tutored in the public use of reason has been shattered; the public is split apart into minorities of specialists who put their reason to use nonpublicly and the great mass of consumers whose receptiveness is public but uncritical.[85] Consequently, it completely lacks the form of communication specific to a public.

19 The Blurred Blueprint: Developmental Pathways in the Disintegration of the Bourgeois Public Sphere

Along the path from a public critically reflecting on its culture to one that merely consumes it, the public sphere in the world of letters, which at one point could still be distinguished from that in the political realm, has lost its specific character. For the "culture" propagated by the mass media is a culture of integration. It not only integrates information with critical debate and the journalistic format with the literary forms of the psychological novel into a combination of entertainment and "advice" governed by the principle of "human interest"; at the same time it is flexible enough to assimilate elements of advertising, indeed, to serve itself as a kind of super slogan that, if it did not already exist, could have been invented for the purpose of public relations serving the cause of the status quo.[86] The public sphere assumes advertising functions. The more it can be deployed as a vehicle for political and economic propaganda, the more it becomes unpolitical as a whole and pseudo-privatized.[87]

The model of the bourgeois public sphere presupposed strict

separation of the public from the private realm in such a way
that the public sphere, made up of private people gathered
together as a public and articulating the needs of society with
the state, was itself considered part of the private realm. To
the extent that the public and private became intermeshed
realms, this model became inapplicable. That is to say, a repoliticized social sphere originated that could not be subsumed
under the categories of public and private from either a sociological or a legal perspective. In this intermediate sphere the
sectors of society that had been absorbed by the state and the
sectors of the state that had been taken over by society intermeshed without involving any rational-critical political debate
on the part of private people. The public was largely relieved
of this task by other institutions: on the one hand by associations in which collectively organized private interests directly
attempted to take on the form of political agency; on the other
hand by parties which, fused with the organs of public authority, established themselves, as it were, *above* the public whose
instruments they once were. The process of the politically relevant exercise and equilibration of power now takes place directly between the private bureaucracies, special-interest
associations, parties, and public administration. The public as
such is included only sporadically in this circuit of power, and
even then it is brought in only to contribute its acclamation. In
so far as they are wage or salary earners and entitled to services,
private people are forced to have their publicly relevant claims
advocated collectively. But the decisions left for them to make
individually as consumers and voters come under the influence
of economic and political agencies to the same degree that any
public relevance can be attributed to them. To the extent that
social reproduction still depends on consumption decisions and
the exercise of political power on voting decisions made by
private citizens there exists an interest in influencing them—
in the case of the former, with the aim of increasing sales; in
the case of the latter, of increasing formally this or that party's
share of voters or, informally, to give greater weight to the
pressure of specific organizations. The social latitude for private decisions is, of course, predetermined by objective factors
like buying power and group membership and by socioeco-

nomic status generally. Yet the more the original relationship between the intimate sphere and the public sphere in the world of letters is reversed and permits an undermining of the private sphere through publicity, the more decisions within this latitude can be influenced. In this fashion the consumption of culture also enters the service of economic and political propaganda. Whereas the relationship of the public sphere in the world of letters to that in the political realm was once absolutely constitutive for that central identification of "property owner" with "human being" as such, without therefore viewing them as coextensive, there prevails today a tendency toward the absorption of the plebiscitary "political" public sphere by one depoliticized through a preoccupation with consumption of culture.

Marx shared the perspective of the propertyless and uneducated masses who, without fulfilling the conditions for admission to the bourgeois public sphere, nonetheless made their way into it in order to translate economic conflicts into the only form holding any promise of success—that is, into political conflict. In Marx's opinion the masses would employ the platform of the public sphere, institutionalized in the constitutional state, not to destroy it but to make it into what, according to liberal pretense, it had always claimed to be. In reality, however, the occupation of the political public sphere by the unpropertied masses led to an interlocking of state and society which removed from the public sphere its former basis without supplying a new one. For the integration of the public and private realms entailed a corresponding disorganization of the public sphere that once was the go-between linking state and society. This mediating function passed from the public to such institutions as have arisen out of the private sphere (e.g., special-interest associations) or out of the public sphere, e.g., parties; these now engage in the exercise and equilibration of power in cooperation with the state apparatus, treating it as a matter internal to their organizations. At the same time they endeavor, via mass media that themselves have become autonomous, to obtain the agreement or at least acquiescence of a mediatized public. Publicity is generated from above, so to speak, in order to create an aura of good will for certain positions. Originally publicity guaranteed the connection between rational-critical public debate and the legislative foundation of domination, including the critical supervision of its exercise. Now it makes possible the peculiar ambivalence of a domination exercised through the domination of nonpublic opinion: it serves the manipulation *of* the public as much as legitimation *before* it. Critical publicity is supplanted by manipulative publicity.

How the idea as well as the reality of a public operating in the political realm were transformed simultaneously with the principle of publicity is demonstrated by the dissolution and obsolescence of the link—still pretended to by liberalism—between public discussion and legal norm. The liberal concept of legal norm (which bound both the executive and the judiciary, although not in the same manner) implied the elements of universality and truth: justice was equivalent to rightness (*Richtigkeit*). The public sphere of civil society was reflected in its structure, for, on the one hand, the generality of laws in the strict sense was guaranteed only so long as the undisturbed autonomy of society as a private sphere made it possible to exclude special interests from the legislative material and to restrict normative regulation to the general conditions of a compromise between interests. The "truth" of the laws, on the other hand, was only guaranteed as long as a public sphere, elevated in the parliament to an organ of the state, made it possible to discover, through public discussion, what was practically necessary in the general interest. In this arrangement it was precisely the formal nature of that universality which guaranteed "truth"—as rightness in the material sense of bourgeois class interest—that was part of the soon to be discovered dialectic of this concept of law. It was based on the dialectic of the public sphere of civil society itself.

Since the separation of state and society was overcome and the government intervened in the social order through advance planning, distribution, and administration, the generality of the norm could no longer be maintained as a principle.[88] The affairs requiring normative regulation now also comprise social conditions in the narrower sense; hence they are concrete, that is, they involve specific groups of persons and transitory situations. Laws, even where they are not explicitly announced as measures pertaining to a special or single case, as non-general norms,[89] under these circumstances often already assume the character of detailed administrative dispositions. The distinction between general law and specific regulatory measure has become blurred. In part legislation sees itself compelled to become so concrete as to penetrate deeply into levels of administrative discretion. More often administrative jurisdictions are expanded in such a way that their activity can hardly any longer be considered a mere execution of the law. Forsthoff summarizes the three typical processes which subvert the classical separation and at the same time complementary interlocking of these two powers. This subversion occurs first inasmuch as the legislator himself takes steps toward implementation and executive measures; he invades the jurisdiction of the administration (in the case of specific regulatory measures). Second, it occurs inasmuch as the lawmaker transfers his functions to the administration; the latter is empowered to legislate supplementary norms by way of administrative ordinances (in the case of enabling-legislation). Finally, it happens inasmuch as the legislator, confronted with a matter in need of regulation, refrains from establishing any norms whatsoever and gives the administration free rein.[90]

In the same degree to which this kind of mutual penetration of state and society dissolved a private sphere whose independent existence made possible the generality of the laws, the foundation for a relatively homogeneous public composed of private citizens engaged in rational-critical debate was also shaken. Competition between organized private interests invaded the public sphere. If the particular interests that as privatized interests were neutralized in the common denominator of class interest once permitted public discussion to attain a certain rationality and even effectiveness, it remains that today the display of competing interests has taken the place of such discussion. The consensus developed in rational-critical public debate has yielded to compromise fought out or simply imposed nonpublicly. The laws that come into existence in this way can no longer be vindicated as regards their elements of "truth," even though in many cases the element of universality is preserved in them; for even the parliamentary public sphere—the place in which "truth" would have to present its credentials—has collapsed.

As has often been described in detail in the literature of the field, discussion loses its creative character. The speeches made in the plenary sessions of the parliament are no longer meant to convince delegates whose opinions differ, but are directed instead—at least as regards the basic issues that dominate political life—directly to the active citizenry. . . . The public sphere that once drew its life from the events occurring in the parliamentary assembly, and that in turn conveyed to it a special glamour, thus assumes a plebiscitary character.[91]

Reflecting these changing realities now even the concept of legal norm itself is positivistically stripped of the marks of universality and truth. Since the 1860s the doctrine of the double concept of law has won out in Germany. Since then "law" in a material sense has come to designate any legal proposition enacted by the proper authorities, regardless of whether it is a general rule or a particular regulation. "Law" in a formal sense, in contrast, refers to all the laws that have come about through parliamentary procedure, no matter what their content.[92] The original connection between the public sphere in the political realm and the rule of law, so clearly formulated by Kant, is captured by neither of these conceptions of law. The altered structure of the law brings out the fact that the task of providing a rational justification for political domination can no longer be expected from the principle of publicity. To be sure, within an immensely expanded sphere of publicity the mediatized public is called upon more frequently and in incomparably more diverse ways for the purposes of public acclamation; at the same time it is so remote from the processes of the exercise and equilibration of power that their rational justification can scarcely be demanded, let alone be accomplished any longer, by the principle of publicity.

VI

The Transformation of the Public Sphere's Political Function

20 From the Journalism of Private Men of Letters to the Public Consumer Services of the Mass Media: The Public Sphere as a Platform for Advertising

The shift in function of the principle of publicity is based on a shift in function of the public sphere as a special realm. This shift can be clearly documented with regard to the transformation of the public sphere's preeminent institution, the press. On the one hand, to the extent that the press became commercialized, the threshhold between the circulation of a commodity and the exchange of communications among the members of a public was leveled; within the private domain the clear line separating the public sphere from the private became blurred. On the other hand, however, to the extent that only certain political guarantees could safeguard the continued independence of its institutions, the public sphere ceased altogether to be exclusively a part of the private domain.[1]

Developed out of the system of private correspondences and for a long time overshadowed by them the newspaper trade was initially organized in the form of small handicraft business. In this beginning phase its calculations were made in accord with the principle of a modest maximization of profit that did not overstep the traditional bounds of early capitalism. The publisher was interested in his enterprise purely as a business. His activity was confined essentially to the organization of the flow of news and the collating of the news itself. As soon as the press developed from a business in pure news reporting to one involving ideologies and viewpoints, however, and the compiling of items of information encountered the competition of literary journalism, a new element—political in the broader sense—was joined to the economic one. Bücher captures the trend succinctly: "From mere institutions for the publication of news, the papers became also carriers and leaders of public opinion, and instruments in the arsenal of party politics. For the internal organization of the newspaper enterprise this had the consequence that a new function was inserted between the gathering and the publication of news: the editorial function. For the newspaper's publisher, however, this meant that he changed from being a merchant of news to being a dealer in public opinion."[2]

The crucial turnabout, of course, had already occurred before the introduction of a special editorial function; it had begun with the "scholarly journals" on the continent and moral weeklies and political journals in Great Britain, as soon as individual authors availed themselves of the new instrument of the periodical press providing a hearing for their critical-rational reflections, pursued with pedagogical intent, by getting them into print. This second phase has been characterized as one of literary journalism.[3] At this point the commercial purpose of such enterprises receded almost entirely into the background; indeed, violating all the rules of profitability, they often were money losers from the start. The pedagogical and later increasingly political impulse could be financed, so to speak, by bankruptcy. In Great Britain newspapers and journals of this sort frequently were the "hobbyhorses of the money-aristocracy";[4] on the continent they arose more often from the initiative of individual scholars and men of letters.

At first the latter bore the economic risk themselves. They procured material as they saw fit, paid their collaborators, and owned the journals whose issues represented for their publishers a continuous series of individual projects. Only gradually did the editors yield their entrepreneurial functions to publishers. This development explains the preeminent position of the editors who continued to be "editor" and "author" in one.

At that time (around the turn of the nineteenth century) the relationship between publisher and editor was not simply one of employer to employee; frequently the latter still shared in the profits. To be sure, the traditional type of newspaper entrepreneur survived right down to the nineteenth century, especially among old style dailies that stayed away from literary and political reflection and debate. Markus Dumont when he took over the *Kölnische Zeitung* in 1805 was still author, editor, publisher, and printer all in one. But the competing periodical press of journalistically active men of letters led, wherever such enterprises were consolidated, to the establishment of specialized and independent editorships. In Germany Cotta led the way by good example. He appointed Posselt as the editor responsible for the *Neueste Weltkunde*; the publicist and economic functions were now divided between "editor" and publisher. In connection with this editorial autonomy, the institution of the lead article came to prevail during the first half of the nineteenth century even in the daily press. Yet Cotta's example shows again how little, with the new form of editorial journalism, the profitability of the enterprise got the upper hand over its publicist intention, how little business outweighed conviction. His *Allgemeine Zeitung* remained a subsidized undertaking for decades, regardless of its significant influence. In the phase of the ascendancy of the public sphere as one with a political function, even the newspaper enterprises consolidated in the hands of publishers continued to give their editors the kind of freedom that in general characterized the communication of private people functioning as a public.

The publishers procured for the press a commercial basis without, however, commercializing it as such. A press that had evolved out of the public's use of its reason and that had merely been an extension of its debate remained thoroughly an institution of this very public: effective in the mode of a transmitter and amplifier, no longer a mere vehicle for the transportation of information but not yet a medium for culture as an object of consumption. Prototypically this type of press can be observed in times of revolution, when the journals of the tiniest political groupings and associations mushroom—in Paris in the year 1789 every marginally prominent politician formed his club, and every other founded his journal; between February and May alone 450 clubs and over 200 journals sprang up.[5] As long as the mere existence of a press that critically-rationally debates political matters remained problematic, it was compelled to engage in continuous self-thematization: before the permanent legalization of the political public sphere, the appearance of a political journal and its survival was equivalent to involvement in the struggle over the range of freedom to be granted to public opinion and over publicity as a principle. To be sure, even the journals in the old style had been rigorously subject to censorship; but the resistance against these restrictions could never be carried on in their own columns as long as the journals exclusively provided news. The regulations of an authoritarian state degraded the press into a mere trade, subject like all other trades to police instructions and prohibitions. In contrast, the editorializing press as the institution of a discussing public was primarily concerned with asserting the latter's critical function; therefore the capital for running the enterprise was only secondarily invested for the sake of a profitable return, if such a consideration played a role at all.

Only with the establishment of the bourgeois constitutional state and the legalization of a political public sphere was the press as a forum of rational-critical debate released from the pressure to take sides ideologically; now it could abandon its polemical stance and concentrate on the profit opportunities for a commercial business. In Great Britain, France, and the United States at about the same time (the 1830s) the way was paved for this sort of transition from a press that took ideological sides to one that was primarily a business. The advertising business put financial calculation on a whole new basis. In a situation of greatly lowered price per copy and a multiplied number of buyers, the publisher could count on selling a correspondingly growing portion of space in his paper for advertisements. Bücher's well-known statement "that the paper assumes the character of an enterprise which produces advertising space as a commodity that is made marketable by means of an editorial section" refers to this third phase of development. These initial attempts at a modern commercial press gave back to the journal the unequivocal character of a private commercial enterprise now, however—in contrast to the handicraft shops of the old "publishers"—on the level of the big business of advanced capitalism. Around the middle of the century a number of newspaper enterprises were already organized as stock companies.[6]

If at first, within a daily press that was primarily politically motivated, the reorganization of individual enterprises on an exclusively commercial basis still represented nothing more than a possibility for profitable investment, it would soon become a necessity for all editors. For the upgrading and perfection of the technical and organizational apparatus demanded an expansion of the capital basis, an increase of the commercial risks, and, necessarily, the subordination of entrepreneurial policy to the demands of business efficiency. Already in 1814 the *Times* was being printed on a new high-speed printing machine that after four and a half centuries replaced Gutenberg's wooden press. A generation later the invention of the telegraph revolutionized the organization of the whole news network.[7] Not only the private economic interests of the individual enterprise gained in importance; the newspaper, as it developed into a capitalist undertaking, became enmeshed in a web of interests extraneous to business that sought to exercise influence upon it. The history of the big daily papers in the second half of the nineteenth century proves that the press itself became manipulable to the extent that it became commercialized. Ever since the marketing of the editorial section became interdependent with that of the advertising section, the press (until then an institution of private people insofar as they constituted a public) became an institution of certain participants in the public sphere in their capacity as private individuals; that is, it became the gate through which privileged private interests invaded the public sphere.

The relationship between publisher and editor changed correspondingly. Editorial activity had, under the pressure of the technically, advanced transmission of news, in any event already become specialized; once a literary activity, it had become a journalistic one.[8] The selection of material became more important than the lead article; the processing and evaluation of news and its screening and organization more urgent than the advocacy of a "line" through an effective literary presentation. Especially since the 1870s the tendency has become manifest: the rank and reputation of a newspaper are no longer primarily a function of its excellent publicists but of its talented publishers. The publisher appoints editors in the expectation that they will do as they are told in the private interest of a profit-oriented enterprise.[9]

The publicist autonomy of the editor, incidentally, is painfully restricted even in the kind of press that does not submit to the laws of the market but serves primarily political goals—and thus is more closely related to the literary journalism of the journals cultivating rational-critical debates. For a while the political press indeed managed to preserve its individualistic style, even after parliamentary factions and parties had constituted themselves in Great Britain and France. A type of party press like the one that with Wirth's *Deutsche Tribüne* entered upon the scene in Germany after the July revolution still held sway around the middle of the century. These publicists were not dependent on any one party or faction but were themselves politicians who around their paper rallied a parliamentary following. Nevertheless, the beginnings of a party-bound press controlled by political organizations go back to the first half of the century, at least in Great Britain and France. In Germany it evolved in the 1860s, first among the conservatives and then among the Social Democrats.[10] The editor was subordinated to a supervisory committee instead of to a director of publishing—in either case he became an employee subject to directives.

Of course, the aspects of the structural transformation of the press that related to the sociology of business enterprise must not be considered in isolation from general tendencies toward concentration and centralization which prevailed here too. In the last quarter of the century the first great newspaper trusts were formed: Hearst in the United States, Northcliffe in Great Britain, and Ullstein and Mosse in Germany. This movement has advanced in our century, although unevenly.[11] Technological development in the means of transmission of news (after the telegraph and the telephone came the wireless telegraph and telephone and shortwave and radio) has in part hastened and in part made possible the organizational unification and economic interlocking of the press. The homogenization of news services by monopolistically organized press agencies[12] was soon followed by the editorial homogenization of smaller papers through the sharing of plates and the advent of factories producing inserts. Matrices were first employed in the Anglo-Saxon countries between 1870 and 1880; by the turn of the century matrix presses also predominated on the continent. Usually this sort of technological unification went hand in hand with organizational unifications in newspaper groups or chains. Parochial papers in the predominantly rural areas were in this way often also made economically dependent on papers in cities nearby and were annexed by them in the form of regional supplementary editorships.[13]

Nevertheless the degree of economic concentration and technological-organizational coordination in the newspaper publishing industry seems small in comparison to the new media of the twentieth century—film, radio, and television. Indeed, their capital requirements seemed so gigantic and their publicist power so threatening that in some countries the establishment of these media was from the start under government direction or under government control. Nothing characterized the development of the press and of the more recent media more conspicuously than these measures: they turned private institutions of a public composed of private people into public corporations (*öffentliche Anstalten*). The reaction of the state to a power-penetrated public sphere that had come under the influence of forces developed in society can already be studied in relation to the history of the first telegraph bureaus. At first, governments brought the agencies into indirect dependence and bestowed on them a semiofficial status not, of course, by eliminating their commercial character but by exploiting it. Meanwhile, Reuters Ltd. is the property of the united British press; however, the consent of the highest court that is required for any change in its statutes lends it a certain public character. The Agence France Press, grown after the Second World War out of the Agence Havas, is a state enterprise whose director general is appointed by the government. The Deutsche Presseagentur is a company with limited liability supported by newspaper publishers, each holding at most a one-percent share of the capital stock; the broadcasting corporations hold 10 percent, but they in turn are under public control.[14] To be sure, newspaper and film industries have been left essentially under private control.[15] But the fact remains that experiences with the tendencies of the press toward concentration gave enough cause to block the development of the "natural monopolies" of radio and television in the form of private business enterprises—as it nonetheless occurred in the United States. In Great Britain, France, and Germany these new media were organized into public or semipublic corporations, because otherwise their publicist function could not have been sufficiently protected from the encroachment of their capitalistic one.[16]

Thus the original basis of the publicist institutions, at least in their most advanced sectors, became practically reversed. According to the liberal model of the public sphere, the institutions of the public engaged in rational-critical debate were protected from interference by public authority by virtue of their being in the hands of private people. To the extent that they were commercialized and underwent economic, technological, and organizational concentration, however, they have turned during the last hundred years into complexes of societal power, so that precisely their remaining in private hands in many ways threatened the critical functions of publicist institutions. In comparison with the press of the liberal era, the mass media have on the one hand attained an incomparably greater range and effectiveness—the sphere of the public realm itself has expanded correspondingly. On the other hand they have been moved ever further out of this sphere and reentered the once private sphere of commodity exchange. The more their effectiveness in terms of publicity increased, the more they became accessible to the pressure of certain private interests, whether individual or collective. Whereas formerly the press was able to limit itself to the transmission and amplification of the rational-critical debate of private people assembled into a public, now conversely this debate gets shaped by the mass media to begin with. In the course of the shift from a journalism of private men of letters to the public services of the mass media, the sphere of the public was altered by the influx of private interests that received privileged exposure in it—although they were by no means *eo ipso* representative of the interests of private people *as* the public. The separation of public and private spheres implied that the competition between private interests was in principle left to the market as a regulating force and was kept outside the conflict of opinions. However, in the measure that the public sphere became a field for business advertising, private people as owners of private property had a direct effect on private people as the public. In this process, to be sure, the transformation of the public sphere into a medium of advertising was met halfway by the commercialization of the press. Conversely, however, the latter was also propelled by the needs of business advertising that independently emerged out of economic configurations.

The flooding of the public sphere with advertising publications is not explained by the liberalization of the market, although business advertising in the old style arose just about simultaneously with it. The incomparably greater efforts of scientifically directed marketing became necessary only as the degree of oligopolistic restriction of the market increased. Especially in the big industrial enterprise a conflict arose between technological and financial optimization, which strengthened the tendency toward so-called monopolistic competition. For to the degree to which the technical aggregates were adapted to mass production, the production process lost in elasticity— "Output can no longer be varied. . . . Output is dictated by the capacity of the unified machine process."[17] Hence a long-term sales strategy was required that ensured the relative stability of markets and market shares. Direct competition via pricing gave way increasingly to an indirect competition via the generation of markets with clienteles oriented to specific firms. The decreasing transparency of the market, usually regarded as the motive for expanded advertising,[18] is in good part actually just the opposite, that is, its consequence. Competition via advertising that replaced competition via pricing is what above all created a confusing multiplicity of markets controlled by specific companies offering brand name products all the more difficult to compare with one another in terms of economic rationality the more their exchange value is codetermined by the psychological manipulation of advertising. There is a transparent connection between the tendency toward capitalist big business and an oligopolistic restriction of the market, on the one hand; and, on the other, the proverbial soap operas, that is, a flood of advertisement which pervades the mass media's integration-oriented culture as a whole.[19]

Business advertising, what in 1820 in France was first called *réclame*,[20] is only a phenomenon of advanced capitalism, however much it has become for us today an obvious ingredient of a market economy. Indeed, it attained a scope worthy of mention only in the processes of concentration that mark industrial capitalism in the second half of the nineteenth century. "Up into the nineteenth century there exists a disinclination among the better companies even toward simple business advertisements";[21] they were considered disreputable. In the eighteenth century advertisements occupied only about one-twentieth of the space in the advertising or intelligence journals; furthermore, they concerned almost exclusively curiosities, that is, unusual commodities. Normal business was still largely face to face; competition relied mostly on propaganda by word of mouth.

Around the middle of the last century advertising agencies arose on the basis of business advertising; Ferdinand Hansenstein founded the first one in Germany in 1855. Close cooperation with the press often led to the sale of advertising space to big advertising agencies on a subscription basis, with the result that these agencies brought an important part of the press in general under their control. In the Federal Republic today over 2,000 firms work in advertising; since the depression their methods are constantly being perfected scientifically in accord with the latest information of economic, sociological, and psychological market research.[22] Yet the advertising handled by these agencies amounts to only about a third of the total expenditure spent on this sort of thing in the entire economy. The other two-thirds are invested by enterprises directly, for the most part in external advertising; every larger business has its own advertising division for this purpose. In the Federal Republic in 1956 the total amount spent on advertising in the entire economy was estimated at about 3 billion

Deutschemarks, which is about 3 percent of all private expenditure.[23] The year before it had already reached a share of 1.3 percent of the gross national product, while in Great Britain and the United States the comparable figures had already reached 1.9 percent and 2.3 percent.[24] Expanded, of course, by the new media, the advertising agencies' activity is now as it was then confined to the design and placement of advertisements, especially in newspapers and illustrated magazines. Naturally, television commercials assume dominant importance in proportion to the proliferation of this means of communication in general and in relation to the kind of organizational structure. In 1957 in the Federal Republic at least half of the regular readers of daily papers also read the ads; 65 percent of the radio audience tuned into the programs specifically designed for advertising (*Werbefunk*), almost a third of them claiming that they listened to them daily.[25] Whereas exposure to the mass media in general increased with a person's position in the stratification system, here this relationship was reversed; advertisements and radio commercials reached lower status groups more extensively and more frequently than higher ones. The trickling down of commodities formerly restricted to the higher strata attracted greater attention among those strata which, through their style of consumption, were trying to elevate themselves at least symbolically.

However, the advertising business not only used the existing publicist organs for its own purposes but also created its own papers, periodicals, and booklets. In 1955 in every fifth household in the Federal Republic there could be found at least one copy of the usual company catalogues (often expensively produced as illustrated brochures).[26] Besides these another special species of publication emerged: at about the same time the number of in-house and customer magazines amounted to almost half of all the periodicals published for the West German market. The number of copies of these was more than a quarter of the total number of copies of all periodicals, a distribution more than twice that of all entertainment periodicals taken together.[27] To this must be added the fact that this entertainment in itself—and surely not only that provided by periodicals—as well as the programs of the mass media, even in their noncommercial portions, also stimulated consumption and channeled it into certain patterns. David Riesman considers it to be practically the essence of the means of mass entertainment that it raises consumers, beginning in childhood and constantly accompanying the grown-ups: "Today the future occupation of all moppets is to be skilled consumers."[28] The culture of harmony infused into the masses per se invites its public to an exchange of opinion about articles of consumption and subjects it to the soft compulsion of constant consumption training.

Of course, even though it has become economically necessary, an invasion of advertising publications into the sphere of the public realm as such would not necessarily have led to its transformation. For instance, just as the daily newspapers roughly since the second third of the last century began to differentiate a classified section from the editorial one, so too a separation of the publicist functions (into a public rational-critical debate of private people as a public and a public presentation of either individual or collective private interests) could have left the public realm essentially untouched. However, such a public sphere as an element in the economic realm split off, as it were, from the political one—a public sphere independent in provenance of commercial advertising—never reached the point of crystallization. Rather, the publicist presentation of privileged private interests was fused from the very start with political interests. For at the time that the horizontal competition among the interests of commodity owners invaded the public sphere via advertising, capitalism's competitive basis as such had already been drawn into the conflict between the parties; and the vertical competition between class interests had also entered the arena of the public realm. In a phase of more or less unconcealed class antagonism, about the middle of the last century, the public sphere itself was torn between the "two nations"—and thus the public presentation of private interests *eo ipso* took on a political significance. Within such a public sphere large-scale advertising almost always also assumed the quality of being more than just business advertising—if only by the fact that it represented per se the most important factor in the financial calculations of the papers and journals and even of the newer media to the degree that they operated on a commercial basis. However, economic advertisement achieved an awareness of its political character only in the *practice of public relations.*

This practice, like the term itself, hails from the United States.[29] Its beginnings can be traced back to Ivy Lee, who developed "publicity techniques on a policy-making level" for the purpose of justifying big business, especially the Standard Oil Company and the Pennsylvania Railroad, then under attack by certain social reformers.[30] Between the two World Wars some of the largest enterprises began to adjust their overall strategies also to considerations of public relations. In the United States this proved quite useful, particularly in the climate of national consensus that prevailed after the entry into the war in 1940. The new techniques diffused widely, including into Europe, only after the end of the war. In the advanced countries of the West they have come to dominate the public sphere during the last decade. They have become a key phenomenon for the diagnosis of that realm.[31] "Opinion management"[32] is distinguished from advertising by the fact that it expressly lays claim to the public sphere as one that plays a role in the political realm. Private advertisements are always directed to other private people insofar as they are consumers; the addressee of public relations is "public opinion," or the private citizens as the public and not directly as consumers. The sender of the message hides his business intentions in the role of someone interested in the public welfare. The influencing of consumers borrows its connotations from the classic idea of a public of private people putting their reason to use and exploits its legitimations for its own ends. The accepted functions of the public sphere are integrated into the competition of organized private interests.

Advertising limited itself by and large to the simple sales pitch. In contrast, opinion management with its "promotion" and "exploitation" goes beyond advertising; it invades the process of "public opinion" by systematically creating news events or exploiting events that attract attention. In doing so it sticks strictly with the psychology and techniques of the feature and pictorial publicity connected with the mass media and with their well tested human interest topics: romance, religion, money, children, health, and animals. By means of a dramatic presentation of facts and calculated stereotypes it aims for a "reorientation of public opinion by the formation of new authorities or symbols which will have acceptance."[33] Either public relations managers succeed in inserting suitable material into the channels of communication, or they arrange specific events in the public sphere that can be counted on to set the communications apparatus into motion; a textbook recommends twenty methods for this kind of "making or creating news."[34]

If one adds the multitude of informations and instructions packaged as solid "documentation" with which the major "distribution centers" are supplied by public relations bureaus, then statements still fixated on the old separation—now serving as occupational ideology—of news reports from advertising appear squarely antiquated.[35] Public relations fuses both: advertisement must absolutely not be recognizable as the self-presentation of a private interest. It bestows on its object the authority of an object of public interest about which—this is the illusion to be created—the public of critically reflecting private people freely forms its opinion. "Engineering of consent"[36] is the central task, for only in the climate of such a consensus does "promotion to the 'public,' suggesting or urging acceptance or rejection of a person, product, organization, or idea," succeed.[37] The awakened readiness of the consumers involves the false consciousness that as critically reflecting private people they contribute responsibly to public opinion.

On the other hand the consensus concerning behavior required by the public interest, or so it seems, actually has certain features of a staged "public opinion." Although public relations is supposed to stimulate, say, the sales of certain commodities, its effect always goes beyond this. Because publicity for specific products is generated indirectly via the detour of a feigned general interest, it creates and not only solidifies the profile of the brand and a clientele of consumers but mobilizes for the firm or branch or for an entire system a quasi-political credit, a respect of the kind one displays toward public authority.

The resulting consensus, of course, does not seriously have much in common with the final unanimity wrought by a time-consuming process of mutual enlightenment, for the "general interest" on the basis of which alone a rational agreement between publicly competing opinions could freely be reached has disappeared precisely to the extent that the publicist self-presentations of privileged private interests have adopted it for themselves. Simultaneously with the double condition of the restriction of the public to private people as members of civil society and the restriction of their rational-critical debate to the foundations of civil society as a sphere of private control, the old basis for a convergence of opinions has also collapsed. A new one is not brought about merely because the private interests inundating the public sphere hold on to its faked version. For the criteria of rationality are completely lacking in a consensus created by sophisticated opinion-molding services under the aegis of a sham public interest. Intelligent criticism of publicly discussed affairs gives way before a mood of conformity with publicly presented persons or personifications; consent coincides with good will evoked by publicity. Publicity once meant the exposure of political domination before the public use of reason; publicity now adds up the reactions of an uncommitted friendly disposition. In the measure that it is shaped by public relations, the public sphere of civil society again takes on feudal features. The "suppliers" display a showy pomp before customers ready to follow. Publicity imitates the kind of aura proper to the personal prestige and supernatural authority once bestowed by the kind of publicity involved in representation.

One may speak of a refeudalization of the public sphere in yet another, more exact sense. For the kind of integration of mass entertainment with advertising, which in the form of public relations already assumes a "political" character, subjects even the state itself to its code.[38] Because private enterprises evoke in their customers the idea that in their consumption decisions they act in their capacity as citizens, the state has to "address" its citizens like consumers. As a result, public authority too competes for publicity.

21 The Transmuted Function of the Principle of Publicity

At the close of the 1920s the topic of public opinion was taken up by a congress of the German Sociological Society.[39] On this occasion for the first time a phenomenon was authoritatively acknowledged that was symptomatic of the transmuted political function of the public sphere—the "journalistic activation" of offices, parties, and organizations. To be sure, Brinkmann constructed an ill-considered antithesis between the "free press" and the "official releases" of public and private bureacracies ("with that relentless extension of its 'publicity' to every sphere of life, the modern newspaper itself has caused the rise of its adversary and perhaps even master of its own insatiable urge for information: the information bureaus and press release specialists that every center of activity exposed to publicity, or desirous of it, now considers requisite."[40]) This antithesis was ill considered because the public relations strategy of the bureaucracies, going far beyond the classical sorts of publications, availed themselves of the existing mass media and bolstered their position. Nevertheless, the observation as such is sound. Beside the great publicist institutions and in connection with them ("an apparatus that surely represents a maximum of publicity, but very little opinion") a second apparatus was established to meet the new publicity needs of the state and the special interest associations. ("We have there . . . another public opinion, which, to be sure, offers 'opinions' that are diverse and quite to the point, but which seeks to shape and hold sway over public opinion in a way that is essentially anything but 'public.'"[41]) The forms of purposive opinion management to which Brinkmann alluded here were of the sorts that "consciously deviate from the liberal ideal of publicity." The state bureaucracy borrowed them from the practice already made current by big private enterprises and interest-group associations; only in conjunction with these did the public administrations acquire their "publicist character" at all.

The increase in the power of the bureaucracy in the social-welfare state—not only in relation to the legislator but to the top of the executive itself[42]—brought one aspect of its mounting autonomy into clear relief, although even in the liberal era

it never functioned as a pure organ of legislative implementation.[43] The other aspect, the countervailing process of a transfer of power from the government to societal groups, remained
less obtrusive; for within the newly acquired latitude for 'dis-
cretionary structuring,' in which the bureaucracy itself also
became a producer, dealer, and distributor, the executive saw
itself forced to act in a fashion that complemented and even
partially replaced authoritarian government from above by an
arrangement with the "public." This led partly to an unofficial
participation of special-interest associations, partly to a routine
transfer of some of the bureaucracy's tasks into their jurisdiction. Werner Weber observed that large jurisdictional areas
were altogether taken away from the state bureaucracy and
have become "components of an estate system of administration that functions alongside the state."[44] But even where the
state maintained or extended its administrative sovereignty, it
had to "adapt" to the dynamics of a field of crisscrossing organized interests. Although agreements here were pursued
and concluded outside the parliament, that is by circumventing
the state's institutionalized public sphere, both sides nevertheless prepared them noisily and accompanied them glaringly by
so-called publicity work. To the extent that state and society
penetrated each other, the public sphere (and along with it the
parliament, i.e., the public sphere established as an organ of
the state) lost a number of its bridging functions. A continuous
process of integration was accomplished in a different fashion.
Correlative to a weakening of the position of the parliament
was a strengthening of the transformers through which the
state was infused into society (bureaucracy) and, in the opposite
direction, through which society was infused into the state
(special-interest associations and political parties). The publicity
effort, however, a carefully managed display of public relations, showed that the public sphere (deprived, for the most
part, of its original functions) under the patronage of administrations, special-interest associations, and parties was now
made to contribute in a different fashion to the process of
integrating state and society.

What made it possible within the political public sphere to
resolve conflicts on the basis of relatively homogeneous inter-

ests and by means of relatively reasonable forms of deliberation, what alone made it possible to encase the parliamentary conflict settlements in a system of abstract and general laws with a claim to rationality and permanence, was a peculiar arrangement. The multitude of substantive decisions within a commercial society neutralized as a private sphere were mediated by the mechanism of the market and were in principle arrived at apolitically. Although limited to a framework of interests common to private people insofar as they owned property, the public was nonetheless kept free from the competition between individual private interests to such an extent that the decisions falling within the domain of political compromise could be handled by the procedures of rational political debate. However, as soon as private interests, collectively organized, were compelled to assume political form, the public sphere necessarily became an arena in which conflicts also had to be settled that transformed the structure of political compromise from the ground up.[45] The public sphere was burdened with the tasks of settling conflicts of interest that could not be accommodated within the classical forms of parliamentary consensus and agreement; their settlements bore the marks of their origins in the sphere of the market. Compromise literally had to be haggled out, produced temporarily through pressure and counterpressure and supported directly only through the unstable equilibrium of a power constellation between state apparatus and interest groups. Political decisions were made within the new forms of "bargaining" that evolved alongside the older forms of the exercise of power: hierarchy and democracy.[46] Admittedly, on the one hand the forum of the public sphere had been expanded. But on the other hand, because the balancing of interests continued to be linked to the liberal claim of this public sphere (which is to say, to legitimation in terms of the common welfare) without being able to fulfill it or to evade it entirely, the haggling out of compromises moved to extraparliamentary sites. This could occur formally by delegating jurisdictional competences of state organs to societal organizations or informally by de facto shifts in jurisdictions, either free from or contrary to regulations.

Wherever a relatively long lasting equilibration of interests or even a "state of peace" between employers and employees (instead of compromises that result in successive waves of regulations) is not to be expected—as in the case of the central conflict of advanced capitalist society—the elimination of coercive state arbitration can create an autonomous domain for a quasi-political exercise of power on the part of conflicting social groups. On the one hand the two sides involved in collective bargaining then no longer act in the exercise of private autonomy; they act within the framework of the public sphere as an element in the political realm and hence are officially subject to the democratic demand for publicity.[47] On the other hand the creation of collective bargaining regulations so shatters the forms of the old style public sphere (founded on trust in the power of reason) and the antagonism between interests which lies at its basis objectively affords so little chance for a legislation in accord with liberal criteria that these compromises are kept away from the procedure of parliamentary legislation and therefore remain altogether outside the realm of jurisdiction of the state's institutionalized public sphere.

This sort of official removal of jurisdictional competence for political compromise from the legislator to the circle of bureaucracies, special-interest associations, and parties is paralleled, to a far greater extent, by a factual divestiture. The increasing integration of the state with a society that is not already as such a political society required decisions in the form of temporary compromises between groups, which is to say, the direct exchange of particularist favors and compensations without detouring through institutionalized processes proper to the political public sphere. Consequently, special-interest associations and parties in principle remain private associations; many are not even organized in the form of bodies with legal standing and nevertheless participate in the filling of public positions. For they also carry out functions allotted to the political public sphere and stand under its claim of providing legitimacy to the pressure exerted by society upon state authority, making it more than a sheer relationship of force. In this way special-interest associations have in fact left the confines established by the statutes regulating the status of associations under civil law; their stated aim is the transformation of the private interests of many individuals into a common public interest, the credible representation and demonstration of the particular association's special interest as the general interest.[48] In this enterprise special-interest associations have far-reaching political power at their disposal not in spite of but on account of their private character; especially, they can manipulate "public opinion" without themselves being controlled by it. For this is the result of the dual necessity of exercising social power, on the one hand, and of claiming legitimation before the traditional standards of a disintegrating public sphere, on the other. These organizations must obtain from a mediatized public an acclamatory consent, or at least benevolent passivity of a sort that entails no specific obligations, for a process of compromise formation that is largely a matter of organization-internal manoeuvering but that requires public credit—whether to transform such consent into political pressure or, on the basis of this toleration, to neutralize political counterpressure.[49]

Publicity work is aimed at strengthening the prestige of one's own position without making the matter on which a compromise is to be achieved itself a topic of *public discussion*. Organizations and functionaries display *representation*: "The special-interest associations under public law do not in fact want to act as legal persons, but as collective organizations; and the reason is, indeed, that these associations *are interested* not so much in their formal representation toward the outside (whereby this representation becomes independent from the association's internal life), but above all *in the representative showing of their members in the public sphere*."[50] Representation, naturally, is less an element in the internal structure of the association than "an expression of its claim to publicity."[51] Representative publicity of the old type is not thereby revived; but it still lends certain traits to a refeudalized public sphere of civil society whose characteristic feature, according to Schelsky's observation, is that the large-scale organizers in state and society "manage the propagation of their positions."[52] The aura of personally represented authority returns as an aspect of publicity; to this extent modern publicity indeed has affinity with feudal publicity. Public relations do not genuinely concern public opinion but opinion in the sense of reputation. The public sphere becomes the court *before* whose public prestige can be displayed—rather than *in* which public critical debate is carried on.

At one time publicity had to be gained in opposition to the secret politics of the monarchs; it sought to subject person or issue to rational-critical public debate and to render political decisions subject to review before the court of public opinion. Today, on the contrary, publicity is achieved with the help of the secret politics of interest groups; it earns public prestige for a person or issue and thereby renders it ready for acclamatory assent in a climate of nonpublic opinion. The very phrase "publicity work" betrays that a public sphere, which at one time was entailed by the position of the carriers of representation and was also safeguarded in its continuity through a firm traditional symbolism, must first be brought about deliberately and from case to case. Today occasions for identification have to be created—the public sphere has to be "made," it is not "there" anymore. Altmann calls this appropriately enough the act of "communification."[53] The immediate effect of publicity is not exhausted by the decommercialized wooing effect of an aura of good will that produces a readiness to assent. Beyond influencing consumer decisions this publicity is now also useful for exerting political pressure because it mobilizes a potential of inarticulate readiness to assent that, if need be, can be translated into a plebiscitarily defined acclamation. The new public sphere still remains related to the one rooted in civil society insofar as the latter's institutional forms of legitimation are still in force. Even staged publicity generates political efficacy only in the measure that it can credibly suggest or even cash in on a capital of potential voting decisions. This "cashing in," to be sure, is then the task of the parties.

This functional transmutation pervades the entire public sphere in the political realm. Even the central relationship between the public, the parties, and the parliament is subject to it. The political public sphere of the liberal era received its imprint from the party run by dignitaries (*Honoratiorenpartei*), as Max Weber described it.[54] Under the leadership of men of the church and professors, lawyers, doctors, teachers and phar-

macists, manufacturers and landowners, the educated and propertied circles founded local political clubs—occasional
associations at first, voter associations held together solely by
the delegates. The number of members who were professional
politicians remained small, and their functions were at first
subordinate; politics was an honorific avocation. The press, as
the single permanent institution, was attached to this informal
enterprise held together, and not in the large towns only, by
associations in the proper sense, which met periodically for the
purpose of bringing delegates to account. There was an unen-
cumbered flow of communication between the local discussion
centers and the sessions of the parliament.[55] It was precisely
the organizationally loose union of the *"Fraktionspartei"* (which
existed practically only in the parliament) via the circle of
dignitaries with the voters in the land that corresponded to the
power-free flow of communication within a single public. The
parity of the educated was not yet fundamentally called into
question by the differentiation of areas of competence. The
parties too understood themselves within this framework of
the bourgeois public sphere as a "formation of opinions." As
Rudolf Haym expressed it in his report on the German National Assembly, they had as their basis political opinions in
their large-scale agglomeration. August Ludwig von Rochau
claimed for the "party spirit" an objectivity of judgment that
allegedly resisted mere (particular) interest.[56] Treitschke, however, abandoned the thesis of a party of opinion: "Especially
the interests of the social classes are far more closely joined to
the partylines than the parties themselves care to admit."[57]
Finally, at the century's end were testimonies that forewent the
illusion of neutrality as regards interests even with respect to
the bourgeois parties. People like Friedrich Naumann demanded precisely a class party for the liberal camp, for "only
a class conscious liberalism has the firmness to put up a good
fight within the general class struggle as it prevails today for
better or worse."[58]

In the meantime the structural transformation of the bourgeois public sphere had set in. The institutions of social-con-
vivial interchange, which secured the coherence of the public
making use of its reason, lost their power or utterly collapsed;

the development toward a commercial mass circulation press had its parallel in the reorganization of the parties run by dignitaries on a mass basis. The advent of equal citizenship rights for all altered the structure of parties. Since the middle of the last century loosely knit voter groups have increasingly given way to parties in the proper sense—organized supralocally and with a bureaucratic apparatus and aimed at the ideological integration and the political mobilization of the broad voting masses. In Great Britain Gladstone introduced the caucus system. With this buildup of an apparatus of professional politicians, organized more or less like a business enterprise and directed centrally, the local committees lost their importance. The parties were now confronted with the job of "integrating" the mass of the citizenry (no longer really "bourgeois"), with the help of new methods, for the purpose of getting their votes. The gathering of voters for the sake of bringing the local delegate to account had to make room for systematic propaganda. Now for the first time there emerged something like modern propaganda, from the very start with the Janus face of enlightenment and control; of information and advertising; of pedagogy and manipulation.[59]

The interdependence of politically relevant events had increased. Along with its communal basis, the public sphere lost its place. It lost its clear boundary over against the private sphere on the one hand and the "world public" on the other; it lost its transparency and no longer admitted of a comprehensive view.[60] There arose as an alternative to class parties,[61] that "integration party" whose form was usually not clearly enough distinguished from them. It "took hold" of the voters temporarily and moved them to provide acclamation, without attempting to remedy their political immaturity.[62] Today this kind of mass-based party trading on surface integration has become the dominant type. For such parties the decisive issue is who has control over the coercive and educational means for ostentatiously or manipulatively influencing the voting behavior of the population. The parties are instruments for the formation of an effective political will; they are not, however, in the hands of the public but in the hands of those who control the party apparatus. This changed relationship of the parties to the public on the one hand and to the parliament on the other can be symptomatically traced by reference to shifts in the status of delegates.

From the very start the rejection of the imperative mandate that had been typical for all kinds of representation in a society structured into estates was implied in the idea of parliamentarianism. As early as 1745 a delegate to the House of Commons declared: "By our constitution, after a gentleman is chosen, he is the representative, or, if you please, the attorney of the people of England"; a generation later this thesis was elaborated by Burke and Blackstone[63] into the classic doctrine of the free mandate. In the formula of the delegate's independence from directives, of the delegate who is responsible only to his conscience and to the people as a whole, it has made its way into all bourgeois constitutions.[64] In the liberal constitutional state this ideology was complemented at least by a process of forming political will that passed through opinion formation on the part of a public making use of its reason. In this phase the free mandate meant, from a sociological point of view, not so much the independence of the representative as such; de facto, the delegate obviously was in far closer contact with his constituency than has been the case ever since. Instead, it was a guarantee of the parity in standing among *all* private people within the public engaged in rational-critical debate. To make sure that the parliament itself would remain part of this public and that the freedom of discussion would be safeguarded *intra muros* as well as *extra muros*, the measures taken to protect the independence of the delegate were not at all supposed to create a privileged status in relation to the rest of the public—representation in the sense of the kind of publicity that antedates bourgeois society—rather, they were only supposed to prevent the status of representative from becoming underprivileged because of delegation.[65]

Of course, this direct mutual contact between the members of the public was lost in the degree that the parties, having become integral parts of a system of special-interest associations under public law, had to transmit and represent at any given time the interests of several such organizations that grew out of the private sphere into the public sphere. Today, as a rule, they are neither class parties (like the old Social Democratic Party) nor interest groups themselves (in the style of the *Bund für Heimatvertriebene und Entrechtete* or BHE). Rather, it is precisely the interlocking of organized interests and their official translation into the political machinery that lends to the parties a paramount position before which the parliament is degraded to the status of a committee for the airing of party lines—and the member of parliament himself "to the status of an organizational-technical intermediary within the party, who has to obey its directives in case of conflict."[66] According to an observation by Kirchheimer this development is linked to the diminishing parliamentary influence of lawyers: the advocate type gives way to that of the functionary.[67] Besides the small group of those considered to be "minister material" and who accumulate leadership positions, a considerable number of party functionaries strictly speaking (apparatchiks, propaganda experts, etc.) and a mass of direct or indirect special-interest association representatives (corporate lawyers, lobbyists, specialists, etc.) get into the parliament. The individual delegate, while called upon to participate in the formation of majority decisions within his party, in the end decides in accordance with the party line. By enforcing the principle that in certain contexts minorities of delegates must make majority opinions their own, the party transforms the pressure toward ever renewed compromise between organized interests into a constraint enabling it to display external unity; de facto, the delegate receives an imperative mandate by his party.[68] The parliament therefore tends to become a place where instruction-bound appointees meet to put their predetermined decisions on record. Carl Schmitt noted a similar trend in the Weimar Republic.[69] The new status of the delegate is no longer characterized by participation in a public engaged in nonpartisan rational debate.

The parliament itself has correspondingly evolved away from a debating body; for the parliamentary rubber-stamping of resolutions haggled out behind closed doors not merely satisfies a formal requirement but serves to demonstrate party consensus toward the outside. The parliament no longer is an "assembly of wise men chosen as individual personalities by privileged strata, who sought to convince each other through arguments in public discussion on the assumption that the subsequent decision reached by the majority would be what was true and right for the national welfare." Instead it has become the "public rostrum on which, before the entire nation (which through radio and television participates in a specific fashion in this sphere of publicity), the government and the parties carrying it present and justify to the nation their political program, while the opposition attacks this program with the same openness and develops its alternatives."[70] Friesenhahn's description, to be sure, captures only one side of this process, namely the expansion of publicity as such, and not the transmutation of its function. Whereas the public nature of the deliberations was once supposed to ensure, and for a while actually did ensure, the continuity between pre-parliamentary and parliamentary discussion, that is, the unity of the public sphere and the public opinion crystallizing within it—in a word, parliamentary deliberation as both part and center of the public as a whole—it no longer accomplishes anything of the sort. Nor can it do so, for the strucure of the public sphere itself, inside and outside of parliament, has been transformed:

Were one to see the sense of the radio and television transmissions of the *Bundestag* [i.e., the German Parliament] sessions in their providing the listener (or viewer) at the receiver with the opportunity for participation in the work of the elected representatives, then one would have to conclude that radio and television are not adequate for this purpose; that instead, by biasing and distorting the debates, they represent a disruption of parliamentary work. Just as deliberation proper has shifted from the full session into committees and party caucuses, so deliberation in parliament has become completely secondary to documentation.[71]

Before the expanded public sphere the transactions themselves are stylized into a show. Publicity loses its critical function in favor of a staged display; even arguments are transmuted into symbols to which again one can not respond by arguing but only by identifying with them.

The transformation of the parliament's function brings the dubiousness of publicity as the organizational principle of the state order into full view. From a critical principle wielded by the public, publicity has been transformed into a principle of managed integration (wielded by staging agencies—the administration, special-interest groups, and above all the parties). A consumer culture's distortion of publicity in the judicial realm matches the plebiscitary distortion of parliamentary publicity. For the trials in criminal court that are interesting enough to be documented and hawked by the mass media reverse the critical principle of publicity in an analogous manner; instead of serving the control of the jurisdictional process by the assembled citizens of the state, publicity increasingly serves the packaging of court proceedings for the mass culture of assembled consumers.

The strength of such tendencies can be gauged in terms of the revisionist endeavors they have called forth. Whereas in post-Napoleonic Germany publicity as the organizational principle of a liberal constitutional state found its first eloquent champions, and whereas at that time Welcker and Feuerbach advocated publicity in the parliament and in the judiciary in conjunction with a freely developing, critically debating political daily press,[72] one is concerned today to shield parliamentary deliberations and judicial processes from a plebiscitary public. The Senior Council of the *Bundestag* has recommended that the sessions of the House no longer be directly transmitted; criminal lawyers and judges demand ever more urgently that every legal means be exhausted or, if these do not suffice, that the trial procedures be changed, for the sake of preventing radio and television reporting in the court room. In both cases the principle of publicity is to be reduced to guaranteeing "public accessibility to those bodily present." To be sure, proceedings are to continue to be open to the public; what is to be avoided is turning parliamentary documentation of internally haggled out resolutions into party grandstanding or criminal trials into show trials for the entertainment of consumers who, strictly speaking, are indifferent. The argument is directed against the plebiscitary deviations from the liberal model. Typical for this purpose is the distinction between public sphere and publicity, a distinction that Eberhard Schmitt would like to see preserved even for criminal trials involving "persons of contemporary significance":

Of what are we really deprived when we do not get to see pictures of defendants or witnesses in the press? There may be a legitimate interest on the part of the public to learn of the acts of which important personalities of our times are being accused, of the court's findings in this respect, and of the sentence. *These* are aspects that are important to know for opinion-forming citizens interested in public life, and that by means of reliable court reporting may also be brought to the attention of those not participating in the deliberations. But what kind of facial expressions defendants and witnesses exhibit when being questioned in the main hearing or at the time of sentencing is a matter of complete indifference for any legitimate interest in information. Only one caught up in the unhappy trend toward publicity that today tramples underfoot everything that a humane mentality naturally feels obligated to respect can here still speak of a legitimate need for information on the part of the public.[73]

It is quite clear that such reactive measures cannot contribute toward reinstating the public sphere in its original function. Any attempt at restoring the liberal public sphere through the reduction of its plebiscitarily expanded form will only serve to weaken even more the residual functions genuinely remaining within it.

Even today the constitution of the welfare-state mass democracy binds the activity of the organs of state to publicity, so that a permanent process of opinion and consensus formation can be influential at least as a freedom-guaranteeing corrective to the exercise of power and domination: "The manifestations of this process that are necessary for the survival of a free democracy, manifestations that consist in the generation of a public opinion concerning state activity in all its ramifications, may legitimately consist in power that is not at all legally sanctioned . . . , presuming that they too are fully public and that they publicly confront the power of the state itself that is obligated to act in public."[74] The public sphere commandeered by societal organizations and that under the pressure of collective private interests has been drawn into the purview of power can perform functions of political critique and control, beyond mere participation in political compromises, only to the extent that it is itself radically subjected to the requirements of publicity, that is to say, that it again becomes a public sphere in the strict sense. Under the changed conditions the intention of the classical demands for publicity can be protected from reactionary misdirection if, supplemented by unorthodox demands for publicity, publicity is also to be extended to institutions that until now have lived off the publicity of the other institutions rather than being themselves subject to the public's supervision: primarily to parties but also to politically influential mass media and special-interest associations under public law. These are all institutions of societal power centers whose actions are oriented to the state—private organizations of society that exercise public functions within the political order.

To be able to satisfy these functions in the sense of democratic opinion and consensus formation their inner structure must first be organized in accord with the principle of publicity and must institutionally permit an intraparty or intra-association democracy—to allow for unhampered communication and public rational-critical debate.[75] In addition, by making the internal affairs of the parties and special-interest associations public, the linkage between such an intraorganizational public sphere and the public sphere of the entire public has to be assured.[76] Finally, the activities of the organizations themselves—their pressure on the state apparatus and their use of power against one another, as well as the manifold relations of dependency and of economic intertwining—need a far-reaching publicity. This would include, for instance, requiring that the organizations provide the public with information concerning the source and deployment of their financial means.[77] In Germany the constitution furnishes the means for extending such publicity requirements from the parties to the special-interest associations under public law as well,[78] because under the constitutional protection of "the multi-party state's institutional freedom of public opinion" they too are legitimated to participate in national opinion and consensus formation.[79] Even political journalism, like all institutions which through display and manipulation exercise a privileged influence in the public realm, should for its part be subject to the democratic demand for publicity. However this may appear from a legal perspective, from the vantage point of sociology such demands make the important dimension of a democratization of societal organizations engaged in state-related activity a topic of discussion. Not only organs of state but all institutions that are publicistically influential in the political public sphere have been bound to publicity because the process in which societal power is transformed into political power is as much in need of criticism and control as the legitimate exercise of political domination over society. Institutionalized in the mass democracy of the social-welfare state no differently than in the bourgeois constitutional state, the idea of publicity (at one time the rationalization of domination in the medium of the critical public debate of private people) is today realizable only as a rationalization—limited, of course, because of the plurality of organized private interests—of the exercise of societal and political power under the mutual control of rival organizations themselves committed to publicity as regards both their internal structure and their interaction with one another and with the state.[80]

Only in proportion to advances in this kind of rationalization can there once again evolve a political public sphere as it once existed in the form of the bourgeois public of private people—that is to say, ". . . [a] society that, beyond the periodic or sporadic state-commandeered elections and referenda, has a real presence in a coherent and permanent process of integration."[81] Of course, how much the political public sphere of the welfare state's mass democracy still lags behind in this dimension, or better, how little it has advanced in this respect, may be analyzed in relation to the public preparation of elections and to the electoral process itself. For the public sphere temporarily created and only intermittently mobilized for this purpose brings just that other publicity of public relations into ascendancy that organizations can all the more successfully install over the heads of the nonorganized public the more they themselves evade the democratic demand of publicity. The most recent election study shows "how advantageous it is for a party to have no members, but rather to come to life only at election time with the centralized freedom to manoeuver that characterizes an advertising firm existing for one purpose only: to carry out the advertising campaign."[82] A process of public communication evolving in the medium of the parties and organizations themselves obviously stands in an inverse relation to the staged and manipulative effectiveness of a publicity aimed at rendering the broad population (and especially the sector of it that is most indifferent as regards politics) infectiously ready for acclamation.

22 Manufactured Publicity and Nonpublic Opinion: The Voting Behavior of the Population

Citizens entitled to services relate to the state not primarily through political participation but by adopting a general attitude of demand—expecting to be provided for without actually wanting to fight for the necessary decisions.[83] Their contact with the state occurs essentially in the rooms and anterooms of bureaucracies; it is unpolitical and indifferent, yet demanding. In a social-welfare state that above all administers, distributes, and provides, the "political" interests of citizens constantly subsumed under administrative acts are reduced primarily to claims specific to occupational branches. The effective representation of these claims, of course, requires that it be delegated to large organizations. Whatever is left over and above this to the initiative of personal decision is appropriated by the parties for an election organized as a vote. The extent to which the public sphere as an element in the political realm has disintegrated as a sphere of ongoing participation in a rational-critical debate concerning public authority is measured by the degree to which it has become a genuine publicist task for parties to generate periodically something like a public sphere to begin with. Election contests are no longer the outcome of a conflict of opinions that exists per se within the framework of an institutionally protected public sphere.

Nonetheless, the democratic arrangement of parliamentary elections continues to count on the liberal fictions of a public sphere in civil society. The expectations that still exercise a normative influence on the citizen's role as voter are a social-psychological mirror image of those conditions under which a public of rationally debating private people once assumed critical and legislative functions. It is expected that the voter, provided with a certain degree of knowledge and critical capacity, might take an interested part in public discussions so that he might help discover what can serve as the standard for right and just political action in rational form and with the general interest in mind.

In an essay entitled "Democratic Theory and Public Opinion" Berelson detailed the components of the voter's "personality structure": interest in public affairs; possession of information and knowledge; of stable political principles or moral standards; ability to observe accurately; engagement in communication and discussion; rational behavior; consideration of community interest.[84] The sociological constituents of a political public sphere have here turned into psychological characteristics. However, if today the mass of the enfranchised population exhibits the democratic behavior patterns to the low degree found by many empirical investigations—even when measured in terms of such superficial criteria as the degree of political activity and initiative and of participation in discussions[85]—then such deviation can only be understood sociologically in connection with the structural and functional transformation of the public sphere itself.

At first sight a remote connection between the voting public in the mass democracies of the social-welfare states, on the one hand, and the public of private people in the bourgeois constitutional states of the nineteenth century, on the other, does seem to exist. Ideally the vote was only the concluding act of a continuous controversy carried out publicly between argument and counterargument; entitled to vote were those who in any case had been admitted to the public sphere: the private people, that is to say, predominantly the heads of households from the urban bourgeois strata who were propertied and well educated. The social composition of the only public that was then entitled to vote is echoed today in that more active portion of a generally enfranchised population that makes use of its voting right. Males usually vote more frequently than females, married people more frequently than the unmarried, and those who belong to the higher status groups (who have a higher income and a higher level of education) more frequently than those belonging to the lower social strata. In this connection, moreover, it is interesting to note that businessmen belonging to the commercial middle classes go to the polls in relatively large numbers. The fact that voter participation is highest in the age groups between thirty-five and fifty-five leads one to assume a strong influence both of the kind of occupation (as in the strata that succeeded the class of bourgeois private people) and of the involvement in relations of social labor through occupational activity per se. Even the participation in rational-critical public debate, at one time the informal condition for taking part in the vote, today seems still to correspond: members of private associations make use of their right to vote to a greater extent than the nonorganized citizens.[86] Such characteristics of a liberal public sphere preserved in the voting behavior of the population can also be demonstrated in the flow of political communication investigated by Katz and Lazarsfeld. In contradistinction to a more horizontal, social stratum-specific spread of fashions and consumption habits in general, the stream of political opinion flows in a vertical direction, from the higher status groups down to the ones just below—the "opinion leader(s) in public affairs" are usually wealthier, better educated, and have a better social position than the groups influenced by them.[87] On the other hand, it has been observed that these politically interested, informed, and active core strata of the public are themselves the least inclined to seriously submit their views to discussion. Precisely among the carriers of this two-tiered process of communication, mediated by these opinion leaders, an opinion once assumed often becomes fixed as a rigid habit.[88] Even those opinions that do not have to bear public exposure do not evolve into a public opinion without the communication flow of a rationally debating public.

Even the well documented fact that those who engage in discussion more frequently (being relatively speaking the best informed) have a tendency to do no more than mutually confirm their ideas and at best to influence only the hesitant and less involved parties—shows how little they contribute to a process of *public* opinion. In addition the political discussions are for the most part confined to in-groups, to family, friends, and neighbors who generate a rather homogeneous climate of opinion anyway. On the other hand, those voters who fluctuate between parties are recruited predominantly from the large reservoir of less interested, less informed, and apathetic citizens, to the extent that they are not altogether indifferent and do not ignore the election.[89] Thus, as a rule, precisely those who are most decisively predisposed to avoid a public opinion formed by discussion are the ones most likely to be influenced in their views—but this time by the staged or manipulatively manufactured public sphere of the election campaign.

The dissolution of the voting constituency's coherence as a public is betrayed in the peculiar immobilization of the larger part of the voters. Of course, the core constituency of one or the other party is composed of two quite distinct groups. On one side there is the small minority of those who with a certain justification may still be called "active" citizens, either members of parties and other social organizations, or unorganized but well informed and strongly involved voters who are usually also influential as opinion leaders. On the other side is the majority of citizens, who, of course, are equally rigid in their decisions, over whom the sands of day-to-day political controversies blow, so it seems, without leaving a trace. This fixation arises partly from the justified but stereotypically ingrained perception of group interests and partly from a layer of cultural common-sense assumptions, from deeply rooted attitudes and prejudices pertaining to experiences usually far in the past and transmitted over generations.[90] Different age groups are guided by experiences specific to their generations; different denominational and ethnic groups by analogous ones. As a result volitional impulses totally heterogeneous in substance and often enough in competition with each other enter into voting decisions that are formally the same and all the more susceptible to being averaged into an illusory consensus as long as the latter's undiscussed presuppositions remain removed from public communication. Between the immobilized blocks stand or fluctuate independent groups of voters composed, according to the findings of Janowitz, partly of compromisers and partly of those who are neutral, ambivalent, or apathetic; depending on how narrowly the criteria are defined, this group amounts to between a fourth and almost half of all those entitled to vote. To their number belong the nonvoters and the so-called marginal voters who vote now for one, now for the other party and who at times cannot be mobilized at all: nonvoters and changers. The characterization of nonvoters as the worst informed and least firmly democratic group[91] also holds true, with certain qualifications, for the bearers of the "floating vote":[92] "Independent voters tend to be those who know and care the least."[93] Nonetheless, these enfranchised voters who are qualified to participate in the public opinion process are the target group for the election managers. Each party tries to draw as much as possible from this reservoir of the "undecided," not through enlightenment but through adaptation to the unpolitical consumer attitude that is especially prevalent in this group. Janowitz is quite right to ask "whether these efforts, which rely heavily on mass media and other promotional devices, do not represent a misuse of limited resources."[94] In any case, campaign advertising also affects the other voter groups. Hence the connection between voter participation and an orientation toward programmatic goals is far weaker than that between voter participation and the successful generation of an appealing image of the leading candidates.[95]

For the periodic staging, when elections come around, of a political public sphere fits smoothly into the constellation representing the decayed form of the bourgeois public sphere. Initially the integration culture concocted and propagated by the mass media, although unpolitical in its intention, itself represents a political ideology; a political program, or any staged announcement whatsoever, must indeed not enter into competition with it but must strive for concordance. The collapse of political ideology as diagnosed decades ago by Mannheim seems to be only one side of that process in reference to which Raymond Aron speaks of the *Fin de l'Age Idéologique* (End of the Ideological Age) altogether.[96] The other side is that ideology accommodates itself to the form of the so-called consumer culture and fulfills, on a deeper level of consciousness, its old function, exerting pressure toward conformity with existing conditions. This false consciousness no longer consists of an internally harmonized nexus of ideas, as did the political ideologies of the nineteenth century, but of a nexus of modes of behavior. As a system of other-directed consumption habits it takes a practical shape in the guise of a practice. To the extent that this involves consciousness, it is exhausted by the pseudo-realistic replication of the status quo as it appears on the surface:

Were one to compress into one sentence what the ideology of mass culture actually amounts to, one would have to present it as a parody of the statement, "Become what you are": as a glorifying reduplication and justification of the state of affairs that exists anyway, while foregoing all transcendence and critique. Inasmuch as the spirit that is active in society limits itself to providing people with no more than a replication of what constitutes the condition of their existence anyway, while at the same time proclaiming this way of life as its own norm, they become confirmed in their faithless belief in pure existence.[97]

Advertising is the other function that has been taken over by the mass media-dominated public sphere. Consequently the parties and their auxiliary organizations see themselves forced to influence voting decisions publicistically in a fashion that has its analogue in the way advertising pressure bears on buying decisions.[98] There emerges the industry of political marketing. Party agitators and old style propagandists give way to advertising experts neutral in respect to party politics and employed to sell politics in an unpolitical way. Although this tendency has been visible for a long time, it prevailed only after the Second World War, with the scientific development of empirical techniques of market and opinion research. The resistance to this trend, which was broken in some parties only after several electoral setbacks,[99] shows that election managers must not only take note of the disappearance of a genuine public sphere in the realm of politics but must in full consciousness promote it themselves. The temporarily manufactured political public sphere reproduces, albeit for different purposes, the sphere for which that integration culture prescribes the law; even the political realm is social-psychologically integrated into the realm of consumption.

The addressees of this kind of public sphere are the type of political consumers to whom Riesman gave the name "new indifferents":

they are not necessarily equivalent to the nonvoters: these indifferents may perform quite a few political chores, for a price or under pressure. Nor are they devoid of political opinions. . . . But . . . these political opinions are connected neither with direct political self-interest nor with clear emotional ties to politics. They resemble, rather, the peer-group exchange of consumption preferences, though unlike the latter, the preferences are seldom taken into the political market and translated into purchases of political commodities. For the indifferents do not believe that, by virtue of anything they do, know, or believe, they can buy a political package that will substantially improve their lives. And so, subject to occasional manipulations, they tend to view politics in most of its large-scale forms as if they were spectators.[100]

The disintegration of the electorate as a public becomes manifest with the realization that press and radio, "deployed in the usual manner,"[101] have practically no effect; within the framework of the manufactured public sphere the mass media are useful only as vehicles of advertising. The parties address themselves to the "people," de facto to that minority whose state of mind is symptomatically revealed, according to survey researchers, in terms of an average vocabulary of five hundred words.[102] Together with the press the second classical instrument of opinion formation, the party meeting, also loses its significance. By now it has been learned that "used in the usual manner," it can at best serve the task of handing out slogans to a small troop of persons who are hard core loyalists to begin with. Party meetings too are useful only as advertising events in which those present may at most participate as unpaid supernumeraries for television coverage.

In the manipulated public sphere an acclamation-prone mood comes to predominate, an opinion climate instead of a public opinion. Especially manipulative are the social-psychologically calculated offers that appeal to unconscious inclinations and call forth predictable reactions without on the other hand placing any obligation whatever on the very persons who in this fashion secure plebiscitary agreement. The appeals, controlled according to carefully investigated and experimentally tested "psychological parameters," must progressively lose their connection with political program statements, not to mention issue-related arguments, the more they are effective as symbols of identification. Their meaning is exhausted in the release of that kind of popularity "that in today's mass society replaces the direct relationship of the individual to politics."[103] Hence the presentation of the leader or the leader's team plays a central role; they too need to be packaged and displayed in a way that makes them marketable. The popularity index is a government's measure of how much it has the nonpublic opinion of the population under its control or of how much publicity that can be translated into popularity its team of leaders must additionally obtain. Popularity is not as such identical with publicity, but it cannot be maintained in the long run without it. The mood it designates is a dependent variable of the temporarily manufactured publicity, although it is by no means dependent on it alone. It is not without reason that ruling parties, in order to survive at the polls, create objective causes, publicity vehicles in the form of genuine concessions to the expectations of the population—say, lowering the taxes on alcohol or cigarettes—to create an abundance of publicity. In order to adjust, however manipulatively, to the scientifically analyzed motives of the voters, it is at times also necessary to take measures, crystallization points of the denied publicity, that satisfy real needs. To that extent the manipulation of even the most inventive election managers has its natural limits. From this, of course, one should not simply draw the converse conclusion that "the better the motives of the voters are known, the more the 'government' is 'manipulated' by the 'people.'"[104]

Certainly the publicist exploitation of given motives must also be accommodating to them; in this connection it may be necessary under certain circumstances to create opportunities for publicity in the form of obligations to satisfy the real needs of the voters. The narrower the "natural" limits of manipulation, the stronger the pressure not only to exploit scientifically analysed motives but to satisfy them as well. In this regard no unambiguous information is available as yet. Even if we hypothetically suppose that in a situation where the limits of manipulation are drawn very narrowly, the acclamation procedure within the framework of the periodically manufactured public sphere guarantees a far-reaching readiness on the part of the government to submit to nonpublic opinion,[105] the conditions for democratic opinion and consensus formation would not be fulfilled. For the offers made for the purposes of advertising psychology, no matter how much they may be objectively to the point, in such a case are not mediated by the will and consciousness but by the subconscious of the subjects. This kind of consensus formation would be more suited to the enlightened absolutism of an authoritarian welfare regime than to a democratic constitutional state committed to social rights: everything for the people, nothing by the people—not accidentally a statement stemming from the Prussia of Frederick II. Strictly speaking, not even welfare would be guaranteed by this procedure. For aside from the attitude of autonomy, a nonpublic opinion having an indirect influence would also lack the attribute of rationality as such. The satisfaction of even a well established motive of the broadest strata does not itself afford any guarantee that it would correspond to their objective interests. Publicity was, according to its very idea, a principle of democracy not just because anyone could in principle announce, with equal opportunity, his personal inclinations, wishes, and convictions—opinions; it could only be realized in the measure that these personal opinions could evolve through the rational-critical debate of a public into public opinion— *opinion publique.* For the guarantee of universal accessibility was understood only as the precondition that guaranteed the truth of a discourse and counter-discourse bound to the laws of logic.

The relationship between the manufactured public sphere and nonpublic opinion can be illustrated by some measures that influenced the elections for the German Bundestag in 1957 in favor of the parties in government. (We focus on this example of a manipulative use of the empirical results of survey research by a certain party only because of the availability of reliable documention, which is lacking with respect to other parties[106].) Four strategic measures were, for the most part, decisive for the publicity work of the party victorious in the electoral campaign. The image of the party leader that had so well stood the test of the Bundestag elections of 1953 had to be restyled to undercut potential apprehensiveness, especially relating to his age: he was presented in the midst of "his team." Next, the propaganda concentrated especially upon anxieties and needs for security, on the one hand, by effectively associating the opponent with the Bolshevik danger and, on the other, by generating the belief that the party that happened to be in control of government (and was without reluctance portrayed as identical with the state as such) represented the only guarantee for security, whether military or social: "no experiments"; "you have what you have." Thirdly, in order to counter the fear of price increases that might have hurt the government at the polls it worked out with industrial leaders a so-called holdback agreement that caused companies to postpone price increases until after the election. In addition, a number of brand-name companies, in advertisements in the daily press, vouched for the stability of the price levels; this was preceded by the advertising campaign of a retailers' association. As the most effective measure, finally, legislation reforming the social security system had been passed. From May of 1957 on about 6 million retired people received higher benefits and retroactive payments; naturally, the material and psychological effect was not limited to retirement benefits. All four measures were carefully tested beforehand and then through calculated advertising techniques publicistically launched ("the soft sell") and exploited ("prosperity for all"). The individual strategic measures were not evaluated with regard to their effectiveness, that is, the amount of acclamation captured; their relative importance is difficult to assess. It is easier to interpret their political content than their effectiveness as propaganda. The only binding obligation assumed by the parties in government was their consent prior to the election to the reform of the social security system. The opposition, to be sure, contributed its own share to the passing of the legislation; but as the Bundestag is identified by many voters with the federal government, the parties in government were in a better position to exploit it as a perfectly timed publicity opportunity.

Thus, on the one hand, even this method of political consensus formation ensures a kind of pressure of nonpublic opinion upon the government to satisfy the real needs of the population in order to avoid a risky loss of popularity. On the other hand, it prevents the formation of a public opinion in the strict sense. For inasmuch as important political decisions are made for manipulative purposes (without, of course, for this reason being factually less consequential) and are introduced with consummate propagandistic skill as publicity vehicles into a public sphere manufactured for show, they remain removed *qua political* decisions from both a public process of rational argumentation and the possibility of a plebiscitary vote of no confidence in the awareness of precisely defined alternatives. To stay with our example, the reform of social security during its preparatory phase was never systematically made into a topic of a process of public opinion formation, although it was thoroughly treated in the great daily press. Population surveys showed that the mass of the population associated no apposite ideas with the notion of dynamic retirement benefits; nor did such benefits afterward, as a central social-political problem, explicitly become an issue in the election campaign (only the indirect psychological effects could be utilized as the basis for propaganda geared to simplistic stereotypes of improvements in the standard of living). In this case too the public sphere as a show set up for purposes of manipulation and staged directly for the sake of that large minority of the "undecided" who normally determine the outcome of an election served a communication process between set symbols and given motives that was social-psychologically calculated and guided by advertising techniques. Even added together the votes resulting from all this did not amount to a public opinion, because two conditions were not fulfilled: informal opinions were not formed rationally, that is, in conscious grappling with cognitively accessible states of affairs (instead, the publicly presented symbols corresponded to unconscious processes whose mode of operation was concealed from the individuals); nor were they formed in discussion, in the pro and con of a public conversation (instead the reactions, although in many ways mediated by group opinions, remained private in the sense that they were not exposed to correction within the framework of a critically debating public). Thus a public of citizens that had disintegrated *as* a public was reduced by publicist means to such a position that it could be claimed for the legitimation of political compromises without participating in effective decisions or being in the least capable of such participation.

The example of social security reform is informative in another respect as well, for social security is part of the complex of social-welfare-state protections against personal life-risks that were once left to private autonomy. The contradiction is obvious: a proliferation of the social conditions of private existence that are maintained and secured by public authority, and therefore ought to be clarified within the communication process of a politically autonomous public of citizens, that is, should be made a topic for public opinion. Although objectively greater demands are placed on this authority, it operates less as a *public* opinion giving a rational foundation to the exercise of political and social authority, the more it is generated for the purpose of an abstract vote that amounts to no more than an act of acclamation within a public sphere temporarily manufactured for show or manipulation.

23 The Political Public Sphere and the Transformation of the Liberal Constitutional State into a Social-Welfare State

The characteristic imbalance between those functions that the political public sphere actually fulfills today and those that, in the context of the changed relation between public sphere and private realm, might be expected of it in relation to the needs of a democratically organized society becomes palpable wherever the transformation of the liberal constitutional state[107] into the so-called social-welfare state is explicitly legislated and, often enough, anticipated in its intention by the letter and spirit of constitutional institutions.

In the first modern constitutions subdivisions in the catalogues of basic rights were the very image of the liberal model of the bourgeois public sphere. They guaranteed society as a sphere of private autonomy. Confronting it stood a public authority limited to a few functions, and between the two, as it were, was the realm of private people assembled into a public who, as the citizenry, linked up the state with the needs of civil society according to the idea that in the medium of this public sphere political authority would be transformed into rational authority. On the assumption of the inherent justice of the market mechanism and the exchange of equivalents (insofar as they implied equal opportunity for the acquisition of property and therewith independence and a voice in political affairs), it seemed that the general interest that was to yield the standard for gauging this kind of rationality would be guaranteed (within a society in which commodities could be freely exchanged) so long as the traffic of private people in the market and in the public sphere was emancipated from domination. As a sphere emancipated from domination all power relationships would be automatically neutralized within a society of small commodity traders.

The injunction-like character of the liberal basic rights corresponded to the following ideas: these rights protected from state interference and encroachment those areas that in principle were the preserve of private people acting in accord with the general rules of the legal system. With regard to their social function (as the framers of constitutions at that time had in mind), however, the basic rights had by no means only an exclusionary effect; according to the basis on which this political order was conceived they necessarily acted as positive guarantees of equal opportunity participation in the process of generating both societal wealth and public opinion. Within the system of a commercial society, as was taken for granted,[108] equal opportunity for social recompense (via the market) and participation in political institutions (in the public sphere) could be assured only indirectly through the guarantee of liberties and securities over against the power concentrated in the state. The positive effect could be ensured only by way of efficacious prohibitions through constitutional rights. In contrast to the view that prevails among the jurists, therefore, it must be concluded that from a sociological perspective the constitution of the liberal constitutional state was from the beginning meant to order not only the state as such and in relation to society but the system of coexistence in society as a whole. The constitutionally determined public order, therefore, also comprised the order that was the object of private law.[109] In consequence, the usual distinction between liberal guarantees of freedom and democratic guarantees of participation appeared in a different light. To be sure, *status negativus* and *status activus* were as clearly separated as the positions and functions of *bourgeois* and *citoyen*, of private person and citizen in general. Yet when one approaches the two types of constitutional right sociologically, by reference to the original relationship between public and private spheres, their indissoluble connection becomes apparent. Status in both the public and private spheres (of civil society and family) was guaranteed in a negative fashion on the basis of a confidence that the public sphere and the market would function in the anticipated way as long as the autonomy of private people was assured in both spheres. Even the constitutionalization of the public sphere in the parliament as an organ of the state obviously did not obscure its origin in the private and autonomous affairs of the public. The right to vote too, directly formulated as a right of participation, was the automatic consequence of the protection, through exemption, of private dealings in the public sphere. Like the order of private law and, in general, the encasing of public order in a constitution, liberal human rights and democratic civil rights diverged in the theory and practice of bourgeois constitutional law only when the fictitious character of the social order hypothetically assumed to be at their basis became conscious and revealed its ambivalence to the bourgeoisie as it gradually actualized its rule..

The transformation of the liberal constitutional state in the direction of a state committed to social rights must be comprehended by reference to this point of departure, for certainly it is characterized by continuity rather than by a break with the liberal traditions. The constitutional social-welfare state (*sozialer Rechtsstaat*) was distinguished from the liberal one not to the extent "that a *state* constitution emerged which also claims to anchor, with legally binding force, the constitution of *societal* organizations in certain basic principles"[110]; instead, matters were reversed. The social-welfare state was compelled to shape social conditions to continue the legal tradition of the liberal state, because the latter too wanted to ensure an overall legal order comprising both state and society. As soon as the state itself came to the fore as the bearer of the societal order, it had to go beyond the negative determinations of liberal basic rights and draw upon a positive directive notion as to how "justice" was to be realized through the interventions that characterize the social-welfare state. As we have seen, the liberal constitutional state's concept of law was so hollow in its two elements—the equality-guaranteeing universality and rightness (in the sense of justice-guaranteeing truth)—that the fulfilling of its formal criteria no longer sufficed for an adequate normative regulation of the new material.[111] Substantive guarantees subjecting compromises between interests to the programmatic rules of *jusititia distributiva* had to replace formal ones. Thus the distribution of increases in the gross national product became ever more a proper concern of political authorities. The special-interest associations under public law wrestled with the legislative and executive branches over the key in accord with which the distribution was to proceed. Thus the state charged with social obligations (*sozialpflichtig*) had to watch out that the negotiated balance of interests stayed inside the framework of the general interest. H. P. Ipsen accordingly interpreted the constitution's welfare-state clause as a definition of the state's goal.[112] With this clause more was posited than just a constitutional recognition of some existing legal institutions in the area of social welfare—there remained "as the normative effect of the constitutional mandate for a state committed to social rights . . . the obligation of all state organs to ensure through legislation, administration, and judicial decisions the adaptation of such legal institutions in the area of social welfare to the ongoing demands."[113]

Somewhat similar programmatic statements hold good for the other Western democracies; and wherever they are not encased in the constitution, they have by now become valid as a kind of political convention. In some cases the traditional catalogues of basic rights have also been expanded in accordance with a program of social welfare, prototypically in the Weimar Constitution.[114] Today basic social rights to welfare are found, apart from the liquidated French Constitution of 1946, in the United Nations Declaration of Human Rights of December 10, 1948.[115] They ensure a share in social services and participation in political institutions: "The freedom secured through demarcation is related to a state that sets limits to itself, that does not interfere with the individual's situation in society, whatever it happens to be. . . . Participation as a right and claim implies an active, allotting, distributing, providing state that does not leave the individual at the mercy of his situation in society, but comes to his aid by offering support. This is the state committed to social rights."[116] This contrast, of course, abstracts from the historical continuity (judged in terms of their social functions) between liberal basic rights and social rights to welfare.

To be sure, in accord with the concept of law proper to the constitutional state, the guarantees of basic rights rest on the demarcation of the private sphere and of a public sphere operative in the political realm not directly subject to interference by public authority; the institutional guarantees concerning property and family serve this purpose as well. They are, however, supplemented by basic social rights only because the positive consequences resulting from the interdictions no longer come about "automatically"; because the demarcation of realms exempted from invasion by the state is no longer honored, through the "accommodating response" of immanent societal mechanisms, with anything that comes even close to equal opportunity in the sharing of social recompenses and in participating in political institutions; these become now explicitly ensured by the state. Only in this way can the political order remain faithful today, under the conditions of a public sphere that itself has been structurally transformed, to that idea of a public sphere as an element in the political realm once invested in the institutions of the bourgeois constitutional state.

This dialectic can be shown with special clarity in the case of the liberal basic rights which, even if their original formulations have been preserved in the currently valid constitutions, have to shift their normative meaning to remain true to their own intention. The very reality that corresponds to a constitution altered in the direction of a social-welfare state causes one to reflect

as to what extent these liberal constitutional rights, originally formulated and conceived as exclusionary rights over against state authority, should now be reconceived as participatory rights, since they pertain to a democratic and constitutional state committed to social rights. . . . [The constitution] is aimed at extending the idea of a substantively democratic constitutional state (which means especially the principle of equality and its combination with the notion of participation in the idea of self-determination) to the entire economic and social order and thereby giving real content to the ideal of the concept of the state committed to social rights.[117]

First of all it has to be demonstrated with regard to those basic rights guaranteeing the effectiveness of a public sphere in the political realm (such as freedom of speech and opinion, freedom of association and assembly, and freedom of the press) that in their application to the factual state of the structurally transformed public sphere they must no longer be interpreted merely as injunctions but positively, as guarantees of participation, if they are to fulfill their original function in a meaningful way. Since the publicist institutions themselves have become a societal force that can be employed both to grant a privileged status to (or to boycott) the private interests flooding into the public sphere and to mediatize all merely individual opinions, the formation of a public opinion in the strict sense is not effectively secured by the mere fact that anyone can freely utter his opinion and put out a newspaper. The public is no longer one composed of persons formally and materially on equal footing. Pushing the interpretation of the social function of the freedom of private opinion to its logical conclusion, Ridder[118] arrived at the formulation of a "freedom of public opinion" aimed at providing citizens with the equal opportunity to participate in the process of public communication to begin with. Correspondingly, he complemented the classical freedom of the press of private people with the institutional commitment of publicist organs to the basic order of the democratic and constitutional state committed to social rights: "It is obvious that freedom of the press cannot be specified in a negative fashion as individual or collective freedom from government interference. What matters before everything else is the public mission of the political press for the sake of which freedoms are subsequently guaranteed."[119] Free expression of opinion by the press can no longer be regarded as part of the traditional expression of opinion by individuals as private people.[120] Equal access to the public sphere is provided to all other private people only through the state's guarantee of active interference to this end (*Gestaltungsgarantie*); a mere guarantee that the state will refrain from intrusion is not longer sufficient for this purpose.[121]

In an analogous way the freedoms of assembly and association change their character. Insofar as they are big, bureaucratized organizations, parties and special-interest associations under public law enjoy an oligopoly of the publicistically effective and politically relevant formation of assemblies and associations. Hence here too freedom of assembly and association needs a guarantee of active promotion (*Gestaltungsgarantie*), which can be effective in assuring citizen participation in the political realm's public sphere only by obligating the organization to fulfill a certain task and to structure its internal order accordingly. To this obligation corresponds the guarantee of certain claims that find expression in the so-called party privilege.[122]

The other group of basic rights which, with the institutional guarantee of private property as its core, confirms the basic liberties of private law and also ensures free choice of occupation, work place, and place of training can no longer be understood as a guarantee of a private sphere based on competitive capitalism. In part these rights take on the character of participatory rights, insofar as they must already be understood (in conjunction with a principle of equality interpreted in a substantive sense) as guarantees of social claims such as an occupational position corresponding to one's performance or an apprenticeship or education corresponding to one's capability. In part they are restricted by other guarantees of the state committed to social rights, so that they lose the character of an area in principle protected from interference. So, for instance, free control over private property finds its limits not only in the social proviso of its compatibility with the interests of society as a whole or in the socialist proviso of its possible transference, in the name of the general interest, into collective property; the social guarantees embedded especially in the legislation concerning work, landlord-tenant relations, and housing construction directly place limits on the liberal guarantee of property.

Even the basic rights that protect the integrity of the family's interior domain and the status of personal freedom (life, liberty, and shelter), together with a substantively interpreted right to free personal development, lose the merely injunction-like character that made them prototypical in the transition from the ancient status-group privileges to civil freedoms.[123] For under the conditions of an industrial society constituted as a social-welfare state the securing of these legal provisions cannot be accomplished by defensive and exemptive measures, or rather can be attained only if these in turn are supported by participatory rights, by guaranteed claims to benefits. The development of personal freedom in a private sphere that has de facto shrunk down to the circle of family and leisure time is itself in need of a status publicly guaranteed through democratic participation—instead of a basis in private property that formerly was adequately protected by liberal exemptionism.

Of course, private autonomy is then only possible as something derivative; the social rights to security, recompense, and free development, reinterpreted within a state committed to social rights, are also no longer grounded in a constitutionality (*Rechtsstaatlichkeit*) stabilized per se by the interest of bourgeois commerce. Instead they are based on the integration of the interests of all organizations that act in a state-related fashion, an integration that according to the prescribed ideal of a state committed to social rights is always to be achieved democratically: "Only from this viewpoint is it possible to reconcile with each other the safeguards of individual rights, protected by impartial judicial decision, and the substantively interpreted idea of equality before the law." In this connection, Abendroth suggests that the real alternative is *not*

whether one wishes to bring about full freedom for each individual to make his own economic and social decisions or his subjection to the planning power of a state that democratically represents society, but rather whether one subjects the great mass of society's members to the power—formally private (and hence oriented toward particular interests, not toward the common good)—of those members of the society who control the society's decisive positions of economic power or whether one removes the planning that is necessary and unavoidable for social production and social life from the haphazardness of the private dispositions of small groups and places it under the collective control of those who participate in the communal process of production as members of a society whose highest decision making unit is the state. In both cases the predictability of legal decisions about the consequences of private dispositions by the society's members is restricted. But in the case of the planning measures of a democratic state committed to social rights this predictability is maintained not in every particular, to be sure, but certainly along general lines and can be made tolerable through regularized procedures and, if warranted, through payment of damages. Within an organization of society irrevocably shot through with oligopolies and monopolies, in contrast, it is subject (on account of private decisions) to changes in scenario that from the individual's point of view are completely accidental. . . . Consequently, the economically weaker members of society are repeatedly exposed to changes in social position for which there are no compensations of any kind. In reality, therefore, the influence of law is not weakened but strengthened when the realm of the publicly controlled sphere is expanded relative to that which formerly was purely a domain of private law.[124]

Forsthoff is admittedly justified in indicating that even the social-welfare state (*Sozialstaat*), as the constitution of a *bourgeois* society, remains in principle a state financed by taxation (*Steuerstaat*) and does not per se normatively posit its transformation into a society under state tutelage (*Staatsgesellschaft*). The social-welfare state, like the liberal one, rests upon the specific foundation of a demarcation of the sovereign right to taxation from the constitutionally granted protection of property: "It is thereby possible to interfere via the right to levy taxes with income and wealth in a fashion which, if it were directed . . . with equal intensity against property, would be qualified as expropriation and would trigger claims to compensation."[125] In the course of the development toward a state committed to social rights, of course, the qualitative difference between interference with income and wealth, on the one hand, and with the control over property on the other is reduced to one of degree, so that taxation can become the instrument for the control of private property. But the state based on taxation would definitely pass over into a society under state tutelage only when all social power that was sufficiently relevant politically was also subjected to democratic control. The model that Abendroth contrasts with the bourgeois public sphere, according to which the direction and administration of all processes of social reproduction are subordinate to a public formation of opinion and will on the part of the citizenry, therefore points up merely the goal of a direction of development—whereby at first not the goal as such but the dimension of development itself is characteristic of the transformation of the bourgeois constitutional state into a social-welfare state.

To the extent that state and society penetrate each other and bring forth a middle sphere of semipublic, semiprivate relationships ordered by social legislation still emerging, the constitutional tenets of a private sphere that precedes the state and of a public sphere that connects society with the state and thus has a function in the political realm are changed in their significance (as regards their sociological import and actual constitutional function) by virtue of a concurrent set of constitutional norms. For what can no longer be vouchsafed indirectly by means of exemption is now in need of being positively granted: a share in social benefits and participation in the institutions of the political realm's public sphere. The legitimate scope of this participation has to be expanded simultaneously to the degree to which this participation is to become effective. Hence societal organizations are active in a state-related fashion in the public sphere of the political realm, be it indirectly through parties or directly in interplay with public administration. In part these are economic associations in the narrower sense that now collectively organize those formerly individual interests of owners operating out of their original private autonomy; in part they are mass organizations that by means of the collective representation of their interests in the public sphere have to obtain and defend a private status granted to them by social legislation. In other words, they have to obtain and defend private autonomy by means of political autonomy. Together with the politically influential representatives of cultural and religious forces this competition of organized private interests in the face of the "neomercantilism" of an interventionist administration leads to a "refeudalization" of society insofar as, with the linking of public and private realms, not only certain functions in the sphere of commerce and social labor are taken over by political authorities but conversely political functions are taken over by societal powers.

Consequently, this refeudalization also reaches into the political public sphere itself. Here organizations strive for political compromises with the state and with one another, as much as possible to the exclusion of the public; in this process, however, they have to procure plebiscitary agreement from a mediatized public by means of a display of staged or manipulated publicity. In opposition to this factual trend toward the weakening of the public sphere as a principle stands the redefinition of the functions of constitutional rights by a state committed to social rights and, in general, the transformation of the liberal constitutional state into a social-welfare state. The mandate of publicity is extended from the organs of the state to all organizations acting in state-related fashion. In the measure that this is realized, a no longer intact public of private people dealing with each other individually would be replaced by a public of organized private people. *Only such a public could, under today's conditions, participate effectively in a process of public communication via the channels of the public spheres internal to parties and special-interest associations and on the basis of an affirmation of publicity as regards the negotiations of organizations with the state and with one another.* The formation of political compromises would have to be legitimated by reference to this process.

The political public sphere of the social-welfare state is marked by two competing tendencies. Insofar as it represents the collapse of the public sphere of civil society, it makes room for a *staged and manipulative* publicity displayed by organizations over the heads of a mediatized public. On the other hand, to the degree to which it preserves the continuity with the liberal constitutional state, the social-welfare state clings to the mandate of a political public sphere according to which the public is to set in motion a *critical* process of public communication through the very organizations that mediatize it. In the constitutional reality of the social-welfare state this form of critical publicity is in conflict with publicity merely staged for manipulative ends.[126] The extent to which the former type prevails gauges the degree of democratization of an industrial society constituted as a social-welfare state—namely, *the rationalization of the exercise of social and political authority.* The state committed to social rights has abandoned the fiction of the liberal constitutional state that with its establishment as an organ of state the public sphere had actually become a reality in the realm of politics. From the very start, indeed, the parliament was rent by the contradiction of being an institution opposing all political authority and yet established as an "authority" itself. In contrast, publicity operating under the conditions of a social-welfare state must conceive of itself as a self-generating process. Gradually it has to establish itself in competition with that other tendency which, within an immensely expanded public sphere, turns the principle of publicity against itself and thereby reduces its critical efficacy.

Naturally, the question of the degree to which the forces active in the political public sphere can effectively be subjugated to the democratic mandate of publicity—and to what extent it is thus possible to achieve the rationalization of political domination and social authority to which the social-welfare state lays claim—ultimately leads back to the problem which from the very beginning was implicit in the idea of the bourgeois public sphere. The notion of society as liberalism's ambivalent conception made evident had supposed the objective possibility of reducing structural conflicts of interest and bureaucratic decisions to a minimum.[127] One aspect of the problem is technical, the other can be reduced to an economic one. Today more than ever the extent to which a public sphere effective in the political realm can be realized in accord with its critical intentions depends on the possibility of resolving these problems. Here I would like to confine myself to two provisional remarks.

With the mounting bureaucratization of the administration in state and society it seems to be inherent in the nature of the case that the expertise of highly specialized experts would necessarily be removed from supervision by rationally debating bodies. Max Weber analyzed this tendency with respect to the inevitably precarious relationship between the parliament and the executive.[128] Against this, however, it must be taken into account that in the meantime a partner equal to the administration has grown within the administration itself: "The control of the state's political bureaucracy today is possible only by means of society's political bureaucracy, in the parties and pressure groups (*Interessenverbände*).[129] Of course, the latter themselves would have to be subject to a control within the framework of their intraorganizational spheres. Inasmuch as this is a matter of the technical aspect within one and the same organization, it should not be impossible on structural grounds to arrive at an appropriate relationship between bureaucratic decisions and a quasi-parliamentary deliberation by means of a process of public communication.[130]

To be sure, this problem does not present itself today as primarily technical. The disappearance of publicity inside large organizations, both in state and society, and even more their flight from publicity in their dealings with one another results from the unresolved plurality of competing interests; this plurality in any event makes it doubtful whether there can ever emerge a general interest of the kind to which a public opinion could refer as a criterion. A structurally ineradicable antagonism of interests would set narrow boundaries for a public sphere reorganized by the social-welfare state to fulfill its critical function. Neutralization of social power and rationalization of political domination in the medium of public discussion indeed presuppose now as they did in the past a possible consensus, that is, the possibility of an objective agreement among competing interests in accord with universal and binding criteria.[131] Otherwise the power relation between pressure and counterpressure, however publicly exercised, creates at best an unstable equilibrium of interests supported by temporary power constellations that in principle is devoid of rationality according to the standard of a universal interest.

In our day, nevertheless, two tendencies are clearly visible which could add a new twist to the problem. On the basis of the high (and ever higher) level of forces of production, industrially advanced societies have attained an expansion of social wealth in the face of which it is not unrealistic to assume that the continuing and increasing plurality of interests may lose the antagonistic edge of competing needs to the extent that the possibility of mutual satisfaction comes within reach. Accordingly, the general interest consists in quickly bringing about the conditions of an "affluent society" which renders moot an equilibrium of interests dictated by the scarcity of means.[132] On the other hand, the technical means of destruction increase along with the technical means of satisfying needs. Harnessed by the military, a potential for self-annihilation on a global scale has called forth risks so total that in relation to them divergent interests can be relativized without difficulty. The as yet unconquered state of nature in international relations has become so threatening for everybody that its specific negation articulates the universal interest with great precision. Kant argued that "perpetual peace" had to be established in a "cosmopolitan order."[133]

Be that as it may, the two conditions for a public sphere to be effective in the political realm—the objectively possible minimizing of bureaucratic decisions and a relativizing of structural conflicts of interest according to the standard of a universal interest everyone can acknowledge—can today no longer be disqualified as simply utopian. The dimension of the democratization of industrial societies constituted as social-welfare states is not limited from the outset by an impenetrability and indissolubility (whether theoretically demonstrable or empirically verifiable) of irrational relations of social power and political domination. The outcome of the struggle between a critical publicity and one that is merely staged for manipulative purposes remains open; the ascendancy of publicity regarding the exercise and balance of political power mandated by the social-welfare state over publicity merely staged for the purpose of acclamation is by no means certain.[134] But unlike the idea of the bourgeois public sphere during the period of its liberal development, it cannot be denounced as an ideology. If anything, it brings the dialectic of that idea, which had been degraded into an ideology, to its conclusion.

On the Concept of Public Opinion

24 Public Opinion as a Fiction of Constitutional Law—and the Social-Psychological Liquidation of the Concept

"Public opinion" takes on a different meaning depending on whether it is brought into play as a critical authority in connection with the normative mandate that the exercise of political and social power be subject to publicity or as the object to be molded in connection with a staged display of, and manipulative propagation of, publicity in the service of persons and institutions, consumer goods, and programs. Both forms of publicity compete in the public sphere, but "the" public opinion is their common addressee. What is the nature of this entity?

The two aspects of publicity and public opinion do not stand in a relationship of norm and fact—as if it were a matter of the same principle whose actual effects simply lagged behind the mandated ones (and correspondingly, the actual behavior of the public lagged behind what was expected of it). In this fashion there could be a link between public opinion as an ideal entity and its actual manifestation; but this is clearly not the case. Instead, the critical and the manipulative functions of publicity are clearly of different orders. They have their places within social configurations whose functional consequences run at cross-purposes to one another. Also, in each version the public is expected to behave in a different fashion. Taking up a distinction introduced earlier it might be said that one version is premised on public opinion, the other on nonpublic opinion.

And critical publicity along with its addressee is more than merely a norm. As a constitutionally institutionalized norm, no matter what structural transformation its social basis has undergone since its original matrix in the bourgeois constitutional state, it nevertheless determines an important portion of the procedures to which the political exercise and balance of power are factually bound. This publicity, together with an addressee that fulfills the behavioral expectations set by it, "exists"—not the public as a whole, certainly, but surely a workable substitute. Further questions, to be decided empirically, concern the areas in which these functions of publicity are in force and to what extent and under which conditions its corresponding public exists today. On the other hand, the competing form of publicity along with its addressee is more than a mere fact. It is accompanied by a specific self-understanding whose normative obligatoriness may to a certain extent also be in opposition to immediate interests of "publicity work." Significantly, this self-understanding borrows essential elements precisely from its publicist antagonist.

Within the framework of constitutional law and political science, the analysis of constitutional norms in relation to the constitutional reality of large democratic states committed to social rights has to maintain the institutionalized fiction of a public opinion without being able to identify it directly as a real entity in the behavior of the public of citizens. The difficulty arising from this situation has been described by Landshut. On the one hand, he registers the fact that "public opinion [is] replaced [by] an in itself indeterminate mood-dependent inclination. Particular measures and events constantly lead it in this or that direction. This mood-dependent preference has the same effect as shifting cargo on a rolling ship."[1] On the other hand, he recalls that the constitutional institutions of large, democratic, social-welfare states count on an intact public opinion because it is still the only accepted basis for the legitimation of political domination: "The modern state presupposes as the principle of its own truth the sovereignty of the people, and this in turn is supposed to be public opinion. Without this attribution, without the substitution of public opinion as the origin of all authority for decisions binding the whole, modern democracy lacks the substance of its own truth."[2] If, without a naive faith in the idea of a rationalization of domination, the mandate implicit in the constitutional norms of a public sphere as an element in the political realm[3] cannot be simply abandoned to the facticity of a public sphere in a state of collapse,[4] two paths toward defining the concept of public opinion become evident.

One of these leads back to the position of liberalism, which in the midst of a disintegrating public sphere wanted to salvage the communication of an inner circle of representatives capable of constituting a public and of forming an opinion, that is, a critically debating public in the midst of one that merely supplies acclamation: "It is obvious that out of the chaos of moods, confused opinions, and popularizing views of the sort spread by the mass media, a public opinion is much more difficult to form than out of the rational controversy between the different great currents of opinion that struggled against one another within society. To this extent it must be conceded that it is harder than ever for public opinion to prevail."[5] Hennis, of course, announces this state of affairs only for the sake of demonstrating the urgency of special arrangements intended to procure authority and obedience for "the view adopted by the relatively best informed, most intelligent, and most moral citizens"[6], as the public in contradistinction to the common opinion. The element of publicity that guarantees rationality is to be salvaged at the expense of its other element, that is, the universality guaranteeing general accessibility. In this process, the qualifications that private people once could attain within the sphere of commerce and social labor as social criteria of membership in the public become autonomous hierarchical qualities of representation, for the old basis can no longer be counted on. Sociologically, a representativeness of this kind can no longer be determined in a satisfactory fashion under the existing conditions.[7]

The other path leads to a concept of public opinion that leaves material criteria such as rationality and representativeness entirely out of consideration and confines itself to institutional criteria. Thus Fraenkel equates public opinion with the view that happens to prevail in the parliament and to be authoritative for the government: "With the help of parliamentary discussion, public opinion makes its desires known to the government, and the government makes its policies known to public opinion"[8]—public opinion reigns, but it does not govern. Leibholz contends that this way of counterposing government and parliament as the mouthpieces of public opinion is incorrect, claiming that the antagonistic political actors always are the parties in their roles as party-in-government and party-in-opposition. The will of the parties is identical with that of the active citizenry, so that the party happening to hold the majority represents the public opinion: "Just as in a plebiscitary democracy the will of the enfranchised citizenry's majority is identified, in a functioning democratic state with a party system, with the collective will of the people on an issue, the will of the parties that happen to hold the majority in government and parliament is identified with the *volonté générale*."[9] Non-public opinion only attains existence as "public" when processed through the parties. Both versions take into account the fact that independently of the organizations by which the opinion of the people is mobilized and integrated, it scarcely plays a politically relevant role any longer in the process of opinion and consensus formation in a mass democracy. At the same time, however, this is the weakness of this theory; by replacing the public as the subject of public opinion with agencies in virtue of which alone it is still viewed as capable of political activity, this concept of public opinion becomes peculiarly nondescript. It is impossible to discern whether this "public opinion" has come about by way of public communication or through opinion management, whereby it must remain undecided again whether the latter refers merely to the enunciation of a mass preference incapable of articulating itself or to the reduction to the status of a plebiscitary echo of an opinion that, although quite capable of attaining enlightenment, has been forcibly integrated. As a fiction of constitutional law, public opinion is no longer identifiable in the actual behavior of the public itself; but even its attribution to certain political institutions (as long as this attribution abstracts from the level of the public's behavior altogether) does not remove its fictive character. Empirical social research therefore returns with positivist pathos to this level, in order to establish "public opinion" directly. Of course, it in turn abstracts from the institutional aspects and quickly accomplishes the social-psychological liquidation of the concept of public opinion as such.

Already a problem for liberalism by the middle of the century, 'public opinion' came fully into view as a problematic entity in the final quarter of the nineteenth century. Striking a note of liberal resignation, a treatise about "Nature and Value of Public Opinion" of 1879 put it in the following fashion:

So for the present the novelty of facts and the need for diversions has become so decisive that the people's opinion is as deprived of the support of a firm historical tradition . . . as it is of that peculiarly energetic spadework in the intellectual laboratory of great men who placed their faith in principles and sacrificed everything to them. What a century ago was, according to the belief of contemporaries, a social principle that placed an obligation upon each individual (namely, public opinion), in the course of time has become a slogan by which the complacent and intellectually lazy mass is supplied with a pretext for avoiding the labor of thinking for themselves.[10]

A half-century earlier Schäffle had characterized public opinion as a "formless reaction on the part of the masses" and defined it as "expression of the views, value judgments, or preferences of the general or of any special public."[11] The normative spell cast by constitutional theory over the concept was therewith broken—public opinion became an object of social-psychological research. Tarde was the first to analyze it in depth as "mass opinion";[12] separated from the functional complex of political institutions, it is immediately stripped of its character as "public" opinion. It is considered a product of a communication process among masses that is neither bound by the principles of public discussion nor concerned with political domination.

When, under the impression of an actually functioning popular government, political theoreticians like Dicey in England and Bryce in the United States[13] nevertheless retained this functional context in their concepts of public opinion (which, to be sure, already show the traces of social-psychological reflection), they exposed themselves to the accusation of empirical unreliability. The prototype of this kind of objection is

A. C. Bentley's early critique. He misses "a quantitative analysis of public opinion in terms of the different elements of the population," which is to say, "an investigation of the exact things really wanted under the cover of the opinion by each group of the people, with time and place and circumstances all taken up into the center of the statement." Hence Bentley's thesis: "There is no public opinion . . . nor activity reflecting or representing the activity of a group or set of groups."[14]

Public opinion became the label of a social-psychological analysis of group processes, defining its object as follows: "Public opinion refers to people's attitudes on an issue when they are members of the same social group."[15] This definition betrays in all clarity what aspects had to be positivistically excluded from the historic concept of public opinion by decades of theoretical development and, above all, of empirical methodological progress. To begin with, "public," as the subject of public opinion, was equated with "mass," then with "group," as the social-psychological substratum of a process of communication and interaction among two or more individuals. "Group" abstracts from the multitude of social and historical conditions, as well as from the institutional means, and certainly from the web of social functions that at one time determined the specific joining of ranks on the part of private people to form a critical debating public in the political realm. "Opinion" itself is conceived no less abstractly. At first it is still identified with "expression on a controversial topic,"[16] later with "expression of an attitude,"[17] then with "attitude" itself.[18] In the end an opinion no longer even needs to be capable of verbalization; it embraces not only any habit that finds expression in some kind of notion—the kind of opinion shaped by religion, custom, mores, and simple "prejudice" against which public opinion was called in as a critical standard in the eighteenth century—but simply all modes of behavior. The only thing that makes such opinion a public one is its connection with group processes. The attempt to define public opinion as a "collection of individual opinions"[19] is soon corrected by the analysis of group relations: "We need concepts of what is both fundamental or deep and also common to a group."[20] A group opinion is considered "public" when subjectively it has come to prevail as the dominant one. The individual group member has a (possibly erroneous) notion concerning the importance of his opinion and conduct, that is to say, concerning how many and which ones of the other members share or reject the custom or view he embraces.[21]

In the meantime Lazarsfeld has pointedly insisted that the price to be paid for the social-psychological concept of public opinion is too high if it is held at the expense of eliminating all essential sociological and politological elements. Using several examples he confronts the social-psychological version with the concept as it derives from traditional political theory[22] but then, unfortunately, does no more than state the desirability of a "classical-empirical synthesis."[23] Nevertheless, the expansion of the field of investigation beyond group dynamics to institutions of public opinion, that is, to the relationship between the mass media and opinion processes, is a first step in this direction. A typical example of the extent to which even these investigations of communication structures are better able to deal with psychological relationships than with institutional conditions is provided by the theorem (which as such is interesting) concerning the two-step flow of communication.[24] A more significant step toward the desired synthesis between the classical concept of public opinion and its social-psychological surrogate occurs only through the recollection of the suppressed relationship to the agencies of political domination. "Public opinion is the corollary of domination . . . something that has political existence only in certain relationships between regime and people."[25]

Yet just as the concept of public opinion oriented to the institutions of the exercise of political power does not reach into the dimension of informal communication processes, a concept of public opinion social-psychologically reduced to group relations does not link up again with that very dimension in which the category once developed its strategic function and in which it survives today, leading the life of a recluse not quite taken seriously by sociologists: precisely as a fiction of constitutional law.[26] Once the subject of public opinion is reduced to an entity neutral to the difference between public and private spheres, namely, the group—thus documenting a structural transformation, albeit not providing its concept—and once public opinion itself is dissolved into a group relationship neutral to the difference between reasonable communication and irrational conformity, the articulation of the relationship between group opinions and public authority is left to be accomplished within the framework of an auxiliary science of public administration. Thus Schmidtchen's approach leads to the following definition: "Accordingly, all those behaviors of population groups would be designated as public opinion that are apt to modify or preserve the structures, practices, and goals of the system of domination."[27] The intention of a political public sphere (to which the mandate of democratic publicity on the part of a social-welfare state refers after all) is so completely ignored by such a concept that if it were applied in empirical research, not even the nonexistence of this sphere would be demonstrated. For it characterizes public opinion as something that, friction-like, might offer resistance to governmental and administrative practice and that in line with the results and recommendations of opinion research can be diagnosed and manipulated by appropriate means. For these results and recommendations "enable the government and its organs to take action with regard to a reality constituted by the reaction of those who are especially affected by a given policy. Opinion research has the task of providing the committees and institutions in charge . . . of aligning the behavior of the population with political goals"[28] with a feedback of reliable soundings of this reality. The author does not fail to produce evidence for his assertion.[29] Public opinion is defined from the outset in reference to the kind of manipulation through which the politically dominant must ever strive "to bring a population's dispositions into harmony with political doctrine and structure, with the type and the results of the ongoing decision process."[30] Public opinion remains the object of domination even when it forces the latter to make concessions or to reorient itself. It is not bound to rules of public discussion or forms of verbalization in general, nor need it be concerned with political problems or even be addressed to political authorities.[31] A relationship to domination accrues to it, so to speak, behind its back. The "private" desires for cars and refrigerators fall under the category of "public opinion" just as much as the behaviors of any given group, if only they are relevant to the governmental and administrative functions of a social-welfare state.[32]

25 A Sociological Attempt at Clarification

The material for opinion research—all sorts of opinions held by all sorts of population groups—is not already constituted as public opinion simply by becoming the object of politically relevant considerations, decisions, and measures. The feedback of group opinions, defined in terms of the categories employed in research on governmental and administrative processes or on political consensus formation (influenced by the display of staged or manipulative publicity), cannot close the gap between public opinion as a fiction of constitutional law and the social-psychological decomposition of its concept. A concept of public opinion that is historically meaningful, that normatively meets the requirements of the constitution of a social-welfare state, and that is theoretically clear and empirically identifiable can be grounded only in the structural transformation of the public sphere itself and in the dimension of its development. The conflict between the two forms of publicity which today characterizes the political public sphere has to be taken seriously as the gauge of a process of democratization within an industrial society constituted as a social-welfare state.[33] Nonpublic opinions are at work in great numbers, and "the" public opinion is indeed a fiction. Nevertheless, in a comparative sense the concept of public opinion is to be retained because the constitutional reality of the social-welfare state must be conceived as a process in the course of which a public sphere that functions effectively in the political realm is realized, that is to say, as a process in which the exercise of social power and political domination is effectively subjected to the mandate of democratic publicity. The criteria by which opinions may be empirically gauged as to their degree of publicness are therefore to be developed in reference to this dimension of the evolution of state and society; indeed, such an empirical specification of public opinion in a comparative sense is today the most reliable means for attaining valid and comparable statements about the extent of democratic integration characterizing a specific constitutional reality.

Within this model, two politically relevant areas of communication can be contrasted with each other: the system of informal, personal, nonpublic opinions on the one hand, and on the other that of formal, institutionally authorized opinions. Informal opinions differ in the degree of their obligatoriness. The lowest level of this area of communication is represented by the verbalization of things culturally taken for granted and not discussed, the highly resistant results of that process of acculturation that is normally not controlled by one's own reflection—for example, attitudes toward the death penalty or sexual morality. On the second level the rarely discussed basic experiences of one's own biography are verbalized, those refractory results of socialization shocks that have again become subreflective—for example, attitudes toward war and peace or certain desires for security. On the third level one finds the often discussed things generated as self-evident by the culture industry, the ephemeral results of the relentless publicist barrage and propagandist manipulation by the media to which consumers are exposed, especially during their leisure time.[34]

In relation to those matters taken for granted in a culture (which as a kind of historical sediment can be considered a type of primordial "opinion" or "prejudice" that probably has scarcely undergone any change in its social-psychological structure), the matters whose taken-for-granted status is generated by the culture industry have both a more evanescent and more artificial character. These opinions are shaped within the medium of a group-specific "exchange of tastes and preferences." Generally, the focus for this stratum of other-directed opinions is the family, the peer group, and acquaintances at work and in the neighborhood—each with its specific structures of information channeling and opinion leadership ensuring the binding nature of group opinions.[35] To be sure, matters that are taken for granted in a culture also become topical in the exchanges of opinion of such groups, but they are of a different sort from the ideas sustained by conviction, which in anticipation of their inconsequentiality circulate, so to speak, until recalled. Like those "opinions," they too constitute systems of norms demanding adaptation, but they do so more in the manner of a social control through "fashions" whose shifting rules require only a temporary loyalty. Just as those things that are taken for granted in a culture because of deep-seated traditions may be called subliterary, so those generated by the culture industry have reached a post-literary stage, as it were. The contents of opinion managed by the culture industry thematize the wide field of intrapsychic and interpersonal relationships first opened up psychologically by the subjectivity which during the eighteenth century, within the framework of an intact bourgeois domain of interiority, required a public and could express itself through literature. At that time the private spheres of life were still protected in their explicit orientation to a public sphere, since the public use of reason remained tied to literature as its medium. In contrast, the integration culture delivers the canned goods of degenerate, psychologically oriented literature as a public service for private consumption—and something to be commented on within the group's exchange of opinions. Such a group is as little a "public" as were those formations of pre-bourgeois society in which the ancient opinions were formed, secure in their tradition, and circulated unpolemically with the effect of "laws of opinion." It is no accident that group research and opinion research have developed simultaneously. The type of opinion that emerges from such intragroup relations—picked up ready-made, flexibly reproduced, barely internalized, and not evoking much commitment—this "mere" opinion, a component of what is only "small talk" anyway, is per se ripe for research. The group's communication processes are under the influence of the mass media either directly or, more frequently, mediated through opinion leaders. Among the latter are often to be found those persons who have reflected opinions formed through literary and rational controversy. However, as long as such opinions remain outside the communication network of an intact public, they too are part of the nonpublic opinions, although they clearly differ from the three other categories.

Over and against the communicative domain of nonpublic opinion stands the sphere of circulation of quasi-public opinion. These formal opinions can be traced back to specific institutions; they are officially or semiofficially authorized as announcements, proclamations, declarations, and speeches. Here we are primarily dealing with opinions that circulate in a relatively narrow circle—skipping the mass of the population—between the large political press and, generally, those publicist organs that cultivate rational debate and the advising, influencing, and deciding bodies with political or politically relevant jurisdictions (cabinet, government commissions, administrative bodies, parliamentary committees, party leadership, interest group committees, corporate bureaucracies, and union secretariats). Although these quasi-official opinions can be addressed to a wide public, they do not fulfill the requirements of a public process of rational-critical debate according to the liberal model. As institutionally authorized opinions, they are always privileged and achieve no mutual correspondence with the nonorganized mass of the "public."

Between the two spheres, naturally, exists a linkage, always through the channels of the mass media; it is established through that publicity, displayed for show or manipulation, with the help of which the groups participating in the exercise and balancing of power strive to create a plebiscitary follower-mentality on the part of a mediated public. We also count this vehicle of managed publicist influence among the formal opinions; but as "publicly manifested" they have to be distinguished from "quasi-public" opinions.

In addition to this massive contact between the formal and informal communicative domains, there also exists the rare relationship between publicist organs devoted to rational-critical debate and those few individuals who still seek to form their opinions through literature—a kind of opinion capable of becoming public, but actually nonpublic. The communicative network of a public made up of rationally debating private citizens has collapsed; the public opinion once emergent from it has partly decomposed into the informal opinions of private citizens without a public and partly become concentrated into formal opinions of publicistically effective institutions. Caught in the vortex of *publicity that is staged for show or manipulation* the public of nonorganized private people is laid claim to not by public communication but by the communication of publicly manifested opinions.

An opinion that is public in the strict sense however can only be generated in the degree that the two domains of communication are mediated by a third, that of *critical publicity*. Today, of course, such a mediation is possible on a sociologically relevant scale only through the participation of private people in a process of formal communication conducted through intraorganizational public spheres. Indeed, a minority of private people already are members of the parties and special-interest associations under public law. To the extent that these organizations permit an internal public sphere not merely at the level of functionaries and managers but at all levels, there exists the possibility of a mutual correspondence between the political opinions of the private people and that kind of quasi-public opinion. This state of affairs may stand for a tendency that for the time being is on the whole insignificant; the extent and actual impact of this tendency need to be established empirically—that is, whether we are dealing in general with a growing or declining tendency. For a sociological theory of public opinion this tendency is nevertheless of decisive importance, for it provides the criteria for a dimension in which alone public opinion can be constituted under the conditions of a large democratic state committed to social rights.

In the same proportion as informal opinions are channeled into the circuit of quasi-public opinions, seized by it, and transformed, this circuit itself, in being expanded by the public of citizens, also gains in publicity. Since, of course, public opinion is by no means simply "there" as such, and since it is at best possible to isolate tendencies that under the given conditions work in the direction of generating a public opinion, it can be defined only comparatively. The degree to which an opinion is a public opinion is measured by the following standard: the degree to which it emerges from the intraorganizational public sphere constituted by the public of the organization's members and how much the intraorganizational public sphere communicates with an external one formed in the publicist interchange, via the mass media, between societal organizations and state institutions.

C. W. Mills, by contrasting "public" and "mass," obtained empirically usable criteria for a definition of public opinion: "In a *public*, as we may understand the term, (1) virtually as many people express opinions as receive them. (2) Public communications are so organized that there is a chance immediately and effectively to answer back any opinion expressed in public. Opinion formed by such discussion (3) readily finds an outlet in effective action, even against—if necessary—the prevailing system of authority. And (4) authoritative institutions do not penetrate the public, which is thus more or less autonomous in its operation."[36] Conversely, opinions cease to be public opinions in the proportion to which they are enmeshed in the communicative interchanges that characterize a "mass":[37]

In a *mass*, (1) far fewer people express opinions than receive them; for the community of publics becomes an abstract collection of individuals who receive impressions from the mass media. (2) The communications that prevail are so organized that it is difficult or impossible for the individual to answer back immediately or with any effect. (3) The realization of opinion in action is controlled by authorities who organize and control the channels of such action. (4) The mass has no autonomy from institutions; on the contrary, agents of authorized institutions penetrate this mass, reducing any autonomy it may have in the formation of opinion by discussion.[38]

These abstract determinations of an opinion process that takes place under the conditions of a collapse of the public sphere can be easily fitted into the framework of our historical and developmental model.[39] The four criteria of *mass* communication are fulfilled to the extent that the informal domain of communication is linked to the formal merely through the channels of a publicity staged for the purpose of manipulation or show; via the "culture industry's unquestioning promulgations," the nonpublic opinions are then integrated through the "publicly manifested" ones into an existing system; in relation to this system the nonpublic opinions are without any autonomy. In contrast to this, under conditions of the large, democratic social-welfare state the communicative interconnectedness of a *public* can be brought about only in this way: through a critical publicity brought to life within intraorganizational public spheres, the completely short-circuited circulation of quasi-public opinion must be linked to the informal domain of the hitherto nonpublic opinions.

In like measure the forms of consensus and conflict that today determine the exercise and equilibration of power would also be altered. A method of public controversy which came to prevail in that manner could both ease the forcible forms of a consensus generated through pressure and temper the forcible forms of conflicts hitherto kept from the public sphere. Conflict and consensus (like domination itself and like the coercive power whose degree of stability they indicate analytically) are not categories that remain untouched by the historical development of society. In the case of the structural transformation of the bourgeois public sphere, we can study the extent to which, and manner in which, the latter's ability to assume *its* proper function determines whether the exercise of domination and power persists as a negative constant, as it were, of history—or whether as a historical category itself, it is open to substantive change.

Notes

Preface

1. Cf. W. Hennis, "Bemerkungen zur wissenschaftsgeschichtlichen Situation der politischen Wissenschaft," *Staat, Gesellschaft, Erziehung* 5:203ff.; *idem., Politik und praktische Philosophie* (Neuwied, 1963); regarding the latter, see my essay, "The Classical Doctrine of Politics in Relation to Social Philosophy," *Theory and Practice*, trans. John Viertel (Boston, 1973), 41–81.

1 Introduction: Preliminary Demarcation of a Type of Bourgeois Public Sphere

1. See below, 238ff.

2. *Deutsches Wörterbuch der Brüder Grimm* (Leipzig, 1889), 7:1183, art. "Öffentlichkeit."

3. *Weigands Deutsches Wörterbuch*, 5th ed. (Giessen, 1910), 2:232.

4. Most recently H. Arendt, *The Human Condition* (Chicago, 1958).

5. See J. Kirchner, *Beiträge zur Geschichte des Begriffs "öffentlich" und "öffentliches Recht"* Ph.D. diss. (Göttingen, 1949), 2. The *res publica* is the property that is universally accessible to the *populus*, i.e. the *res extra commercium*, which is exempted from the law that applies to the *privati* and their property; e.g., *flumen publicum, via publica*, etc. *Ibid.*, 10ff.

6. Otto Brunner, *Land und Herrschaft* (Brünn, 1943), 386f.

7. Kirchner, *Beiträge zur Geschichte des Begriffs*, 22.

8. We leave aside the problem of late medieval town sovereignty. On the level of the "territory" we encounter the towns (which usually belonged to the prince's crown land) as an integral component of feudalism. In early capitalism, however, the free towns assumed a decisive role in the evolution of the bourgeois public sphere. See below, section 3, 25ff.

9. *The Oxford Dictionary* (1909), 7:2.

10. On the history of the concept of "representation," see the remarks in H. G. Gadamer, *Truth and Method* (New York, 1975), p.125, n. 53 (on 513–14): "The history of this word is very informative. The Romans used it, but in the light of the Christian idea of the incarnation and the mystical body it acquired a completely new meaning. Representation now no longer means 'copy' or 'representation in a picture' . . . but 'replacement.' The word can obviously have this meaning because what is represented is present in the copy. *Repraesentare* means 'to make present.' . . . The important thing about the legal idea of representation is that the *persona repraesentata* is only the person represented, and yet the representative, who is exercising the former's right, is dependent on him." See also the supplementary observation on p.514: "*Repraesentatio* in the sense of 'representation' on the stage—which in the middle ages can only mean in a religious play—can be found already in the thirteenth and fourteenth centuries. . . . this does not mean that *repraesentatio* signifies 'performance' but signifies, until the seventeenth century, the represented presence of the divine itself."

11. C. Schmitt, *Verfassungslehre*, 3rd ed. (Berlin, 1957), 208ff.; on the localization of this medieval concept of publicity in the context of intellectual history, see A. Dempf, *Sacrum Imperium* (Darmstadt, 1954), esp. ch. 2, pp. 21ff., on the "Forms of Publicity."

12. Carl Schmitt observes that the rhetorical formula is as intimately connected to representative publicity as discussion is linked to the bourgeois version: "It is not speech in the form of discussion and argumentation but, if the expression be permitted, representative speech [that is] decisive. . . . Slipping neither into discourse, nor dictate, nor dialectic, it moves along in its architecture. Its grand diction is more than music; it is human dignity become visible in the rationality of speech as it assumes form. All this presupposes a hierarchy, for the spiritual resonance of grand rhetoric comes from faith in the representation to which the orator lays claim." *Römischer Katholizismus und politische Form* (München, 1925), 32f.

13. Arnold Hauser, *The Social History of Art* (New York, 1951) 1:209–10.

14. Schmitt, *Römischer Katholizismus und politische Form*, 26.

15. J. Huizinga, *The Waning of the Middle Ages* (Garden City, NY, 1952).

16. For a view that differs from Jacob Burckhardt's famous interpretation, see the exposition by O. Brunner, *Adeliges Landleben* (Salzburg, 1949), 108ff.

17. On the plane of intellectual history Gadamer develops the connection between this early tradition of educational humanism and those formulae of *sensus communis* and of "taste" (a category in moral philosophy) whose sociological implications reveal the significance of courtly humanism for the formation of the "public sphere." With regard to Gracian's educational ideal, he comments: "It is remarkable within the history of Western ideals of Bildung for being independent of class. It is the ideal of a society based on Bildung. . . . Taste is not only the ideal created by a new society, but we see this ideal of 'good taste' producing what was subsequently called 'good society.' Its criteria are no longer birth and rank but simply the shared nature of its judgments or, rather, its capacity to rise above the narrowness of interests and private predilections to the title of judgment. The concept of taste undoubtedly includes a mode of knowing. It is through good taste that we are capable of standing back from ourselves and our private preferences. Thus taste, in its essential nature, is not private, but a social phenomenon of the first order. It can even counter the private inclinations of the individual like a court of law, in the name of a universality that it represents." Gadamer, *Truth and Method*, 34.

18. R. Alewyn, *Das grosse Welttheater. Die Epoche der höfischen Feste* (Hamburg, 1959), 14.

19. "On all public occasions, victory celebrations, and peace treaties, illuminations and fireworks are merely the finale of a day that started at dawn with rounds of cannon fire and the blowing of the town pipers from every tower, a day on which wine filled the fountains of the city and entire oxen were publicly roasted on a spit, a day that was given over, until late into the night, to the dancing and games and merriment of a crowd that had flocked together from far and wide. In the baroque period this was no different than in ages past, and only the era of the bourgeoisie wrought a gradual change." Alewyn, *Das grosse Welttheater*, 43.

20. Ibid.

21. See P. Joachimsen, "Zur historischen Psychologie des deutschen Staatsgedankens," *Die Dioskuren. Jahrbuch für Geisteswissenschaften*, vol. 1 (1921).

22. *Weigands Deutsches Wörterbuch*, 475.

23. *Deutsches Wörterbuch der Brüder Grimm*, 2137f.

24. *The Oxford Dictionary*, 1388f.

25. *Dictionnaire de la Langue Française* (1875), vol. 3, art. "privé."

26. In his contribution, "Der soziale Gehalt von Goethes Roman Wilhelm Meisters Lehrjahre," *Erinnerungsgabe für Max Weber*, ed. Melchior Palyi (München und Leipzig, 1919), 2:279ff., Werner Wittich has drawn attention to this letter from a sociological perspective. [Translator's note: For the passages from Goethe cited in the text I have used Johann Wolfgang von Goethe, *Wilhelm Meister's Apprenticeship (Wilhelm Meisters Lehrjahre)*, trans. Thomas Carlyle (Boston, 1901), vol. 2, bk. 5, ch. 3, pp.13–15.]

27. W. Sombart, *Der Moderne Kapitalismus*, 3rd ed. (München und Leipzig, 1919), vol.2, bk.1, p.33.

28. M. Dobb, *Studies in the Development of Capitalism* (London, 1954), 160f.: "At any rate, it is clear that a mature development of merchant and financial capital is not of itself a guarantee that capitalist production will develop under its wing."

29. Ibid., 83ff.

30. H. Sée, *Modern Capitalism: Its Origin and Evolution* (New York, 1968).

31. In Germany especially Strassburg, Nuremberg, Augsburg, Frankfurt, Cologne, Hamburg, Lübeck, and Leipzig.

32. This occurred quite early on in Venice through the writers of news letters, *scrittori d'avisi*; in Rome they were called *gazettani*, in Paris *nouvellistes*, in London *writers of letters*, and in Germany *Zeitunger* or *Novellisten*. In the course of the sixteenth century they became suppliers of formal weekly reports, the newsletters, of which the so-called *Fuggerzeitungen* were typical in Germany. (The approximately 40,000 reports from the years between 1565 and 1605, however, originated not only in such news offices but also among employees and business friends of the House of Fugger.)

33. W. Sombart, *Der Moderne Kapitalismus*, 2:369.

34. For a long time the reports of the Strassburg printer and merchant Johann Carolus

were held to be the oldest newspaper; see, however, the investigation by Helmut Fischer, *Die ältesten Zeitungen und ihre Verleger* (Augsburg, 1936).

35. The traditional form of authority included as one of its elements the right to represent and interpret whatever was held to be "the ancient truth." Communications concerning actual events remained anchored in this knowledge of the tradition. Anything novel appeared under the aspect of a more or less marvelous event. "New facts," if only they were sufficiently unusual, were transformed in the court of the "ancient truth" into something "extraordinary"—into signs and miracles. Facts were transfigured into ciphers. Since they could only be representations of knowledge vouched for by tradition, the novel and the surprising assumed an enigmatic structure. In this respect no distinction was made between events in the world of nature and in human history; natural catastrophes and historical incidents were considered equally suitable for miraculous stories. The fifteenth-century broadsheets and sixteenth-century single-sheet prints called *New Journals* still bore witness to the strength with which an unbroken traditional knowledge was able to assimilate communications whose rising stream, to be sure, already pointed to a new form of public sphere. Such sheets indiscriminately spread the news of religious wars, campaigns against the Turks, and Papal decrees as well as news of rains of blood and fire, freaks, locust plagues, earthquakes, thunderstorms, and heavenly phenomena; of Papal Bulls, electoral agreements, and discoveries of new continents as well as of baptisms of Jews, punishments by the devil, divine judgments, and resurrections of the dead. Often the *New Journals*, like the broadsheets before them, were written in the form of songs or dialogues, i.e., were meant to be declaimed or sung, alone or with others. In this process, the novelty moved out of the historical sphere of "news" and, as sign and miracle, was reintegrated into that sphere of representation in which a ritualized and ceremonialized participation of the people in the public sphere permitted a merely passive acceptance incapable of independent interpretation. Characteristically, even songs were published as *New Journals*, e.g., the so-called historical folk songs that at once transported the political events of the day into the sphere of the heroic epic. See E. Everth, *Die Öffenlickeit in der Aussenpolitik* (Jena, 1931), 114. In general, cf. Karl Bücher, "Die Grundlagen des Zeitungswesens," *Gesammelte Aufsätze zur Zeitungskunde* (Tübingen, 1926), 9ff. The content of some broadsheets has survived until today in the form of nursery rhymes.

36. G. Schmoller, *Umrisse und Untersuchungen* (Leipzig, 1898), 37.

37. In the founding charter of 1553 the "Adventurers" called themselves a "mysterie and Company of the Marchants Adventurers for the Discovery of regions, dominions, islands, and places unknown." Cf. Sée, *Modern Capitalism*, 55f.

38. See E. F. Heckscher, *Merkantilismus* (Jena, 1932), 1:108ff. [English version: *Mercantilism* (New York: Macmillan, 1935).]

39. In the areas where Roman Law was adopted, the fiction of the *fiscus* became the legal expression for a state household independent from the prince's person; at the same time it furnished subjects with the advantage of being able to raise private legal claims against the state.

40. "Greater export meant greater opportunity for the employment of labour in home manufacture; and increased employment of labour represented a widened scope for investments of capital in industry." Dobb, *Studies in The Development of Capitalism*, 218.

41. The classic expression were Colbert's regulations for the industrial techniques of textile manufacturing. But even in Great Britain regulations regarding raw materials, the manner of their processing, and the quality of the finished products existed until

the second half of the eighteenth century. See Heckscher, *Merkantilismus*, 1:118ff. and 201ff.

42. J. Schumpeter, *Die Krise des Steuerstaates* (Leipzig, 1918), 16.

43. H. Arendt, *The Human Condition*, 46: "Civil society," *Zivilsozietät, societé civile*, in the eighteenth-century usage of the words, often still betray the older tradition of political theory, which does not yet differentiate "civil society" from the "state." On this, see M. Riedel, "Aristotelestradition am Ausgang des 18. Jahrhunderts," *Alteuropa und die moderne Gesellschaft. Festschrift für Otto Brunner*, ed. Alexander Bergengruen and Ludwig Deike (Göttingen, 1963), 276ff.; Riedel, "Hegels Bürgerliche Gesellschaft und das Problem ihres Ursprungs," *ARS Bel* 48 (1962): 539ff. Much earlier the new sphere of the social received its apt apolitical conceptualization in modern natural law. See my essay referred to above in note 1 to the Preface.

44. O. Brunner, *Adeliges Landleben*, 244ff.

45. See K. Kempters, *Die wirtschaftliche Berichterstattung in den sog. Fuggerzeitungen* (München, 1936).

46. Hermann Bode, *Anfänge der wirtschaftlichen Berichterstattung* (Heidelberg, 1908), 25: "The newspaper was a secondary news organ compared to the letter, which in the seventeenth century was quite generally considered the faster and more reliable news source." See also Heinrich Goitsch, *Entwicklung und Strukturwandlung des Wirtschaftsteils der deutschen Tageszeitung.* Ph. D. diss. (Frankfurt, 1939).

47. O. Groth, *Die Zeitung* (Berlin-Leipzig, 1928), 1:580.

48. Cited after Groth, *Die Zeitung*, 1:585.

49. E. Everth, *Die Öffenlickeit in der Aussenpolitik*, 202.

50. Stanley Morrison, *The English Newspaper* (Cambridge, 1932).

51. W. Sombart, *Der Moderne Kapitalismus*, 2:406ff.; also K. Bücher *Gesammelte Aufsätze zur Zeitungskunde*, 87. As in the first intelligence sheets so too in eighteenth-century advertisers the advertisements still referred to the commodities and deadlines outside the usual business routines, to special offers, books, medicine, travel companionships, domestic servants, etc. Commercial advertising in the proper sense was rare: the local market for goods and services was still a matter of face-to-face contact.

52. Groth, *Die Zeitung*, 1:598.

53. R. Stadelmann and W. Fischer, *Die Bildungswelt des deutschen Handwerks* (Berlin, 1955), 40. Compare also Br. Kuske, "Der Einfluss des Staates auf die geschichtliche Entwicklung der sozialen Gruppen in Deutschland," *Kölner Zeitschrift für Soziologie und Sozialpsychologie* 2 (1949): 193ff.

54. Percy Ernst Schramm, *Hamburg, Deutschland und die Welt* (München, 1943), 37, stresses this difference precisely in comparing the social development of Hamburg with that of the rest of the Reich: "The feature that constituted the authentic townsman (*Bürger*) is precisely what they (i.e., the 'bourgeois') lacked, namely, membership in a town community confirmed by an oath of citizenship. . . . These others, who were not 'citizens' but 'bourgeois,' served their masters, their church, and their employers or were 'free' as members of a liberal profession; but they had nothing more in common among themselves than that they belonged to the 'bourgeoisie'—which did not mean

a whole lot more than that this label distinguished them from nobility, peasantry, and the lower strata of the town. For the use of this expression did not even require that one had made the town one's home; the pastor in his country parish, the engineer in his mining district, and the petty official in the prince's palace also belonged to the 'bourgeoisie.' They too were counted among the educated bourgeoisie, in the wider sense, which was strictly distinguished from the people, *le peuple*."

55. See below, sect. 5, pp. 31ff.

56. Heckscher, *Merkantilismus*, 1:258; also on this W. Treue, "Das Verhältnis von Fürst, Staat, Unternehmer in der Zeit des Merkantilismus," *Vierteljahreshefte für Sozial- und Wirtschaftsgeschichte* 44 (1957): 26ff.

57. Sombart, *Der Moderne Kapitalismus*, 1:365.

58. Cited after Groth, *Die Zeitung*, 1:623.

59. Cited after W. Schöne, *Zeitungswesen und Statistik* (Jena, 1924), 77.

60. *Wörterbuch der hochdeutschen Mundart* (Wien, 1808), pt. 3, p.856.

II Social Structures of the Public Sphere

1. Kant used "reasoning" (*räsonieren*) and "use of rational argument" (*Räsonnement*) naively in the Englightenment sense. He still stood, as it were, on this side of the barricades; Hegel crossed them. Reasoning thought (*das räsonierende Denken*), as mere use of the understanding (*Verstandesbetrachtung*), did not penetrate to the concrete universality of the concept; Hegel, faithful to the Platonic tradition, found its most exemplary development in the Sophists. Concerning their use of rational argumentation he stated "that it makes duty, that which has to be done, not come from the notion of the thing as determined in and for itself; for it brings forward external reasons through which right and wrong, utility and harmfulness, are distinguished." *Hegel's Lectures on the History of Philosophy*, trans. E. S. Haldane and Frances H. Simson (New York: Humanities Press, 1974), 1:366–67. Hegel downgraded the use of rational arguments, especially their public use, in order to justify political authority (with which the reasoning public, of course, was involved in a polemical way) as an element on a higher level. "The conception of the monarch is therefore of all conceptions the hardest for ratiocination, i.e., for the method of reflection employed by the Understanding. This method refuses to move beyond isolated categories. . . ." *Hegel's Philosophy of Right*, trans. T. M. Knox (Oxford, 1964), 182.

2. Such status contracts, usually concluded on the occasion of a knight's rendering hommage to his Lord's successor, are naturally not to be compared with contracts in the sense of modern private law; see Brunner, *Land und Herrschaft*, 484ff.

3. See W. Naef, "Frühformen des modernen Staates im Spätmittelalter," *Historische Zeitschrift* 171 (1951): 225ff.

4. E. Auerbach finds the word, in the sense of a theater audience, documented as early as 1629; until then, the use of "public" as a noun referred exclusively to the state or to the public welfare. See *Das französische Publikum des 17. Jahrhunderts* (München, 1933), 5.

5. At that time it still referred to the state room, in the sense of the Italian Renaissance, and not to the cabinet, the circle, the reduite, etc.

6. A. Hauser, *The Social History of Art*, 2:505–6.

7. Unlike Paris, London was never directly subject to the king. The city, which administered itself by means of elected councillors and maintained public order through its own militia, was less accessible to the court's and Parliament's administration of justice than any other town in the country. Around the turn of the eighteenth century its approximately 12,000 taxpayers, almost all of whom were members of the 89 guilds and companies, elected 26 councillors and 200 council members—a broad, almost "democratic" base without equal during this period. Nevertheless, after the Glorious Revolution a shift occurred in the relationship between court and town that was comparable, say, to the development under the regency.

8. G. M. Trevelyan, *English Social History: A Survey of Six Centuries from Chaucer to Queen Victoria* (London, 1944), 338.

9. L. Stephen, *English Literature and Society in the 18th Century* (London, 1903; most recently, 1947), 47. See also H. Reinhold, "Zur Sozialgeschichte der Kaffees und des Kaffeehauses," *Kölner Zeitschrift für Soziologie und Sozialpsychologie* 10 (1958): 151ff. (review of a group of works).

10. H. Westerfrölke, *Englische Kaffeehäuser als Sammelpunkte der literarischen Welt* (Jena, 1924), 24f.

11. As early as 1674 there appeared a pamphlet, "The Women's Petition against Coffee, representing to Public Consideration of the Grand Inconveniences according to their Sex from the Excessive use of that Drying, Enfeebling Liquor."

12. Trevelyan, *English Social History*, 324, footnote.

13. See "The Clubs of London," *National Review* 4, no. 8 (April 1857): 301. "Every profession, trade, class, party, had its favourite coffee-house. The lawyers discussed law or literature, criticised the last new play, or retailed the freshest Westminster-Hall 'bite' at Nando's or the Grecian, both close on the purlieus of the Temple.... The cits met to discuss the rise and fall of stocks, and to settle the rate of insurances at Garraway's or Jonathan's; the parsons exchanged university gossip, or commented on Dr. Sacheverell's last sermon at Truby's or at Child's in St. Paul's Churchyard; the soldiers mustered to grumble over their grievances at Old or Young Man's, near Charing Cross; the St. James's and the Smyrna were the head-quarters of the Whig politicians, while the Tories frequented the Cocoa-Tree or Ozinda's, all in St. James's Street; Scotchmen had their house of call at Forrest's, Frenchmen at Giles's or old Slaughter's in St. Martin's Lane; the gamesters shook their elbows in White's, and the Chocolate-houses, round Covent Garden; the *virtuosi* honoured the neighbourhood of Gresham College; and the leading wits gathered at Will's, Button's, or Tom's, in Great Russell Street, where after the theatre, was playing at piquet and the best of conversation till midnight."

14. Hauser, *The Social History of Art*, 2:506–7.

15. "Nos écrits n'opèrent que sur une certaine classe de citoyens, nos discours sur toutes" (Our writings have an impact only on a certain class of citizens, our speech on all).

16. E. Manheim, *Die Träger der öffentlichen Meinung* (Wien, 1923), 83.

17. Language is considered "the organ of a transcendental communal spirit" and "the

medium of a public consensus"; see Manheim, *Die Träger der öffentlichen Meinung*, 88 and 92.

18. Lessing, Ernst, and Falk, *Gespräche für Freimaurer* (1778). On the entire complex, see E. Lennhoff and O. Posner, *Internationales Freimaurerlexikon* (Zürich-Leipzig-Wien, 1932); also B. Fay, *La Franc-maçonnerie et la révolution intellectuelle du XVIIIe siécle* (Paris, 1935).

19. Manheim, *Die Träger der öffentlichen Meinung*, 11.

20. H. Plessner, admittedly in a different context, defines the public sphere as the "sphere in which tact rules." Diplomatic relations arise between role bearers, relationships of tact between natural persons; see his *Grenzen der Gemeinschaft* (Bonn, 1924), esp. 100.

21. R. Williams, *Culture and Society 1870–1950* (London, 1958), xv, xvi: "An *art* had formerly been any human skill [art in the sense of artfulness, ability. J.H.]; but *Art*, now, signified a particular group of skills, the 'imaginative' or 'creative' arts. . . . From . . . a 'skill,' it had come . . . to be a kind of institution, a set body of activities of a certain kind." To this corresponded the change in the meaning of "culture": ". . . it had meant, primarily, the 'tending of natural growth' [culture in the sense of the cultivation of plants. J.H.], and then, by analogy, a process of human training [e.g., a 'man of culture.' J.H.]. But this latter use, which had usually been a culture *of* something, was changed . . . to *culture* as such, a thing in itself." Also R. Wittram, *Das Interesse an der Geschichte* (Göttingen, 1958), 40ff., who offers several observations on the history of the concept of culture.

22. See R. D. Altick, *The English Common Reader: A Social History of the Mass Reading Public* (Chicago, 1957), especially the first chapter, the results of which are summarized on p. 30. "If, speculating from such little information as we have, we tried to chart the growth of the reading public in the first three centuries after Caxton, the line would climb slowly for the first hundred years. During the Elizabethan period its rate of ascent would considerably quicken. The line would reach a peak during the Civil War and Commonwealth, when interest in reading was powerfully stimulated by public excitements. But during the Restoration it would drop, because of the lessening of popular turmoil, the damage the war had done to the educational system, and the aristocratic domination of current literature in the age of Dryden. A fresh ascent would begin in the early eighteenth century, the time of Addison and Steele, *and thereafter the line would climb steadily.*"

23. I. Watt, "The Reading Public," *The Rise of the Novel* (London, 1957).

24. A. Hauser, *The Social History of Art*, 2:548: "The patron's place is taken by the publisher; public subscription, which has very aptly been called collective patronage, is the bridge between the two. Patronage is the purely aristocratic form of the relationship between author and public; the system of public subscription loosens the bond, but still maintains certain features of the personal character of the relationship; the publication of books for a general public, completely unknown to the author, is the first form of the relationship to correspond to the structure of a middle-class society based on the anonymous circulation of goods."

25. Parfaict even reports a playwright who proudly measured the success of his piece by the fact that four ushers were killed at the premiere. See Auerbach, *Das französische Publikum*, 13.

26. Trevelyan, *English Social History*, 260.

27. Cited after Groth, *Die Zeitung*, 1:620.

28. Hauser, *The Social History of Art*, 2:574f. See also L. Balet, *Die Verbürgerlichung der deutschen Kunst, Literatur und Musik im 18. Jahrhundert* (Leyden, 1938), 38: "Regular public concerts had been performed in Frankfurt since 1723, in Hamburg since 1724, in Strassburg since 1730, and in Lübeck since 1733. In Leipzig the *Grosse Konzerte* were founded in 1743 by some enterprising merchants. Later on these were expanded into the famous *Gewandhauskonzerte* still in existence today."

29. They took place, under open skies in the courtyard of the Royal Palace, on the occasion of the Academy's annual meeting; in 1699 the first *salon* moved to the Louvre. After 1704, however, these exhibitions entirely ceased for a generation.

30. La Font, *Refléxions sur quelques causes de l'état présent de la peinture*, cited after A. Dresdner, *Die Entstehung der Kunstkritik im Zusammenhang des europäischen Kunstlebens* (München, 1915), 161.

31. Especially epoch-making were the critiques of the *salons* of 1765 and 1767; however, all of them were published only after the revolution.

32. In principle anyone was called upon and had the right to make a free judgment as long as he participated in public discussion, bought a book, acquired a seat in a concert or theater, or visited an art exhibition. But in the conflict of judgments he was not to shut his ears to convincing arguments; instead, he had to rid himself of his "prejudices." With the removal of the barrier that representative publicity had erected between laymen and initiates, special qualifications—whether inherited or acquired, social or intellectual—became in principle irrelevant. But since the true judgment was supposed to be discovered only through discussion, truth appeared as a process, a process of enlightenment. Some sectors of the public might be more advanced in this process than others. Hence, if the public acknowledged no one as privileged, it did recognize experts. They were permitted and supposed to educate the public, but only inasmuch as they convinced through arguments and could not themselves be corrected by better arguments.

33. As soon as the press assumed critical functions, the writing of news letters developed into literary journalism. The early journals, called *Monthly Conversations, Monthly Discussions*, etc., had this journalism's origin in convivial critical discussion written all over them. Their proliferation may be observed in exemplary fashion in Germany. The beginning was made with the *Gelehrte Anzeigen* which, developing out of the Thomasian journals, through articles and reviews submitted philosophy and the sciences to public discussion. After 1736 the well-known *Frankfurtische Gelehrte Zeitungen* too concerned themselves with the "fine arts and sciences." Following upon Gottsched's efforts, the journals devoted to literary criticism reached their point of fullest development with the *Bibliothek der schönen Wissenschaften und der freyen Künste*, founded in Berlin in 1757 by Nicolai. Beginning with Lessing's and Mylius's *Beiträge zur Historie und Aufnahme des Theaters* in 1750 a journalistic theater criticism arose. Journals for music criticism were also founded, although less frequently than those dealing with the stage, once Adam Hiller in Leipzig had created the model with his *Wöchentliche Nachrichten und Anmerkungen die Musik betreffend* in 1767.

34. Dresdner, *Die Entstehung der Kuntskritik*, 17.

35. L. Stephen, *English Literature and Society*, 76: "The periodical essay represents the most successful innovation of the day . . . because it represents the mode by which the most cultivated writer could be brought into effective relation with the genuine interests of the largest audience."

36. The *Tatler* expressly addressed the "worthy citizens who live more in a coffeehouse than in their shops." *Tatler*, 17 May 1709.

37. The *Tatler* immediately reached an edition of 4,000. How strong the interest was is demonstrated by the universal regret expressed when the *Tatler* suddenly ceased publication in 1711. For details, see Westerfrölke, *Englische Kaffeehäuser*, 64.

38. From then on the submitted letters were published weekly as the "Roaring of the Lion."

39. The British models remained valid for three generations of moral weeklies on the continent, too. In Germany *Der Vernünftler* was published in 1713 in Hamburg. Later on the *Hamburger Patriot* was much more successful, lasting from 1724 until 1726. In the course of the entire century the number of these journals grew to 187 in Germany; during the same period in Great Britain the number is reported to have been 227; in France, 31.

40. Trevelyan, *English Social History*, 246.

41. W. H. Riehl, *Die Familie*, 10th ed. (Stuttgart, 1889), 174 and 179.

42. *Ibid.*, 187: "In the old style house, the architectural symbol of the individual's relation to the family was the oriel. In the oriel, which essentially was part of the family room or living hall, the individual had indeed his corner for work, play, and sulking; he could withdraw there, but he could not close himself off since the oriel was open to the room."

43. *Ibid.*, 185.

44. See Hans Paul Bahrdt, *Öffentlichkeit und Privatheit als Grundformen städtischer Sozi-ierung* (Manuscript, 1956), 32: "The interiorization and cultivation of family life; a culture of life in the home that involves the conscious shaping of the most intimate material environment; private possession of the means of education, and their common use by the smallest social group; intellectual exchange as the normal and integrative form of life with one's kin; a religious life within the circle of the family, relatively independent of the Church; individual eroticism; and freedom of choice of marriage partner, which in its final stage of development grants legitimate veto power not even to the parents—all these are typical phenomena of the expansion of the private sphere and, at the same time, of bourgeois culture and mores." Meanwhile published in expanded form in H. P. Bahrdt, *Die moderne Grossstadt* (Hamburg, 1961), 36ff.

45. See especially Erich Fromm in Max Horkheimer, *Autorität und Familie* (Paris, 1936), 77ff.

46. See my gloss "Heiratsmarkt" in the journal *Merkur* (November 1956).

47. The sociological roots of the humanism of the Renaissance differed from those of the Anglo-French humanism of the Enlightenment and of the neohumanism of the German classic period with which we are dealing here.

48. See M. Horkheimer, *Autorität und Familie*, 64: "The reification of the human being in the economy as the mere function of an economic variable is, of course, also continued in the family to the extent that the father becomes the breadwinner, the woman a sex object or domestic slave, and the children one's heirs or living insurance from whom one expects a later return, with interest, for the pains one has taken. Nonetheless, since relations inside the family are not mediated by the market and

individuals do not oppose one another to be competitors, human beings have always also had the opportunity for acting not merely as determined by a function but as human beings. Whereas in bourgeois life the communal interest has an essentially negative character, concerning itself only with the defense against danger, it assumes a positive character in sexual love and, above all, in maternal care. Within this unity . . . the development and happiness of the other is desired. To this extent, the bourgeois family leads not only to bourgeois authority but to a premonition of a better human condition."

49. G. Steinhausen, *Geschichte des deutschen Briefes* (Berlin, 1889), esp. 245ff.

50. *Ibid.*, 288.

51. In Germany, in any event, Pietism had prepared the way for these forms of secularized sentimentality.

52. See Hauser, *The Social History of Art*, 2:565–66; on the role of the narrator, see W. Kayser, *Entstehung und Krise des modernen Romans* (Göttingen, 1954).

53. G. D. Levis, *Fiction and the Reading Public* (London, 1932), 130; also Altick, *The English Common Reader*, 30ff.

54. On the classical concept of *societas civilis*, see M. Riedel, "Aristotelestradition am Ausgang des 18. Jahrhunderts," *Festschrift für Otto Brunner*, 278ff.

55. C. Schmitt, *Die Diktatur* (München-Leipzig, 1928), 14ff.

56. Concerning the eighteenth-century's rigorous notion of law, see E. Lask, *Fichtes Geschichtsphilosophie* (1902); most recently, from a legal perspective, E. W. Böckenförde, *Gesetzgebende Gewalt* (Berlin, 1958), 20ff.

57. J. Locke, *Two Treatises of Civil Government* (London, 1953), 182.

58. *Ibid.*, 191.

59. Baron de Montesquieu, *The Spirit of the Laws*, trans. Thomas Nugent (New York and London, 1949), bk. 1, ch.1, p.1.

60. *Ibid.*, bk. 1, ch.17, p.169.

61. See below. sect. 12.

62. On the "natural system of the seventeenth-century *Geisteswissenschaften*," see the well-known investigation by Wilhelm Dilthey, *Gesammelte Schriften*, 5th ed. (Göttingen, 1957), vol. 2; F. Borkenau clarifies the social-philosophic meaning and sociological context of the rationalist concept of "nature" in *Der Übergang vom feudalen zum bürgerlichen Weltbild* (Paris, 1934).

III Political Functions of the Public Sphere

1. Most of the seats in parliament were "attached" to landed estates; see K. Kluxen, *Das Problem der politischen Opposition* (München, 1956), 71.

2. Dobb, *Studies in the Development of Capitalism*, 193.

3. As we know, the specific form of modern capitalism became dominant only in the measure that finance and merchant capital first subjugated the old mode of production in town (petty commodity production) and country (feudal agrarian production) and transformed it into a production on the basis of wage labor. Capitalist forms of commodity exchange (finance and merchant capitalism) seemed to be able to get *established firmly* only where labor power was also exchanged as a commodity, which is to say, where production took place on a capitalist basis.

4. For the first time the King appointed a cabinet composed entirely of Whigs (1695–1698). The period from the accession to the throne of William III to that of the Hannoverian dynasty was a transitional period in which the Crown selected its ministers partly in accord with its own free judgment, partly according to the mood in the House of Commons. See W. Hasbach, *Die parlamentarische Kabinettsregierung* (Stuttgart-Berlin, 1919), 45ff.

5. Cited after C. S. Emden, *The People and the Constitution* (Oxford, 1956), 33. Similar proclamations were issued in 1674 and 1675. Hans Speier's "The Historical Development of Public Opinion," *Social Order and the Risks of War* (New York, 1952), 323ff. establishes the connection between the coffee houses and the beginnings of "public opinion."

6. It was replaced only in 1792 by Fox's liberal Libel Act.

7. The "tax on knowledge," as it has been called, existed until 1855. See L. Hanson, *Government and the Press (1695–1763)* (London, 1936), 11f.

8. Under the pseudonym Cato, two Whigs wrote lead articles that, especially during the so-called Panama Scandal, indulged "in the loudest cries for justice." The newspaper stirred up attention when in August of 1721 it publicized and commented on the proceedings of the investigative commission instituted by Parliament: a first act of political journalism in the strict sense.

9. Kluxen, *Das Problem der politischen Opposition*, 187.

10. Most recently, see M. Schlenke, *England und das Friderizianische Preussen 1740–1763* (Freiburg-München, 1963).

11. W. Bauer, *Die Öffentliche Meinung in der Weltgeschichte* (Berlin-Leipzig, 1950), 227f.

12. In general, these parliamentary reports had, since 1641, constituted the first daily newspapers.

13. Hanson, *Government and the Press*, 81.

14. Which could be additionally based on the traditional rule of order concerning the "exclusion of strangers."

15. K. Löwenstein, "Zur Soziologie der parlamentarischen Repräsentation in England," *Erinnerungsgabe für Max Weber*, ed. M. Palyi, vol. 2, (München-Leipzig, 1923), 94.

16. Every male taxpaying householder had the right to vote there.

17. For details, see Löwenstein, "Zur Soziologie der parlamentarischen Repräsentation," 95ff.

18. Kluxen, *Das Problem der politischen Opposition*, 103ff.

19. In 1733 and 1734 on the issue of the Septennial Bill and in 1739 on the issue of the War with Spain.

20. See the balanced assessment in Emden, *The People and the Constitution*, 194–96.

21. *Parliamentary History* 29:974.

22. Emden, *The People and the Constitution*, 205.

23. Louis XIV already had to prohibit the importation of foreign newspapers in 1679, 1683, and 1686. At that time the *Gazettes de Hollande*, Europe's least censored papers, earned the reputation that they maintained throughout the eighteenth century. Through these publicist channels too the Huguenots forced into exile by the abolition of the Edict of Nantes exercised an influence upon their homeland. See E. Everth, *Die Öffentlichkeit in der Aussenpolitik*, 229.

24. See the sociological analysis of the *noblesse de robe* in Borkenau, *Der Übergang*, 172ff.

25. E. G. Barber, *The Bourgeoisie in 18th Century France* (New York, 1959).

26. In 1750 appeared Diderot's *Prospectus*, a prepublication announcement that was soon echoed throughout Europe; one year later came D'Alembert's *Discours Préliminaire*, a brilliant outline of the entire work. His essay was expressly addressed to the *public éclairé*. It spoke in the name of a *societé de gens de lettres*. And in 1758 Diderot underscored in a letter to Voltaire the obligations to the public. In the meantime 4,000 subscribers had come forward, two to three times as many as the most widely read newspaper at that time had.

27. At the emigré Bolingbroke's urging a private society had been established at the home of the Abbé Alary, located on a mezzanine (*entresol*) (hence the name *Club d'Entresol*). This was an informal academy of scholars, clerics, and officials who exchanged news, developed plans, and analyzed the constitution of the state as well as the needs of society. Walpole too frequented it, as did the Marquis d'Argenson and the old Abbé de St. Pierre. See R. Koselleck, *Kritik und Krise* (Freiburg-München, 1959), 53ff. (now in English translation, *Critique and Crisis*. Cambridge, MA, 1988).

28. On the eve of the revolution it was Necker who noticed the bourgeois public's degree of maturity: "The spirit of convivial life, the predilection for respect and praise, have instituted a court of appeal in France before which all who draw attention to themselves are obliged to appear: it is public opinion (*opinion publique*)." And he continued: "For the majority of foreigners it is difficult to obtain a correct idea of the authority that public opinion exercises in France. Only with difficulty do they understand that there is an invisible power that, without treasury, without bodyguard, without army, lays down laws—laws obeyed even in the palace of the King; and yet there exists nothing that would be more true." From then on people talked about "Monsieur Necker's public opinion," and it even made its way into the reports to the King. Cited after Bauer, *Die Öffentliche Meinung*, 234, and M. von Böhm, *Rokoko, Frankreich im 17. Jahrhundert* (Berlin, 1921), 318.

29. On this, in greater detail, see Bauer, *Die Öffentliche Meinung*, ch.13, pp.239ff.

30. The verse is found in R. Smend, "Zum Problem des Öffentlichen und der Öffentlichkeit," *Forschungen und Berichte aus dem öffentlichen Recht. Gedächtnisschrift für Walter Jellinek*, ed. O. Bachof et al. (München, 1955).

31. F. Hartung, ed., *Die Entwicklung der Menschen- und Bürgerrechte* (Göttingen, 1954),

33, 35. The first to grant similar guarantees was the state of Virginia in its Bill of Rights of June 12, 1776, art. 12: "The freedom of the press is one of the great bulwarks of liberty and can never be restricted except by despotic governments." *Ibid.*, 27.

32. *Ibid.*

33. Hartung, *Die Entwicklung der Menschenrechte*, 45.

34. "Le roi règne et ne gouverne pas" (The king rules and does not govern.)

35. See the contemporary report, "Schreiben von München, betreffend den bayerischen Landtag von 1831," *Historisch-Politische Zeitschrift* 1 (Hamburg, 1832): 94ff.

36. E. Heilborn, *Zwischen zwei Revolutionen* (Berlin, 1929), vol. I, *Der Geist der Schinkelzeit 1789 bis 1848*, 97ff.

37. So, for instance, the *Journal von und für Deutschland* (1790): 2:55; or the *Jenaische Allgemeine Literaturzeitung*, no. 30 (1797): 255. In general, on the emergence of a public sphere in the political realm of late eighteenth-century Germany, see F. Valjavec, *Die Entstehung der politischen Strömungen in Deutschland 1770–1815* (München, 1951).

38. See the abundant material in the Ph.D. dissertation by I. Jentsch, *Zur Geschichte des Zeitungswesens in Deutschland* (Leipzig, 1937). The same holds true of Switzerland; *ibid.*, 33, n. 10. See also the detailed study by M. Braubach, "Ein publizistischer Plan der Bonner Lesegesellschaft," *Aus Geschichte und Politik. Festschrift zum 70. Geburtstag von Ludwig Bergsträsser*, ed. A. J. M. Herrmann (Düsseldorf, 1954), 21ff.

39. In the famous reading room of the *Hamburger Harmonie* around the turn of the century 47 German, 8 French, and 2 British journals were available. Journals for light reading, following upon the old moral weeklies, did not really belong to the repertoire; women read these at home.

40. Groth, *Die Zeitung*, 1:706.

41. On this, see Balet, *Die Verbürgerlichung*, 132f.: "For one year Schubart lay upon a bed of straw in the cell of the old tower (of the Hohenasperg fortress). His night robe had finally disintegrated on his body. . . . After 2¼ years of incarceration he was allowed to exercise outside in the fresh air. In 1780 he was for the first time permitted to correspond with his wife and children, and in the same year the lock-down in his cell was converted to confinement within the fortress. After ten years of imprisonment he was finally released. . . ." Incidentally, Schiller received his first political impulses from this Schubart; the *Robbers* too belonged in its own way to the beginnings of political publicity.

42. On the history of this concept from the point of view of legal theory, see Hermann Coing, *Der Rechtsbegriff der menschlichen Person und die Theorie der Menschenrechte*, special issue of *Zeitschrift für ausländisches und internationales Privatrecht* (Berlin and Tübingen, 1950): 191ff. H. Conrad, "Individuum und Gemeinschaft in der Privatrechtsordnung," *Juristische Studiengesellschaft*, Heft 18 (Karlsruhe, 1956), traces the progressive establishment of "general legal capacity" in the private law codifications of the eighteenth and early nineteenth centuries.

43. Namely, the stock company, mortgage debentures, bonds, elements of legislation for trade and navigation, mining statutes, and the entire legislation regulating competition.

44. E.g., codes regulating dress, weddings, prostitution, usury, blasphemy, adulteration of food, etc.. See F. Wieacker, *Privatrechtsgeschichte der Neuzeit* (Göttingen, 1952), 108ff.

45. *Ibid.*, 110.

46. L. Brentano, *Geschichte der wirtschaftlichen Entwicklung Englands* (Jena, 1927–1928), vol. 3, pt.1, pp.223ff.

47. W. Ashley, *The Economic Organization of England: An Outline History* (London, 1923), 141: "Long before 1776, by far the greater part of English industry had become dependent on capitalistic enterprise in the two important respects that a commercial capitalist provided the actual workmen with their materials and found a market for their finished goods." See also H. O. Meredith, *Economic History of England* (London, 1949), 221ff.

48. R. Hilferding, *Das Finanzkapital* (Berlin, 1955), 447ff.

49. "The victory of Trafalgar, and the consequent establishing of the unrivalled maritime power of Britain, seemed to render it unnecessary to pay any special attention to the political aspects of national wealth or to raise any question as to what trades were good for the community. All ground for interference on the part of the State with the manner in which a man employed his capital seemed to be taken away, and when the nineteenth century opened public opinion was inclined to leave the capitalist perfectly free to employ his wealth in any enterprise he chose, and to regard the profit which he secured as the best proof that his enterprise was beneficial to the State." W. Cunningham, *The Progress of Capitalism in England* (Cambridge, 1916), 107.

50. The liberalization of foreign trade began with the treaty that William Pitt concluded with the French in 1786.

51. This did not hold for Germany to the same extent as it did for Great Britain and France. At the close of the eighteenth century the separation of state and society in Prussia was only virtual. On this, see the social-hisorical study by W. Conze, "Staat und Gesellschaft in der frührevolutionären Epoche Deutschlands," *Historische Zeitschrift* 186 (1958): 1–34; see also W. Conze, ed., *Staat und Gesellschaft im deutschen Vormärz* (Stuttgart, 1963).

52. "The man who is moved to exploit his consumers through unduly high prices will survive only long enough to discover that they have deserted him in favor of his numerous competitors. To pay a worker less than the going wage is to invite him to go where the going wage is paid. It requires only a moment's reflection to conclude that a businessman with power neither to overcharge his customers nor to underpay his labor (and for similar reasons his other suppliers) has very little power to do anybody ill. To minimize the exercise of private power, and especially the opportunity for its misuse, was to remove most of the justification for exercise of government authority over the economy." J. K. Galbraith, *American Capitalism* (Boston, 1952), 31.

53. Max Weber, *Economy and Society* (Berkeley, 1978) 2:1095: "Industrial capitalism must be able to count on the continuity, trustworthiness and objectivity of the legal order, and on the rational, predictable functioning of legal and administrative agencies."

54. I am speaking of the "bourgeois constitutional state" (*bürgerlicher Rechtsstaat*) in the substantive sense of a distinctive political constitution; the formalization of this concept in late nineteenth-century German jurisprudence was an adaptation, itself to be explained sociologically, that belonged in the context to which I alluded. For further

information, see U. Scheuner, "Die neuere Entwicklung des Rechtsstaats in Deutschland", *Festschrift des deutschen Juristentages* (Karsruhe, 1960) 2:229ff.

55. Whereby the administration of justice in turn called for a scientific jurisprudence; see Wieacker, *Privatrechtsgeschichte der Neuzeit*, 257: "The neutrality of a science of jurisprudence responsible to its own principles has a direct function for the attainment of justice. Inasmuch as it binds the judge to established and verifiable doctrines, approved by public opinion, it forces the competing, self-interested political, social, and economic interests in a free society (whose functional principle is the regulated struggle, i.e., competition) to remain outside the realm of jurisprudence. Hereby, however, it realizes precisely this society's rule of the game, namely, arbitration and formal correctness instead of the dominance of power.

56. L. Brentano, *Geschichte der wirtschaftlichen Entwicklung Englands*, 209ff.

57. C. Schmitt, *Verfassungslehre*, 148.

58. *Ibid.*, 139.

59. Böckenförde, *Gesetzgebende Gewalt*, 35.

60. See *Theory and Practice*, 113ff.

61. See Hartung, *Die Entwicklung der Menschen- und Bürgerrechte*.

62. If one conceives of the basic rights in the context of the link established, within the constitutional state, between a public sphere that is an element in the political realm and a private sphere that is free from political interference, their genealogy becomes transparent as well. Civil rights of man are clearly distinct from the privileges enjoyed by estates. No direct path led from the Magna Charta Libertatum of 1215 over the Petition of Rights of 1628, the Habeas Corpus Act of 1679, and the Bill of Rights of 1689 to Virginia's first Declaration of the Rights of Man of 1776. The liberties granted to estates were essentially treaties between corporations that established limits of legally permissible interference; they did not guarantee the autonomy of a private sphere through the political functions of a public composed of private people, that is, of the public sphere. To the extent that in the course of the evolution of civil society (and of the patriarchal conjugal family as one of its preeminent institutions), the Church too lost the character of representative publicity, and religion after the Reformation became a private affair (and the private practice of religion therewith at once function and symbol of the new intimate sphere)—to that extent the so-called freedom of religion may be considered the historically earliest "basic right." However, when G. Jellinek in *Die Erklärung der Menschen- und Bürgerrechte* (Leipzig, 1909) derived the origin of the basic rights purely from the struggle over religious freedom, he was hypostatizing a connection on the level of intellectual history that itself can only be clearly understood as part of a more comprehensive system of social interdependencies. In those conflicts between colonies and mother country from which the first formulation of the rights of man resulted, it was not religious freedom that played the decisive role but the issue of whether private people, assembled into a public, had the right to political input regarding such laws as invaded their private sphere: no taxation without representation (see the introductory remarks by Hartung, *Die Entwicklung der Menschenrechte*, 2ff., who summarizes the controversy surrounding Jellinek). The protection of the intimate sphere (with the freedom of the person and, especially, of religious worship) was the early expression of the protection of the private sphere in general that became necessary for the reproduction of capitalism in the phase of liberalized markets. See the collection of texts by R. Schnur, ed., *Zur Geschichte der Erklärung der Menschenrechte* (Darmstadt, 1964).

63. The demands concerning legal policy that arose in the public sphere of civil society found their first precise expression in the Napoleonic code for civil suits, the *Code de Procédure*. On the left bank of the Rhine it went into effect immediately; from 1815 on, however, its maxims came to prevail also in the rest of the German territories.

64. Cited after Groth, *Die Zeitung*, 1:721.

65. At this level of generality we disregard national differences between Great Britain, France, and Germany, which are simultaneously differences in the level of capitalist development. The conditions in the United States, of course, are incomparable in this regard, as their social structure and political order did not have to come to terms with the traditional European elements of the feudal manorial regime and of absolutist monarchy. Generally our analysis, oriented toward European conditions, neglects the specific features of American development; on that political system, see recently Ernst Fraenkel, *Das amerikanische Regierungssystem* (Köln-Opladen, 1960).

66. On the analysis of economic theories in terms of the sociology of knowledge, see G. Eisermann, Ökonomische Theorien und sozioökonomische Struktur," *Zeitschrift für die Gesamte Staatswissenschaft* 110 (1954): 457ff.

67. For a polemic against landed interests see, for instance, Richardo's treatise attacking high grain prices, *An Essay on the Influence of a Low Price of Corn on the Profits of Stock* (London, 1815). Ricardo reached the conclusion that indeed the interest of the land-owner was opposed to that of every other class in society.

68. On the history of the concept of ideology, see most recently the text collection by Kurt Lenk, ed., *Ideologiekritik und Wissenssoziologie*, 2nd ed. (Neuwied, 1964), including its references.

IV The Bourgeois Public Sphere: Idea and Ideology

1. In this context we skip the ramified history of the concept of *"sensus communis"*; see Gadamer, *Truth and Method*, 19ff. and 40f. Similarly there exists a connection, mediated by the concept of "common opinion," between the phrase "public opinion" and the classical tradition of the *consensus omnium*: see Klaus Oehler, "Der consensus omnium als Kriterium der Wahrheit in der antiken Philosophie und der Patristik," *Antike und Abendland* 10 (1961); 103ff. Such interconnections, although certainly relevant in terms of *intellectual* history, skip over specific ruptures in the *social* evolution, ruptures which are at the same time thresholds in the formation of polemical concepts—as, for instance, in the case of the transition from "opinion" to "public opinion."

2. R. Mischke, *Die Entstehung der öffentlichen Meinung im 18. Jahrhundert* (Ph.D. diss., Hamburg, 1958) neglects the English development. I am indebted to the outstanding investigation by R. Koselleck, *Critique and Crisis*, for many references.

3. The nuances emerge clearly in Shakespeare's usage. For example, the great repute, even fame (*Julius Caesar*, act 1, sc. 2, l. 323: "all tending to the great opinion that Rome holds of his name"); via the good reputation of a gentleman (*Henry IV*, 5.4.48: "Thou hast redeem'd thy lost opinion"); and the already mercenary good will one enjoys from others (*Julius Caesar*, 2.1.145: "Purchase us a good opinion"); to the dubious and precarious brilliance of merely superficial valor (*Othello*, 1.3.225: "Opinion, a sovereign mistress of effects"); the two basic meanings flow into one another. Shakespeare characterized them in that contrast between the "craft of great opinion" and the "great truth of mere simplicity" (*Henry VIII*, 4.4.105).

4. J. Bartlett, *A Complete Concordance of Shakespeare* (London, 1956), see entries under "opinion" and "spirit."

5. Indeed, "critique" was also taken over into the English language around 1600; the humanists applied the word initially in the philological-historical context of their studies in source criticism; after Shaftesbury to engage in "criticks" meant to know how to judge in accord with the rules of good taste. Here, however, opinion was not opposed to criticism. Incidentally, in Germany at that time too *Kritikus* was the judge of art and of language; see A. Bäumler, *Kants Kritik der Urteilskraft* (Halle, 1923), 46ff.

6. Hobbes, *The Elements of Law, Natural and Political*, ed. Ferdinand Tönnies (Cambridge, 1928) 1, 6: 8: "Men, when they say things upon their conscience, are not therefore presumed certainly to know the truth of what they say. Conscience therefore I define to be opinion of evidence."

7. Ibid., 2. 6: 12.

8. See C. Schmitt, *Der Leviathan* (Hamburg, 1933), 94: "At the moment when the distinction between inward and outward is acknowledged, the superiority of the inward over the outward and hence that of the private over the public is, at its core, already decided." In another context I hope to show how, along the path from Luther and Calvin to Hobbes, the Reformation's distinction between the *regnum spirituale* and the *regnum politicum* shifted in meaning and ultimately came to refer to the *inner-worldly* opposition of a privatized society to political authority, of society to government.

9. Locke, *An Essay Concerning Human Understanding*, bk. 2, ch. 28, sec. 11; see Koselleck, *Kritik und Krise*, 41. (English translation, *Critique and Crisis*. Cambridge, MA, 1988.)

10. Locke, *An Essay Concerning Human Understanding*, bk. 2, ch. 28, sect. 12.

11. See Koselleck, *Kritik und Krise*, 89ff.

12. In 1695 Bayle's *Dictionnaire historique et critique* was published.

13. D'Alembert, *Discours Préliminaire, Einleitung zur Enzyklopädie von 1751*, ed. Köhler (Hamburg, 1955), 148.

14. *Ibid.*, 149.

15. J. J. Rousseau, "Discourse on the Sciences and Arts (First Discourse)," *The First and Second Discourses*, trans. R. D. and J. R. Masters (New York, 1964), 50.

16. *Spectator*, no. 204 (1712).

17. *Craftsman*, 27 July 1734.

18. Recently, D. Hilger, *Edmund Burke und seine Kritik der französischen Revolution* (Stuttgart, 1960), 122ff.; I am leaving aside the interesting doctrines regarding the public sphere in the political realm with which the Scottish moral philosophers at the same period supplemented their evolutionary theory of civil society. See the references in *Theory and Practice*, 76ff.

19. *Burke's Politics*, ed. Hoffmann and Levack (New York, 1949), 106.

20. *Ibid.*, 119.

21. On this see Jürgen Kuczynski, "Zur Theorie der Physiokraten," *Grundpositionen der französischen Aufklärung* (Berlin, 1955), 27ff.

22. R. Mischke, *Die Entstehung,* 170ff.; already Carl Schmitt, *Die Diktatur,* 109ff., directed attention to this connection.

23. L. S. Mercier, *Notions claires sur les gouvernements* (Amsterdam, 1797), vi ff.

24. *Ibid.,* vii.

25. Cited after L. Say, *Turgot* (1891), 108; Koselleck directs attention to this characteristic passage, *Kritik und Krise,* 123. (English translation, *Critique and Crisis.* Cambridge, MA, 1988.)

26. "The commitments that bind us to the body politic are obligatory only because they are mutual, and their nature is such that in fulfilling them one cannot work for someone else without also working for oneself." J. J. Rousseau. *On the Social Contract,* trans. and ed. Donald A. Cress (Indianapolis, 1983) bk. 2, ch. 4, p. 33.

27. See Weigand's footnote to bk. 3, p. 15, in Rousseau, *Contrat Social,* trans. Weigand (München, 1959), 164.

28. Rousseau, *On the Social Contract,* bk. 2, ch. 12, p. 48.

29. On what follows, see *On the Social Contract,* bk. 4, chs. 1 and 2, pp. 79–83.

30. *Ibid.,* bk. 3, ch. 1, pp. 49–52.

31. *Ibid.,* bk. 3, ch. 4, p. 56.

32. *Ibid.*

33. *Ibid.,* bk. 4, ch. 7, p. 95.

34. *Ibid.*

35. *Ibid.,* bk. 2, ch. 7, p. 40.

36. W. Hennis in "Der Begriff der öffentlichen Meinung bei Rousseau," *Archiv für Rechts- und Sozialphilosophie* 43 (1957): 111ff. does not realize that Rousseau identifies *opinion publique* with nonpublic opinion. Precisely the mistrust, in terms of his critique of culture, toward the accomplishments of "public opinion" in the strict sense of his physiocrat contemporaries forced the democratic idea of the *Social Contract* to incorporate certain elements of a dictatorship. See most recently I. Fetscher, *Rousseaus politische Philosophie* (Neuwied, 1960) and references to further literature there.

37. *On the Social Contract,* bk. 3, ch. 20, p. 74: "Sovereignty cannot be represented. . . . It consists essentially in the general will, and the will does not allow of being represented. It is either itself or it is something else. . . . Any law that the populace has not ratified in person is null."

38. Characteristic of this usage is the broadsheet of the Abbé Sieyès, published in 1788, entitled, "What is the Third Estate?" See my essay "Natural Law and Revolution," *Theory and Practice,* 82–120.

39. Cited after R. Redslob, *Staatstheorien der französischen Nationalversammlung* (Leipzig, 1912), p. 65, n. 1.

40. These proposals, however, were not able to exercise any influence on the authors of the French constitution. The original was written in French; it was first published in Geneva in 1816. Cited after "An Essay on Political Tactics," *Jeremy Bentham's Works,* ed. Bowring (Edinburgh, 1843) 2: 299–373. See esp. ch. 2, "Of Publicity."

41. *Ibid.*, 310.

42. *Ibid.*, 311.

43. *Ibid.*

44. *Ibid.*, 312.

45. *Ibid.*, 316. At another place was the expression of a safeguard in "the protection of the people"; the French edition read instead: "Il n'y a de sauve garde que dans la protection de l'opinion publique." "Tactic des Assemblées Legislatives," ed. Dumont, 2nd ed., (Paris 1822), 28.

46. M. Guizot, *History of the Origin of Representative Government in Europe* trans. A. R. Scoble (London, 1852), 264. C. Schmitt also remarked on the significance of this passage in *Die geistesgeschichtliche Lage des Parlamentarismus* (München, Leipzig, 1923), 22, footnote. (English translation, *The Crisis of Parliamentary Democracy.* Cambridge, MA, 1985.)

47. Forster wrote about the origin of public opinion in France in his *Parisische Umrisse*: "Not without reason do I place its first transformations still in the final years of the monarchy. For the greatness of the capital city, the amount of information, taste, wit, and imagination concentrated in it; the ever more gnawing needs in this place for an education providing Epicurean titilation; the independence from prejudices in the higher and more or less also in the middle strata; the power of the parliaments ever opposing the Court; the ideas about government, constitution, and republicanism brought into currency by America's attainment of independence and by France's role in this achievement. . . . All of this paved the way for freedom of thought and freedom of will in such way that already for a considerable time before the Revolution, a firm public opinion held almost limitless sway throughout Paris and, reaching out from this center, nearly over the whole of France." Cited after Bauer, *Die öffentliche Meinung,* 238.

48. *Georg Forsters sämtliche Schriften*, ed. Gervinus (Leipzig, 1843), vol. 5, ch. 2 ("Über öffentliche Meinung"), p. 249.

49. Posselt's *Europäische Annalen*, the first volume of which was published in 1795 with an article entitled, "Frankreichs Diplomatie oder Geschichte der öffentlichen Meinung in Frankreich," still betrayed the uncertainty in terminological usage.

50. C. M. Wieland, *Sämtliche Werke* (Leipzig, 1857), 32:191ff.

51. *Ibid.*, 200.

52. *Ibid.*, 218.

53. *Ibid.*, 192.

54. *Ibid.*, 198.

55. *Ibid.*, 193: Public opinion is the opinion that, "without being noticed has taken

over most heads, and even in cases when it does not yet dare to be uttered, yet like a beehive about to swarm, announces itself by a rumbling that grows ever stronger;" similarly, *ibid.*, 212f. R. Flad demonstrated the connection of the notion of public opinion with the teaching of the spirit of a nation developed especially in the anti-Napoleonic journalism. See *Der Begriff der öffentlichen Meinung bei Stein, Arndt, Humboldt* (Berlin-Leipzig, 1929).

56. "As long as morality is an exclusive office of the priesthood and politics is the presumptuous secret of courts and cabinet, both the former and the latter must needs be misused as tools of deception and suppression. The people become victims of outrageous games of words, and the powers-that-be do as they please and get away with it unpunished, since it depends only on their arbitrary will to stamp what is just unjust, and what is unjust just. What they fear most, the promulgation of the truth, they make a crime, and they punish it as such. Not so when reason has again recouped its inveterate rights to bring to light all truths the knowledge of which is the first desire of everyone, and to obtain for these truths the greatest possible popularity with the help of all the Muses' arts, and in every imaginable shape and guise. A multitude of corrected notions and facts then gains currency, a multitude of prejudices fall from the eyes like scales. . . ." *Ibid.*, 208f.

57. See I. Kant, "Perpetual Peace", *On History* ed. and trans. Lewis White Beck (Indianapolis, 1957), 85–135; see p. 128.

58. *Ibid.*, 115ff.

59. Kant, "What is Enlightenment," *ibid.*, 3–10; see p. 3.

60. *Ibid.*, 4.

61. I. Kant, "On the Common Saying: 'This May be True in Theory, but it Does not Apply in Practice,'" *Kant's Political Writings*, ed. Hans Reiss, trans. H. B. Nisbet (Cambridge, England, 1970), 61–92; see 84, 85. Henceforth: "Common Saying."

62. I. Kant, "What is Orientation in Thinking?", *Critique of Practical Reason and Other Writings in Moral Philosophy*, ed. Lewis White Beck (Chicago, 1949), 293–305; see 303.

63. I. Kant, *The Conflict of the Faculties*, trans. Mary J. Gregor (New York, 1979), 57.

64. *Ibid.*, 55.

65. *Ibid.*, 29.

66. "What is Enlightenment?", 5.

67. *Ibid.*

68. *Ibid.*, 6.

69. *Immanuel Kant's Critique of Pure Reason*, trans. Norman Kemp Smith (London, 1963), 658, note. Henceforth: *Pure Reason*.

70. I. Kant, *Critique of Practical Reason*, trans. L. W. Beck (New York, 1956), 250–51.

71. A distinction which certainly did not coincide with that between public and private law. In the Kantian sense, civil law as a whole was public; see I. Kant, *The Metaphysical*

Elements of Justice: Part I of the Metaphysics of Morals, trans. J. Ladd (Indianapolis-New York, 1965).

72. "Common Saying," 129ff.

73. *Ibid.*, 85: "*Whatever a people cannot impose upon itself cannot be imposed upon it by the legislator either.*"

74. *Ibid*, 85–86.

75. In the section: "Opining, Knowing, and Believing," *Pure Reason*, 645.

76. Kant called this "The harmony which the Transcendental Concept of Public Right Establishes Between Morality and Politics," in "Perpetual Peace", 129ff.

77. See R. Koselleck, *Kritik und Krise*, esp. 81ff. (English translation, *Critique and Crisis.* Cambridge, MA, 1988.)

78. Kant, *The Conflict of the Faculties*, 165.

79. I. Kant, "Idea for a Universal History With a Cosmopolitan Purpose," *Kant's Political Writings*, 41–53; see 44–45.

80. "Perpetual Peace," 112.

81. "Common Saying," 78.

82. "The domestic servant, the shop assistant, the labourer, or even the barber, are merely labourers (*operarii*), not *artists* (*artifices*, in the wider sense) or members of the state, and are thus unqualified to be citizens"; they can only be co-beneficiaries who enjoy the protection of the laws, but not the right to legislate itself—"although the man to whom I give my firewood to chop and the tailor to whom I give material to make into clothes both appear to have a similar relationship towards me, the former differs from the latter in the same way as the barber from the wig-maker (to whom I may in fact have given the requisite hair) or the labourer from the artist or tradesman, who does a piece of work which belongs to him until he is paid for it. For the latter, in pursuing his trade, exchanges his property with someone else (*opus*), while the former allows someone else to make use of him (*operam*)." *Ibid.*, 78, footnote.

83. In another context, Kant made an anecdotal reference to the slogan, "laisser faire," just put in currency at that time: "A minister of the French government summoned a few of the most eminent merchants and asked them for suggestions on how to stimulate trade. . . . After one had suggested this and another that, an old merchant who had kept quiet so far said: 'Build good roads, mint sound money, give us laws for exchanging money readily, etc.; but as for the rest, leave us alone.!'" *The Conflict of the Faculties*, 27–29, note.

84. "Common Saying," 76–77.

85. *Pure Reason*, 409ff.

86. "Perpetual Peace," 134–35.

87. *Ibid.*, 126–27.

88. "Common Saying," 88.

89. *Ibid.*, 89.

90. "Idea for a Universal History from a Cosmopolitan Point of View," *On History*, 15.

91. *The Conflict of the Faculties*, 163, 165.

92. *Pure Reason*, 485.

93. *Ibid.*, 486–87.

94. "Idea for a Universal History," 23.

95. *Ibid.*

96. *The Conflict of the Faculties*, 161.

97. *Ibid.*

98. G. W. F. Hegel, *Hegel's Philosophy of Right*, trans. T. M. Knox (Oxford, 1952), sect. 301, p. 195. Hegel commented upon this paragraph: "The phrase, 'the Many' . . . denotes empirical universality more strictly than 'All,'" which is in current use. If it is said to be obvious that this 'all' prima facie excludes at least children, women, etc., then it is surely still more obvious that the quite definite word 'all' should not be used when something quite indefinite is meant."

99. *Hegel's Philosophy of Right*, sect. 316, p. 204.

100. *Ibid.*, addition to sects. 116 and 117, p. 294.

101. *Ibid.*, addition to sect. 315, p. 294.

102. *Ibid.*, sect. 319, p. 207.

103. *Ibid.*, sect. 200, p. 130.

104. *Ibid*, sects. 243 and 245, pp. 149–150.

105. *Ibid.*, sect. 258, p. 156.

106. *Ibid.*, sect. 303, p. 198.

107. *Ibid.*, sect. 302, p. 197.

108. *Ibid.*, sect. 236, pp. 147–48.

109. *Ibid.*, sect. 317, p. 204.

110. *Ibid.*, sect. 314, p. 205.

111. *Ibid.*, sect. 315, pp. 203–4.

112. *Ibid.*, sect. 318, p. 205.

113. *Ibid.*, sect. 320, p. 208.

114. *Ibid.*, sect. 317, p. 205. See also G. W. F. Hegel, *Phenomenology of Mind*, trans. J. B. Baillie (London, New York, 1966), 428–29.

115. *Hegel's Philosophy of Right*, sec. 337, p. 215.

116. See M. Riedel, "Hegels 'bürgerliche Gesellschaft' und das Problem ihres Ursprungs," *Studien zu Hegels Rechtsphilosophie* (Frankfurt, 1969), 135–66.

117. K. Marx, "Critique of Hegel's Doctrine of State," *Early Writings*, ed. Quentin Hoare, trans. R. Livingstone and G. Benton (New York, 1975), 57–198; see 147.

118. *Ibid.*, 90.

119. K. Marx, "On the Jewish Question," *Early Writings* trans. and ed. T. B. Bottomore, *The Marx-Engels Reader* (New York, 1963), 28–29.

120. *Ibid.*, 25.

121. *Ibid.*, 15.

122. Marx, "Critique of Hegel's Doctrine," 143.

123. *Ibid.*, 188.

124. K. Marx, *The Eighteenth Brumaire of Louis Bonaparte* (New York, 1963), 66.

125. "Critique of Hegel's Doctrine," 191.

126. K. Marx and Fr. Engels, *Manifesto of the Communist Party* (New York, 1983), 52 (end of sect. 2).

127. *The Poverty of Philosophy* (New York, 1963), 175.

128. F. Engels, *Herr Eugen Dühring's Revolution in Science (Anti-Dühring)* (New York, 1966), 283.

129. K. Marx, *Capital* (New York, 1967), 3:820.

130. F. Engels, "Principles of Communism," *Birth of the Communist Manifesto*, ed. D. J. Struik (New York, 1971), 169–89; see 185.

131. K. Marx, "On a Proposed Divorce Law," *Writings of the Young Marx on Philosophy and Society*, ed. L. D. Easton and K. H. Guddat (Garden City, NY: 1967), 136–42; see 139.

132. H. Kesting, *Geschichtsphilosophie und Weltbürgerkrieg* (Heidelberg, 1959), 24ff. and 219ff.

133. In connection with issues of the emancipation of women, one even reads: "In all things the presumption ought to be on the side of equality. A reason must be given why anything should be permitted to one person and interdicted to another. But when that which is interdicted includes nearly everything which those to whom it is permitted most prize, and to be deprived of which they feel to be most insulting; when not only political liberty but personal freedom of action is the prerogative of a caste; when even in the exercise of industry, almost all employments which task the higher faculties in an important field, which lead to distinction, riches, or even pecuniary independence, are fenced round as the exclusive domain of the predominant section, scarcely any doors being left open to the dependent class, except such as all who can enter elsewhere disdainfully pass by; the miserable expediencies which are advanced as excuses for so

grossly partial a dispensation, would not be sufficient, even if they were real, to render it other than a flagrant injustice." Harriet Taylor Mill, "Enfranchisement of Women," in J. S. Mill, *Collected Works*, ed. J. M. Robson, vol. 21 (London, 1984), 393–415; see 398.

134. A. de Tocqueville, "Question Financière," *Ooeuvres Complètes*, ed. J. P. Mayer vol. 3, pt. 2 (Paris, 1985), 734–37; see 735.

135. J. S. Mill, "On Liberty," *Collected Works*, 18:213–310; see 268–69.

136. A. de Tocqueville, *Democracy in America*, trans. G. Lawrence (New York, 1969), 399–400.

137. *Ibid.*, 233.

138. Mill, "On Liberty," 269.

139. *Ibid.*, 254.

140. J. S. Mill, "Bentham," *Collected Works*, 10:75–115; see 107–8. Also in J. S. Mill, *Dissertations and Discussions*, vol. 1 (Boston, 1868), 355–417; see 404, 406.

141. Most recently, E. Fraenkel, "Die repräsentative und die plebiszitäre Komponente im demokratischen Verfassungsstaat," *Recht und Staat*, nos. 219–20 (Tübingen, 1958).

142. Mill, "On Liberty," 251.

143. *Ibid.*, 247.

144. A. de Tocqueville, *Democracy in America*, 644; also 645, 656.

145. *Ibid.*, 672.

146. J. S. Mill, "Appendix," *Dissertations and Discussions*, 1:648–53 in *Collected Works*, 19:650.

147. See the observation of the conservative constitutional specialist Friedrich Julius Stahl, *Die gegenwärtigen Parteien in Staat und Kirche* (Berlin, 1863), 73: "The liberal party affirms the idea of equality against the nobility, against all estates as such, because on the basis of the revolution it cannot admit to an organic structure of society. However, when it comes to giving the propertyless class the same rights as the propertied, then it abandons the idea and makes political-legal distinctions in favor of those with means. It wants a census for representation and payment of security for the press; it admits only the fashionable to its salons; it does not extend honor and courtesies to the poor as it does to the rich. This stopping halfway in the implementation of the principles of the revolution is what characterizes the party stance of the liberals." Of course, this was aimed specifically at conditions in Germany. To be sure, in Germany on the eve of the revolution too a more courageous liberal theory provided the puny constitutional actuality with the vision of the classical idea of publicity: "Complete publicity therefore consists," according to Welcker's programmatic definition, "in treating all affairs of state as matters of common concern to the entire state and all its citizens, and accordingly in making them accessible to public opinion by arranging that they may be seen and heard to the greatest possible extent, through public presentation and the freedom of all publicistic organs." *Staatslexikon oder Enzyklopädie der Staatswissenschaften*, 15 vols. (1834–1848; 15th ed., 1855), art. "Öffentlichkeit und öffentliche Meinung." And Niebuhr insisted rigorously on the convergence

of public opinion and reason: "Public opinion is what emerges in minds on its own and in congruence despite diversities of individuality and varieties of condition, undisturbed by the personal influences that can lead those in power astray; and if in fact it is a judgment, it can be deemed a representation of universal reason and truth, a voice of God." Bluntschli, however, quoted this statement only to expound, in contrast to it, a liberalism adapted to national particularities: "It is a radical exaggeration if public opinion is declared to be infallible and even our rightful ruler. The men who possess a deeper insight into political life and its needs too are never numerous in any age; and it is far from certain whether they are successful in diffusing their opinion so that it becomes public opinion. The knowing and wise minority by no means always agrees with the majority of the middle classes. The general judgment even of the educated classes will almost always be superficial. It is not possible for them to know all the circumstances and to have uncovered all the reasons upon which decision in important matters depends. Public opinion can be confused by the momentary passions of the crowd; it can even be artificially misled. A single remarkable individual may see things correctly, while all the world about him has wrong views." *Bluntschlis Staatswörterbuch in drei Bänden*, ed. Löhning (Zürich, 1871), 2:745f., art. "Öffentliche Meinung." Inasmuch as Bluntschli definitely viewed public opinion as the correlate of one among several classes ("it is above all the opinion of the great middle class"), he broke with the principle of publicity, i.e., with the principle of the universal accessibility of that domain in which is to be rationally decided what is practically necessary in the general interest. Inasmuch as he located publicity sociologically within the framework of a class society taken as a natural given, he treated it as an ideology without criticizing it as such. In his opinion, the class of manual laborers should fittingly refrain from participation in political life: "Indeed, upon the opposition between mental and manual labor, between intellectual and physical activity, rests the distinction which is of great importance also for the organization of the state and its political life. . . . For the liberal professions of the third estate higher education is a necessary requirement, and hence only these persons usually also have the capacity and the leisure to work intellectually for the state. In contrast, the large classes preoccupied with the material cultivation of the soil, with crafts, small trade, and factory work, are throughout lacking in the education and leisure needed to dedicate themselves to the affairs of the state," *Ibid.*, 3:879. But even the bourgeoisie was not to exercise the political functions of a truncated public sphere closed to the people at large. Instead, public opinion was to be confined to the criticism and control of an authority which from the outset was granted as the preserve of the monarch, supported by the landowning nobility: "The aristocracy is inclined by nature to share power with the monarchy; the third estate is inherently inclined to criticize and to control," *Ibid.*, 881. On the basis of a class compromise between the bourgeoisie and the feudal powers which were still politically dominant in Germany, it was not only access to the public realm that became a privilege; this realm too no longer viewed itself as a sphere in which the state, through the critical debate of a public comprised of private people, was penetrated by society and in which authority was dissolved to the extent to which its substance was domination: "It is not true that public opinion rules, since it neither can rule, nor does it want to rule. It leaves government to the organs entrusted with it. Not a creative power, it is first and foremost a controlling force," *Ibid.*, 2:747. T. Schieder analyzed the connection of this deformed liberal ideology to the specific relationship between state and society in nineteenth-century, Prussian Germany in "Das Verhältnis von Staat und gesellschaftlicher Verfassung und die Kritik des bürgerlichen Liberalismus," *Historische Zeitschrift* 177 (1954): 49–74.

148. Tocqueville, *Democracy in America*, 667.

149. Tocqueville, *Oeuvres Complètes* (publiées par Mme. de Tocqueville). (Paris, 1866), vol. 9, *Etudes Economiques, Politiques et Litéraires*, 537–38.

150. K. Marx, *The Eighteenth Brumaire of Louis Bonaparte*, 121f.

151. K. Marx, *The Civil War in France* (New York, 1940), 54.

152. *Ibid.*

153. M. L. Goldschmidt, "Publicity, Privacy, and Secrecy," *Western Political Quarterly* 7 (1954): 401.

V The Social-Structural Transformation of the Public Sphere

1. W. Hallgarten, *Vorkriegsimperialismus* (Paris, 1935).

2. G. Lukacs, "On Some Characteristics of Germany's Historical Development," *The Destruction of Reason*, trans. P. Palmer (London: Merlin Press, 1980), ch. 1; further, see: H. Plessner, *Die verspätete Nation* (Stuttgart, 1959) and my review in *Frankfurter Hefte*, Nov. 1959; most recently, R. Dahrendorf, "Demokratie und Sozialstruktur in Deutschland," *Europäisches Archiv für Soziologie* 1 (1960): 86ff.

3. Dobb, *Studies in the Development of Capitalism*, 258 (quoting J. R. Hicks).

4. *Ibid.*, 257: "An age of technical change which rapidly augmented the productivity of labour also witnessed an abnormally rapid natural increase in the ranks of the proletariat, together with a series of events which simultaneously widened the field of investment and the market for consumption goods to an unprecedented degree. We have seen how straitly in previous centuries the growth of capitalist industry was cramped by the narrowness of the market, and its expansion thwarted by the low productivity which the methods of production of the period imposed; these obstacles being reinforced from time to time by scarcity of labour. At the industrial revolution these barriers were simultaneously swept away; and, instead, capital accumulation and investment were faced, from each point of the economic compass, with ever-widening horizons to lure them on."

5. T. H. Bunzel, "Liberal Theory and the Problem of Power," *Western Political Quarterly*, 13 (1960): 374–88.

6. The term, which comes from Lasalle, is always associated with Wilhelm von Humboldt's famous treatise, "Ideen zu einem Versuch, die Grenzen der Wirksamkeit des Staates zu bestimmen," *Werke*, ed. Flitner (Darmstadt, 1960), 1:56ff.

7. F. Neumann, "Der Funktionswandel des Gesetzes im Recht der bürgerlichen Gesellschaft," *Zeitschrift für Sozialforschung*, 6:542ff., and Neumann, "Okonomie und Politik," *Zeitschrift für Politik* 2 (1955): 1ff.

8. H. Achinger, *Sozialpolitik als Gesellschaftspolitik* (Hamburg, 1958), 155.

9. J. Strachey, *Contemporary Capitalism* (New York, 1956), 185.

10. J. K. Galbraith, *American Capitalism: The Concept of Countervailing Power* (Boston, 1952). For a critique, see the outstanding essay by A. Schweizer, "A Critique of Countervailing Power," *Social Research* 21 (1954): 253ff.

11. Well documented for the United States by Berle and Means, *The Modern Corporation*

and Private Property (New York, 1932); *The Structure of the American Economy*, vol. 1 (National Resources Planning Board, U.S. Government Printing Office, 1939); idem., *The Concentration of Productive Facilities* (1947); idem., *A Survey of Contemporary Economics* (1948). For Germany: H. König. "Konzentration und Wachstum, eine empirische Untersuchung der westdeutschen Aktiengesellschaften," *Zeitschrift für die gesamte Staatswissenschaft* 115 (1959): 229ff.

12. S. Fabricant, *The Trends of Government Activities in the U.S.A. Since 1900* (New York, 1952); Urs Hicks, *British Public Finances: Their Structure and Development 1880–1952* (London, 1954). In his *Lehrbuch der politischen Ökonomie*, 3rd ed. (Leipzig, 1883), 5:76ff. Adolf Wagner already discusses the "law" of an expanding need for capital.

13. F. Neumark, *Wirtschafts- und Finanzpolitik des Interventionsstaates* (Tübingen, 1961); from the legal perspective, see U. Scheuner, "Die staatliche Intervention im Bereich der Wirtschaft," *Veröffentlichung des Vereins deutscher Rechtslehrer* 11 (Berlin, 1954): 1ff.

14. Strachey, *Contemporary Capitalism*, 30f.

15. The transition here between merely regulative and formative functions was fluid but clear enough in its tendency. Legally this process found expression in the extension and hence the transformation of the older police law; on this see H. Huber, *Recht, Staat und Gesellschaft* (Bern, 1954), 32: "Police law is the law which for the maintenance of public order protects the public from danger. It has a negative, defensive character. Until not long ago it was a branch of public law which, so to speak, clung to private law. Presently there is a growing inclination toward either replacing or complementing the defense against dangers with a positive shaping of social life. So, for instance, building codes used to be designed to protect against traffic, health, and fire hazards, environmental legislation aimed at preventing the disfiguring of urban and rural landscapes. Today urban, regional, and super-regional planning do not merely want to fight detrimental developments but to take a hand in shaping something positive, namely, the use of space for housing and industry."

16. K. Littmann, *Zunehmende Staatstätigkeit und wirtschaftliche Entwicklung* (Köln, 1947), 164. Here we shall not consider costs for armaments, since military protection already belonged among the classical functions of the state.

17. Since the capitalist system tended to restrict the private sector as little as possible, at the expense of the sector of public services, a disequilibrium between the two arose which has been recently analyzed by Galbraith; see his study, *The Affluent Society* (Boston, 1958). Also A. Downs, "Why Government Budget Is too Small in a Democracy," *World Politics* 12 (1960): 541–63.

18. E. Forsthoff, *Die Verfassungsprobleme des Sozialstaates* (München, 1954). W. Friedmann, in *Law and Social Change* (London, 1951), 298, distinguished five functions: ". . . they result from the activities of the State: Firstly, as Protector; secondly, as Dispenser of Social Services; thirdly, as Industrial Manager; fourthly, as Economic Controller; fifthly, as Arbitrator."

19. See Strachey, *Contemporary Capitalism*, 155–81.

20. J. M. Clark, "The Interplay of Politics and Economics," *Freedom and Control in Modern Society*, ed. P. Berger et al. (New York, 1954), 192ff; A. Berle, *Power without Property* (London, 1960).

21. See A. Menger, *Das bürgerliche Recht und die besitzlosen Volksklassen*, 2nd ed. (Tübingen, 1890).

22. K. Renner, *Die Rechtsinstitute des Privatrechts und ihre Funktion*, 2nd ed. (Tübingen, 1929).

23. J. W. Hedemann, *Einführung in die Rechtswissenschaft*, 2nd ed. (Tübingen, 1927), 229.

24. Huber, *Recht, Staat und Gesellschaft*, 34.

25. F. Wieacker, "Das Sozialmodell der klassischen Privatrechtsgesetzbücher und die Entwicklung der modernen Gesellschaft," *Juristische Studiengesellschaft Karlsruhe*, Heft 3 (Karlsruhe, 1953), 21ff.

26. Huber, *Recht, Staat und Gesellschaft*, 33.

27. *Ibid.*, 37f.

28. Spiros Simitis, *Die faktischen Vertragsverhältnisse* (Frankfurt, 1958).

29. German law contains the fiction of the *Fiskus*, which qualifies the state as a subject of private law and hence as a possible partner for contractual relationships with private people. At one time, under absolutism, the good reason for this was that it granted a certain measure of legal security to the subjects even without the guarantee of a share in legislation. Similarly, French law distinguishes between the state as a subject of private law involved in *gestions privées* from the state as a subject of public law involved in *gestions publiques*. The two functions were relatively transparent in the liberal era and hence easily separable; however, the distinction becomes harder the more the state takes over functions in the private sphere of society itself and regulates its relationships with private economic subjects by contract: "Predominantly industrial, commercial, and managerial operations, such as the provision of transport, electricity, or gas, or the management of health services, are now normally carried out by incorporated public authorities, which are subject to the rules of private law, although responsible to ministers and parliaments for the general conduct of the operation." Friedmann, *Law and Social Change*, 63.

30. Huber, *Recht, Staat und Gesellschaft*, 40.

31. On the following, see W. Siebert, "Privatrecht im Bereich der öffentlichen Verwaltung," *Festschrift für Hans Niedermeyer*, ed. Universität Göttingen, Rechts- und Staatswissenschaftliche Fakultät (Göttingen, 1953), esp. 223f.

32. Spiros Simitis, *Der Sozialstaatsgrundsatz in seinen Auswirkungen auf das Recht von Familie und Unternehmen* (Manuscript: Habilitationsschrift der Juristischen Fakultät, Frankfurt, 1963) provides an exhaustive analysis of this whole complex.

33. H. Schelsky, *Schule und Erziehung in der industriellen Gesellschaft* (Würzburg, 1957), 33.

34. It is uncertain whether a strong position of the industrial bureaucracy vis-à-vis the shareholders has also been accompanied by a prevalence of management-specific interests, say, in the expansion of the enterprise at the expense of a possible increase in the amount of profits, and whether this has already diluted the private capitalist form of accumulation.

35. Then it played a role in the reformist ideology of the unions as well as in the fascist practice of the so-called Labor Front. In both cases, although opposite in political intent, the isolation of the institutional elements of large enterprise from their eco-

nomic functions led naturally to illusions concerning the extent to which an enterprise that operates in a capitalist way in accord with the principles of profit maximization also has to serve private interests. It fails to acknowledge, therefore, that the purpose of the enterprise cannot *eo ipso* coincide with the interests of the personnel or even of society as a whole.

36. H. P. Bahrdt, *Öffentlichkeit und Privatheit als Grundformen städtischer Soziierung*, 43ff.

37. L. von Friedeburg, *Soziologie des Betriebsklimas* (Frankfurt, 1963).

38. In the German Federal Republic more than three-fourths of the population are entitled to social security and pension benefits; at present, every other household contains at least one member receiving such payments.

39. "The question of how the individual manages his life has become an object of uninterrupted *public* concern only in our age. If one wants to bring into relief the changes that resulted from this in the forms of life of individuals, or more precisely, of private households, one has to look at all the forms of insurance, public aid, and welfare benefits predicated on social welfare considerations as they arrive in individual households." H. Achinger, *Sozialpolitik als Gesellschaftspolitik*, 79f.

40. *Ibid.*

41. H. Schelsky, *Wandlungen der deutschen Familie in der Gegenwart* (1953), 20, esp. 253ff.; Schelsky, "Gesellschaftlicher Wandel," *Auf der Suche nach Wirklichkeit* (Düsseldorf, 1965), 337ff.

42. R. König, *Materialien zur Soziologie der Familie* (Bern, 1946); Burgess and Locke, *The Family* (New York, 1953); Winch and Ginnis, *Marriage and Family* (New York, 1953).

43. See H. Marcuse, "Trieblehre und Freiheit," *Frevel in der Gegenwart* (Frankfurt, 1957), 401–24. "For the younger generation the reality principle is supplied less by the family than outside the family; they learn the socially normal behavior and reactions outside the protected sphere of the family," p. 413.

44. For more details, see my essay: "Pädagogischer Optimismus vor Gericht einer pessimistischen Anthropologie," *Neue Sammlungen*, vol. *Elternhaus und Schule* (Stuttgart, 1963).

45. W. H. Whyte, *The Organization Man* (New York, 1956), 280.

46. *Ibid.*, 352.

47. *Ibid.*

48. *Ibid.*, 353.

49. H. P. Bahrdt, "Von der romantischen Grossstadtkritik zum urbanen Städtebau," *Schweizer Monatshefte* (1958): 644f.

50. Helmuth Plessner, *Das Problem der Öffentlichkeit und die Idee der Entfremdung* (Göttingen, 1960), 9: "Since the increasingly intensified means of mass communication are open to all kinds of propagandistic influence and create a public sphere inside the house itself, as newspapers and books were never capable of doing, the insecurity of

the private sphere approaches crisis proportions, at least emotionally." In the same vein: M. J. Goldschmidt, "Publicity, Privacy, Secrecy," 404ff.

51. See my study, "Zum Verhältnis von Arbeit und Freizeit," *Konkrete Vernunft. Festschrift für E. Rothacker*, ed. G. Funke (Bonn, 1958), 219ff.

52. See H. Marcuse, *Eros and Civilization.*

53. L. L. Schücking, *Die Soziologie der literarischen Geschmacksbildung* (München, 1923), 60.

54. B. J. Fine, *Television and Family Life: A Survey of Two New England Communities* (Boston, 1952), defined the televiewing family as a "unity without conversation." On the basis of her case studies, E. E. Maccoby, "Television: Its Impact on School Children," *Public Opinion Quarterly* 15, no. 3 (1951): 421f, came to the conclusion that in nine out of ten families no conversations took place: "It appears that the increased family contact brought about by television is not social except in the most limited sense: that of being in the same room with other people. Whether the shared experience of television programs gives family members a similar perceptual framework with which to view the world, so that there are fewer differences in point of view among family members and fewer grounds for conflicts, is a matter which cannot be appraised with the data on hand."

55. D. Riesman, "The Tradition, the Written Word, and the Screen Image," *Antioch Founders Day Lecture* (Yellow Springs, Ohio, 1955).

56. On modern art's need for commentary, see A. Gehlen, *Zeitbilder* (Bonn, 1960).

57. A study of the sociological aspects of the conferences organized by the Evangelische Akademien is still needed. For some hints, see H. Schelsky, "Ist die Dauerreflexion institutionalisierbar?", *Zeitschrift für evangelische Ethik* 4 (1957), Heft 4, pp. 153ff.

58. According to a contemporary source, there were about 200 in Germany around 1800. J. A. Weiss, *Über das Zunftwesen* (Frankfurt, 1798), 229.

59. R. Meyersohn, "Commercialism and Complexity in Popular Culture." (Paper presented at the fifty-fifth Meeting of the American Sociological Association, New York, 1960).

60. Meyersohn, "Commercialism and Complexity," 5: "The average American has by now watched television for perhaps eighteen hours a week for ten years, but this enormous buildup of time has had no apparent consequences for his performance in front of a television set."

61. On this see T. W. Adorno, "Über den Fetischcharakter in der Musik und die Regression des Hörens," *Dissonanzen* (Göttingen, 1956), 9ff.

62. H. M. Enzensberger, "Bildung als Konsumgut. Analyse der Taschenbuchproduktion," *Einzelheiten* (Frankfurt, 1962), 110ff.

63. W. Kayser, Das literarische Leben der Gegenwart," *Deutsche Literatur in unserer Zeit*, ed. Kayser (Göttingen, 1959), 22.

64. *Ibid.* Kayser reckons a membership of about 3 million for the book clubs in West Germany; they purchase about 30 million books a year—far more than half the entire yearly production in the field of *belles lettres.*

65. In 1955 there were no books in more than a third of all West German households; 58 percent of all households *owned* at least one book. See *Jahrbuch der öffentlichen Meinung* (Allensbach, 1957), 102.

66. On the sociology of book consumption, see recently: R. Escarpit, *Das Buch und der Leser* (Köln, 1961), esp. 120ff.; for an economist's analysis: P. Meyer-Dohm, *Der west-deutsche Büchermarkt* (Stuttgart, 1957).

67. R. E. Park, "The Natural History of the Newspaper," *Mass Communication*, ed. W. Schramm (Urbana, 1944), 21: "It was in the *Sunday World* that the first seven-column cut was printed. Then followed the comic section and all the other devices with which we are familiar for compelling a dull-minded and reluctant public to read. After these methods had been worked out, they were introduced into the daily. The final triumph of the Yellow journal was Brisbane's Heart to Heart Editorial—a column of predigested platitudes and moralizing, with half-page diagrams and illustrations to reinforce the text. Nowhere has Herbert Spencer's maxim that the art of printing is the economy of attention been so completely realized." On the German mass newspapers of the nineteenth century, see: J. Kirchner, "Redaktion und Publikum," *Publizistik* 5 (1960): 463ff.

68. W. G. Bleyer, *History of American Journalism* (Boston, 1927), 184.

69. According to a study done a few years ago in Germany, of the adults whose daily papers contain such contributions 86 percent read the local section but only 40 percent read the editorial; 52 percent read the political news inside the paper and 59 percent the featured political article. At the end of 1957 more than 70 percent of the adult population in West Germany read at least one newspaper daily: 17 percent read a tabloid regularly, 63 percent read a local newspaper, 2.4 percent one of the great super-regional daily newspapers. Almost half the adults read illustrated weeklies regularly, and another quarter read chiefly entertainment magazines, weekend magazines, magazines for women, and radio and television guides. DIVO, *Der westdeutsche Markt in Zahlen* (Frankfurt, 1958), 145ff.

70. W. Schramm and D. M. White, "Age, Education, and Economic Status as Factors in Newspaper Reading," *Mass Communication*, 402ff.

71. G. Seldes, *The Great Audience* (New York, 1951).

72. H. M. Hughes, "Human Interest Stories and Democracy," *Public Opinion and Communication*, ed. Berelson and Janowitz (Glencoe, 1950), 317ff.

73. "Television and radio, because they appear, among all of the media, to have the most direct line of communication to individuals are perhaps the most influential. At its best the newspaper exerts a tremendously powerful influence. But it is less personalized than the broadcast media, and certainly less intimate in concept. The press, however, allows for privacy of thought, for only one person can read a speech in the newspaper, but several may watch and listen to it. . . . A televised speech is directed electronically 'to you,' the listener. The same speech reprinted in the morning paper is one step removed from immediacy and directness." C. S. Steinberg, *The Mass Communicators* (New York, 1958), 122.

74. On this see G. Anders, *Die Antiquiertheit des Menschen* (München, 1957); also L. Bogart, *The Age of Television* (New York, 1958).

75. D. Riesman, *The Lonely Crowd* (New Haven, 1950), 356ff. See also the contributions

on this in the volumes: White and Rosenberg, eds., *Mass Culture* (New York, 1955); Larabee and Meyersohn, eds., *Mass Leisure* (New York, 1959).

76. L. Löwenthal, "Die biographische Mode," *Sociologica* (Frankfurt, 1955), 363ff.; and *idem.*, *Literatur und Gesellschaft* (Neuwied, 1964).

77. On the basis of empirical studies, Elisabeth Noelle reported on the astonishing influence of "advice" columns in newspapers: "Die Wirkung der Massenmedien," *Publizistik* 5 (1960): 532ff., esp. 538f.: "When there was advice given in an issue of the magazine *Constanze* on how to repair damaged shirt collars, a million readers of this issue tried it out. . . . Nearly two and a half million readers propped their legs up for five minutes each hour for several days or weeks because this was suggested in an issue of *Constanze.*"

78. H. J. Knebel used the example of group tourism to analyze the similar complementarity of trends toward a "de-interiorization" on the one hand, and toward a differentiation and individualization on the other, which reactively created the illusion of privacy. *Soziologische Strukturwandlungen im modernen Tourismus* (Stuttgart, 1960), 124ff.

79. DIVO, *Der Westdeutsche Markt in Zahlen*, 145ff. and *Jahrbuch der öffentlichen Meinung*, 51ff. The frequency of moviegoing, of course, depends primarily on age level. On the whole matter, see also G. Kieslich, *Freizeitgestaltung in einer Industriestadt* (Dortmund, 1956).

80. C. E. Swanson and R. D. Jones, "Television Owning and Its Correlates," *Journal of Applied Psychology* (October 1951): 352ff.

81. This is R. Meyersohn's interpretation; cf. his "Social Research in Television," *Mass Culture*, 347.

82. Hauser, *The Social History of Art*, 2:838.

83. R. König demonstrates this in the case of sociologists, in "Wandlungen in der Stellung der sozialwissenschaftlichen Intelligenz," *Soziologie und moderne Gesellschaft. Verhandlungen des 14. Deutschen Soziologentages* (Stuttgart, 1959), 53ff.; in general, see T. Geiger, *Aufgaben und Stellung der Intelligenz in der Gesellschaft* (Stuttgart, 1949).

84. T. W. Adorno, "Das Altern der neuen Musik," *Dissonanzen*, 102ff.

85. See A. Gehlen, "Bemerkungen zum Thema 'Kulturkonsum und Konsumkultur,'" *Tagungsbericht des "Bundes"* (Wuppertal, 1955), 6ff.

86. H. M. Enzensberger, "Bewusstseinsindustrie," *Einzelheiten*, 7ff.

87. See W. Thomssen, *Zum Problem der Scheinöffentlichkeit, inhaltsanalytisch dargestellt an der Bildzeitung* (Manuscript, Frankfurt, 1960). This study was based on 69 daily issues of the Hamburg national edition, of which 23 issues covered the half-years 2/1953, 1/1956, and 2/1958 respectively. This study gives an indication of the magnitude of the trend under discussion in terms of an extreme example: The newspaper selected for this purpose, i.e., the *Bildzeitung*, was quite suitable from a diagnostic point of view because within the daily press (which is to say, the classic genre of journalism) it represented a stage of development in which the daily paper already took on the form of a magazine that appeared every day. The diversification of the page makeup has advanced to such an extent that only 40 percent of the column total was devoted to the text itself, while roughly one-fourth was reserved for headlines and another fourth

for pictures; advertising took up the rest of the space. About half of the total text was divided between news and reportage, about a fourth went to entertainment; sports news got 12 percent and editorial statements 7 percent. The latter were certainly not devoted to critical reflection but to direct contact with readers through advice columns, prize competitions, questionnaires, etc. Of the news and reportage hardly more than a fourth covered areas that could be considered politically relevant—in the broadest sense. Politics (including the main editorial) got 19 percent and clarifying information 8 percent. The remaining area was divided among crime, accidents, and reports about everyday life (32 percent), trials (13 percent), "society," film, fashion, beauty contests, etc. (21 percent), advice concerning problems of life and instruction (7 percent). These articles were done in such a style that in one half, text was predominant, in the other, illustration. Only a third of the total news columns was taken up by contributions that provided straightforward factual information; two-thirds provided such information incidentally through the vehicle of "human-interest" stories; among the front page articles, the proportion of articles made up as human-interest stories increased to 72 percent. Hence, the final conclusion of this study comes as no surprise. The news and reports of all categories that could be classified as "publicly relevant" (reports or assessments of events that by reason of their significance in the life process of the society attained importance beyond the single instance), got no more than a quarter of the area devoted to news; this corresponded to about one-third of the total number of all reports and news. Among the front page articles, the proportion of contributions classified as "not publicly relevant" increased to 73 percent; only 18 percent could be considered "publicly relevant" while not distracting the reader from the material content through packaging as human-interest stories. Table 6, p. 50 gives a total overview.

88. The "generality" of the norm in the strict sense of the bourgeois concept of law was not bestowed solely by the *formal* criterion of universality. This sense was only met adequately if the universal formulation, which excluded dispensations and privileges, was also, under the given social conditions, factually not addressed only to some specific group within the society. The legal effect of a law that was universal according to substantive criteria was not to be selective. It had to be "elementary" or a matter of "principle" in such a fashion that it applied to the foundations of the social order as a whole and, to that extent, to a circle of persons that might possibly include *all* members of society. Legal norms that regulated not mere principles of social intercourse as a whole but concrete states of affairs within the framework of the total order were called "specific" (in contrast to the general ones), no matter whether or not they were formulated in a universal form. Only during the liberal phase of capitalism was civil society a a sphere of private autonomy "separated" from the state to such an extent that legislation tended to be confined to a system of general norms; and only in this phase did the universality of the formulation also necessarily imply the generality of the actual effect of the law as well. See F. Neumann, *Der Funktionswandel des Gesetzes im Recht der bürgerlichen Gesellschaft,*; see also my essay, "Natural Law and Revolution," *Theory and Practice,* 82–120.

89. On the conceptual distinction see (among others) H. Schneider, "Über Einzelfallsgesetze," *Festschrift für Carl Schmitt,* ed. H. Barion, E. Forsthoff, and W. Weber (Berlin, 1959), 197ff.

90. E. Forsthoff, *Lehrbuch des Verwaltungsrechts* (München, 1955), 1:9f.; on this, see F. Neumann, *Der Funktionswandel des Rechtsgesetzes,* 577. Neumann also analyzed the political function of Carl Schmitt's efforts to restore the exclusive validity of the classical concept of law for the legislation in the Weimar Republic. Today the preoccupations of the Carl Schmitt School have the *analogous* function of restoring the exclusive validity, at the level of constitutional law, of the classical concept of the constitutional state. See, for instance, E. Forsthoff, "Begriff und Wesen de sozialen Rechtsstaates,"

Veröffentlichungen des Vereins Deutscher Staatsrechtslehrer, Heft 12 (Berlin, 1954). Thesis 15: "The social-welfare state and the constitutional state cannot be fused at the level of the constitution. The field of action of the social-welfare state is legislation and administration. 'Constitutional social-welfare state' is the typological characterization of a state, and it encompasses constitution, legislation, and administration. It is not a legal concept."

91. G. Leibholz, "Strukturwandel der modernen Demokratie," *Strukturprobleme der Demokratie* (Karlsruhe, 1953), 94f.

92. See Böckenförde, *Gesetzgebende Gewalt*, pt. 3, pp. 210ff.

VI Transformation of the Public Sphere's Political Function

1. See the schema above, p. 30.

2. K. Bücher, "Die Anfänge des Zeitungswesens," *Die Entstehung der Volkswirtschaft* (Tübingen, 1917), 1:257.

3. D. P. Baumert, *Die Entstehung des deutschen Journalismus (München-Leipzig, 1921)*.

4. U. DeVolder, *Soziologie der Zeitung* (Stuttgart, 1959), 22.

5. Groth, *Die Zeitung*, 4:8ff.

6. In Germany in 1848 this was a matter of the *Nationalzeitung*, the *Kreuzzeitung*, and the *Neue Rheinische Zeitung*; see F. Lenz, *Werden und Wesen der öffentlichen Meinung* (München, 1956), 157.

7. Earlier than that stock exchange interests, especially under the aegis of rapidly growing capital investment in industrial stock, had already motivated the Parisian Charles Havas, who between 1830 and 1840 united older correspondence services in one hand, to institute mail services by carrier pigeon. He distributed above all London stock exchange news to banks, firms, and newspapers. In 1849 he could use the first telegraph line. At the same time, the head of the Berlin *Nationalzeitung*, Bernhard Wolff, attempted to lower the telegram expenses for his paper by reselling the messages to subscribers; thus originated, after the Agence Havas, the Wolffsche Telegrafenbüro; following both in 1857 was the famed Reuters Ltd. in London. These three, initially organized as private economic enterprises, dominated the European market for over half a century. First they provided economic news exclusively and then political news as well. See E. Dovifat, *Zeitungslehre* (Berlin, 1955), 1:62ff. The stimulus provided by these agencies for the stock market interests, and not just their great need for capital, quickly led to the interlocking of telegraph offices with the most important banking institutions. Wolff joined with Bleichröder and Delbrück, Schickler & Co., Havas with the Crédit Lyonnais, and Reuters with the Union Bank of Scotland as well as with the London and Provincial Bank. Thus, under certain circumstances, the insiders who came into the possession of important news with a headstart or who for their part channeled reports into the public sphere could gain advantages in speculation. Just as importantly, the intimate informal ties of the agencies with their governments also proved important; they could from case to case be utilized for propaganda purposes.

8. See Groth, *Die Zeitung*, 4:14ff.

9. Reports are available about the Berlin newspaper market at this time which emphasize the weakening in the position of the editor in relation to the publisher. "It is no longer the editor who determines the character of the paper, not even the so-called editor-in-chief, who earlier had been in daily intimate contact with the publisher and exchanged views with him. In his place is the publisher's director or department head who looks at the whole enterprise only in terms of the business aspect, with an eye to sales or to general propaganda purposes, or even to considerations regarding the advertising business. The publisher's representative presides over staff conferences, criticizes the latest issues, and gives directives for upcoming ones." Karl Mischke, "Der Berliner Zeitungsmarkt," *Das Buchgewerbe in der Reichshauptstadt* (Berlin, 1914), 129.

10. Groth, *Die Zeitung*, 2:335ff.

11. On present conditions in the United States and Great Britain, see the studies by the Commission on the Freedom of the Press, *A Free and Responsible Press* (Chicago, 1947); also R. B. Nixon, "Concentration and Absenteeism in Daily Newspaper Ownership," *Public Opinion and Communication*, ed. Berelson and Janowitz (Glencoe, 1950), 193ff. and the Royal Commission on the Press, the so-called *Ross Report* (London, 1949). Comparable analyses are lacking for France and Germany; in general, however, conditions are unlikely to differ fundamentally from those in Anglo-Saxon countries. In 1932 there were 2,483 daily papers in the Reich; in 1956, 1,479 in the Federal Republic; see the manual, *Die deutsche Presse 1956*, ed. Institut für Publizistik der Freien Universität (Berlin, 1956), 30.

12. Havas, Reuters, Wolff, and the Associated Press soon set up an international cartel which divided up the world into four spheres of interest and inside national borders permanently granted to one agency the distribution of the news reports of the other agencies.

13. In 1956 there were 1,479 daily papers in West Germany; of these almost half, accounting for 28 percent of all copies printed, were organized into 62 joint networks. At that time the regional and branch editions of the 693 major papers accounted for 53 percent of total copies printed (whereby 2.3 percent of the central papers, each having more than ten different local editions attained a share of 16 percent of total copies). In 1954 only 225 papers were not connected with either a major paper or with one of the joint networks. See *Die deutsche Presse 1956*, 30ff.

14. Dovifat, *Zeitungslehre*, 1:69ff.

15. Beyond censorship in questions of taste, the various organizations concerned with self-control had not yet obtained any central supervisory rights on behalf of the public interest.

16. This development has been confirmed most recently in West Germany by the Bundesverfassungsgericht's so-called "television verdict."

17. Dobb, *Studies in the Development of Capitalism*, 360.

18. From more recent positions one can discern that even the advertising business distanced itself from the institutional ideology that advertising promoted the transparency of the market. See *Jahresbericht 1962*, Zentralausschuss der Werbewirtschaft (Bad Godesberg, 1963), 13.

19. Galbraith, *American Capitalism*, 46ff.

20. H. Wuttke, "Die Reklame," *Die deutschen Zeitschriften und die Entstehung der öffentlichen Meinung*, 3rd ed. (Leipzig, 1875), 18ff.

21. W. Sombart, *Der Bourgeois*, 204.

22. G. Töpfer, "Mittler der Werbung," *Der Volkswirt* 55 (1952); supplement *Die deutsche Werbewirtschaft*, 40ff.

23. F. Greiser, "Die Kosten der Werbung," 82ff.

24. Between 1880 and 1948 advertising expenditure per capita in the United States increased sevenfold. See Schramm, *Hamburg, Deutschland und die Welt*, 548.

25. DIVO, *Der westdeutsche Markt in Zahlen*, 156.

26. *Jahrbuch der öffentlichen Meinung*, 53.

27. *Handbuch: Die deutsche Presse 1956*, 47. On this type of periodicals, see the analysis of H. J. F. Kropff, "Synthese von Journalismus, industrieller Publizität und Public Relations," *Publizistik*, 5 (1960): 491ff.

28. D. Riesman, *The Lonely Crowd*, 81.

29. E. L. Bernays, *Crystallizing Public Opinion* (New York, 1923); see also S. Kelley, *Professional Public Relations and Political Power* (Baltimore, 1956).

30. C. S. Steinberg, *The Mass Communicators*, 16ff.

31. "Industry, business, and labor realize that they cannot survive in a healthy state and meet their competitive problems without some means of achieving and maintaining the good will of the public." *Ibid.*, 19; also ch. 3, pp. 115ff.

32. H. Gross, *Moderne Meinungspflege* (Düsseldorf, 1952); for a summary, cf. C. Hundhausen, *Industrielle Publizität als Public Relations* (Essen, 1957).

33. Steinberg, *The Mass Communicators*, 92; also ch. 3, pp. 115ff.

34. Ranging from the usual organized affair (reports, talks, meetings, the formation of committees and conventions, etc.) to the skilled exploitation of suitable vehicles (such as vacations or holy days with which special campaigns can be associated) to publicity-attracting endowments, contests, gifts, stipends and all the way to the systematic arranging of news events (parades, exhibitions, bicycle races, vacation camps, gardening contests, beauty contests, etc.). *Ibid.*, 237ff.

35. "The press . . . has two major sources of news: its own reporters and the public relations man. The press also has two related audience potentials: the number of readers in the receiving audience who form opinions based on the content in the newspaper and the number of persons in the receiving audience who are motivated to buy the products advertised in the newspaper." *Ibid.*, 137.

36. *The Engineering of Consent*, ed. E. L. Bernays (Oklahoma, 1955).

37. Steinberg, *The Mass Communicators*, 74.

38. A 1953 report names far more than 100 institutions in West Germany engaged in publicity work, whereby it is at times difficult to distinguish between civic education and advertising. H. E. Jahn, *Verantwortung und Mitarbeit* (Oberlahnstein, 1953).

39. *Verhandlungen des 7. Deutschen Soziologentages. Schriften der deutschen Gesellschaft für*

Soziologie, vol. 3 (Tübingen, 1931). A few years earlier F. Tönnies had summarized the studies of the older German sociology on this topic: *Kritik der öffentlichen Meinung* (Berlin, 1922).

40. C. Brinkmann, "Presse und öffentliche Meinung," *Verhandlungen*, 27ff.

41. *Ibid.*, 30.

42. Administrative operations became increasingly independent from general political programs; under the guise of rational-technical adaptation to changing situations, government was replaced by administration to the extent that conservatives complained about a "thinning out of the element of rulership."

43. Forsthoff, *Lehrbuch des Verwaltungsrechts*, 1:65.

44. W. Weber, *Spannungen und Kräfte im westdeutschen Verfassungssystem* (Stuttgart, 1951), 38 and 53; on the abundant literature about interest groups, see O. Stammer, "Interessenverbände und Parteien," *Kölner Zeitschrift für Soziologie und Sozialpsychologie* 9 (1957): 587ff,; on the historical side: G. Schulz, "Über Entstehung und Formen von Interessengruppen in Deutschland seit Beginn der Industrialisierung," *Politische Vierteljahresschrift* 2 (1961): 124ff.

45. O. Kirchheimer, "Changes in the Structure of Political Compromise," *Studies in Philosophy and Social Science* 9 (1941): 456.

46. R. A. Dahl, "Hierarchy, Democracy and Bargaining in Politics and Economics," *Research Frontiers in Politics and Government* (Washington, 1955), 47ff.

47. H. Ridder, *Zur verfassungsrechtlichen Stellung der Gewerkschaften im Sozialstaat nach dem Grundgesetz für die Bundesrepublik Deutschland* (Stuttgart, 1960).

48. See J. M. Kaiser, *Die Repräsentation organisierter Interessen* (Berlin, 1956).

49. This incidental mobilization of "public" opinion for the purposes of supporting or securing compromises negotiated nonpublicly also reacts back on the structure of the compromises themselves. In a "genuine" compromise both parties typically reserve the right to maintain the goals that reflect the unreconciled interest situations and interest directions of a continuing basic conflict of interests. To abandon this sort of reservation renders the compromise ideological, for it reduces it to a status contract within the fictive framework of an order in principle free from conflict. With regard to the verdict of the Federal Labor Court, these tendencies have been analyzed by Abendroth, Ramm, Ridder, et al.: "Innergewerkschaftliche Willensbildung, Urabstimmung, und 'Kampfmassnahme,'" *Arbeit und Recht* 7 (1959): 262ff. Just as remarkable as the legal critique is the sociological fact (documented by the criticized verdict) brought to light by it: the obligation of the bureaucracies of umbrella organizations to achieve cooperative integration within the framework of a substantively fixed order while at the same time abandoning all consciousness of a compromise involving merely temporary adjustment of divergent interests in a situation of continuing conflict of interests. Analogous to this were the phenomena of the "vanishing opposition" inside the parliament, as noted by O. Kirchheimer: "The Waning of Opposition in Parliamentary Regimes," *Social Research* 24 (1957): 127–56. This state of affairs was symptomatic not only of the political ambivalence [neglected in our context] of the development of the welfare state in general [on this see my introductory chapter to *Student und Politik* (Neuwied, 1961), 34ff.] but specifically of the structural transformation of the public sphere. For that kind of integration-bound cooperation of organization bureaucracies that tended to become independent from their member-

publics could only win out to the extent that the forms of a critically debating public in the political realm—in this case, the organization-internal public of organization members—were replaced by the depoliticized sphere of a mediatized public whose explicit acclamation or implicit toleration was brought about by a manipulative or staged publicity issuing 'from above.'

Important in this context were the tendencies we have analyzed above in relation to the process of concentration of the press: first, the centralization of the political press along with an increased dependence of the newspaper on party bureaucracies; later on, the weakening in the position of the partisan political press as such; and finally, the depoliticization of the press as a whole. Abendroth confirmed this as far as the Social Democrats' press was concerned, in connection with a remark in Hermann Heller's *Staatslehre* (Leiden, 1934), 137: "When Heller points to the fact that the workers remain intellectually capable of resistance only by means of their own newspapers, it must not be forgotten that in the Federal Republic the characteristic element of the partisan press set up by the democratic parties, which was of tremendous significance in Germany in the period before 1933, no longer exists; and for economic and technical reasons it is unlikely to arise again to the former extent." Sultan und Abendroth, *Bürokratischer Verwaltungsstaat und soziale Demokratie* (Hannover, 1955), p. 92, n. 45. In 1933 about half of all German daily newspapers were politically committed. In the Federal Republic by 1956, their share had fallen to about a quarter: 65 percent of all newspapers declared themselves to be nonpartisan; 10 percent were undefined. These two categories comprised over 32 percent of the total output of copies (see *Die Deutsche Presse 1956*. 35ff.

50. R. Altmann, "Zur Rechtsstellung der öffentlichen Verbände," *Zeitschrift für Politik*, 2 (1955): 214.

51. *Ibid.*, 226.

52. Schelsky, *Familie*, 357.

53. R. Altmann, *Das Problem der Öffentlichkeit und seine Bedeutung für die Demokratie*, (Ph.D. diss., Marburg, 1954), 72.

54. M. Weber, "Politics as a Vocation," *From Max Weber*, ed. H. H. Gerth and C. W. Mills (New York, 1946), 77–128; see 100ff.

55. Weber spoke of the quite limited number of those participating directly on account of the mechanism of the selection of dignitaries, but then went on to admit: "However, the number of those who indirectly had a stake in the management of politics, especially a material one, was very large. For all administrative measures of a ministerial department, and especially all decisions in matters of personnel, were made partly with a view to their influence upon electoral chances. The realization of each and every kind of wish was sought through the local delegate's mediation. For better or for worse the minister had to lend his ear to this delegate. . . . The single deputy controlled the patronage of office, and, in general, any kind of patronage in his election district. In order to be reelected the deputy, in turn, maintained connections with the local notables." *Ibid.*, 102.

56. A von Rochau, *Grundsätze der Realpolitik* (Stuttgart, 1853), 91f.; on the entire topic, see T. Schieder, "Die Theorie der Partei im älteren deutschen Liberalismus," *Aus Geschichte und Politik. Festschrift zum 70 Geburtstag von Ludwig Bergsträsser*, ed. Kommission für Geschichte des Parlamentarismus und der Politischen Parteien (Düsseldorf, 1954), 183ff.

57. H. von Treitschke, *Parteien und Franktionen* (1871); cited by Schieder, "Das Verhältnis von Staat," 194.

58. In *Die Hilfe* 10, no. 2 (1904).

59. D. Hilger, "Die demokratischen Parteien und Parteiendemokratie," *Hamburger Jahrbuch für Wirtschafts- und Gesellschaftspolitik* 1 (1956): 176ff., with reference to the text prepared by W. Mommsen, *Deutsche Parteiprogramme vom Vormärz bis zur Gegenwart* (München, 1952), drew attention to the change of formulation: considerations, occasionally of a wide-sweeping nature, addressed to small, highly educated strata gave way increasingly to political clichés.

60. H. Plessner, *Das Problem der Öffentlichkeit*, 8.

61. Here we neglect this type, which was representative for the Social Democrats of the Wilhelminian era. It was no longer characteristic of the contemporary party system. On the typology of modern parties, see: M. Duverger, *Les Parties Politiques* (Paris, 1951), and S. Newmann "Towards a Comparative Study of Political Parties," *Modern Political Parties* (Chicago, 1956), 395ff.

62. "The common voter, who does not belong to any organization and is wooed by the parties, is completely inactive; the parties take notice of him mostly during the elections, otherwise only through propaganda directed at him." M. Weber, "Parliament and Government in a Reconstructed Germany," *Economy and Society*, ed. G. Roth and C. Wittich (New York, 1968), 1381–1469; see 1445.

63. Blackstone, *Commentaries of the Laws of England* (London, 1783).

64. *Grundgesetz*, art. 38.

65. The two protective clauses, right to immunity and the foregoing of financial compensation, were simply more extreme versions of specifications which generally qualified participation in the bourgeois public sphere. For the latter was understood as a sphere emancipated from public authority and protected from private force. The protective clauses were intended to preserve for delegates the status of private people who were part of the public, even on the parliamentary level; their purpose was definitely not to endow them with the additional qualities of lords whose office was to represent authority—parliamentary publicity was exactly the contrary of "representative" publicity.

66. Leibholz, "Strukturwardel der modernen Demokratie," 97.

67. O. Kirchheimer, "Majoritäten und Minoritäten in westeuropäischen Regierungen," *Die Neue Gesellschaft* (1959), 256ff.; also *idem.*, "Parteistruktur und Massendemokratie in Europa," *Archiv für öffentliches Recht* 79 (1954); 307ff.; and *idem.*, *The Party in Mass Society* (New York, 1958).

68. This was precisely the state of affairs invoked by the parties to support their (legally unfounded) demand that a delegate who refused to vote according to the party line resign from his mandate.

69. C. Schmitt, *The Crisis of Parliamentary Democracy* (Cambridge, MA, 1985).

70. E. Friesenhahn, "Parlament und Regierung im modernen Staat," *Veröffentlichungen des Vereins deutscher Staatsrechtslehrer*, Heft 16 (Berlin, 1958), 31.

71. Just how much the connection between parliamentary discussion and critical reasoning about political issues by private people *extra muros* has been severed is demonstrated, with reference to the trends in parliamentary reporting, by H. Haftendorn,

Das Problem von Parlament und Öffentlichkeit, dargestellt am Beispiel der Parlamentsberichter-stattung (Ph.D. diss., Frankfurt, 1960), 146ff. The work of the parliament itself, as is well known, is nowadays taking place in the party offices and caucuses as well as in the specialized parliamentary committees. These negotiations cannot be considered substitutes for public critical parliamentary debate because they do not compensate for the latter's disjunction from the public. Even where the committees are declared by the rules of order to be publicly proceeding institutions, they are not established as substitutes for a parliamentary publicity. Symptomatically, precisely "a growing interest on the part of the public in their proceedings makes it necessary to find opportunities for confidential contacts. Publicity seeps into the proceedings of the committees only to witness the relocation of the object of its interest to ever new levels of nonpublicity." *Ibid.*, 89; see also B. Dechamps, *Macht und Arbeit der Ausschüsse* (Meisenheim/Glan, 1954); on the historical aspect, see W. Steffani, "Funktion und Kompetenz parlamentarischer Untersuchungsausschüsse," *Politische Vierteljahresschrift* 1 (1960): 153ff.

72. C. T. Welcker, *Die vollkomene und ganze Pressefreiheit, nach ihrer sittlichen, rechtlichen und politischen Notwendigkeit, und ihre Übereinstimmung mit dem deutschen Fürstenwort, und nach ihrer völligen Zeitgemässheit* (Freiburg, 1830); A. Feuerbach, Betrachtungen über die Öffentlichkeit und Mündlichkeit der Gerechtigkeitspflege (Siegen, 1821).

73. E. Schmidt, "Öffentlichkeit oder Publizität," *Festschrift zum 70. Geburtstag von Walter Schmidt-Rimpler*, ed. Rechts-und Staatswissenschaftliche Fakultät der Universität Bonn (Karlsruhe, 1957), 351ff.

74. Ridder, *Stellung der Gewerkschaften*, 27.

75. O. Stammer and H. Schelsky, "Über die 'Organisationswirklichkeit.' A discussion," *Neue Gesellschaft* 2, no. 2 (1955): Heft 3, 4, 6; for relevant references, O. Stammer, "Politische Soziologie- und Demokratie-Forschung," *Kölner Zeitschrift für Soziologie und Sozialpsychologie* 8 (1956): 380ff.

76. T. Ramm, *Die Freiheit der Willensbildung* (Stuttgart, 1960), 108: "The threatening collapse of society into countless, practically uncontrollable special orders can be coun-teracted relatively simply by a public opinion that is informed about, and has a critical impact on, what is going on inside organizations."

77. On questions regarding party finances in West Germany, see T. Eschenburg, *Probleme der modernen Parteifinanzierung in Deutschland* (Opladen, 1962); for the United States, A. Heard, *The Costs of Democracy* (University of North Carolina, 1960); on the legal aspect, W. Grundmann, "Die Finanzierung der politischen Parteien," *Zeitschrift für die gesamte Staatswissenschaft* 115 (1959): 113–30.

78. Altmann, *Rechtsstellung der öffentlichen Verbände*, 225.

79. H. Ridder, "Meinungsfreiheit," *Die Grundrechte*, ed. Neumann, Nipperdey, and Scheuner (Berlin, 1954), 2:257. See also M. Löffler, "Der Verfassungsauftrag der Publizistik," *Publizistik* 5 (1960): 517ff.; H. Copic, "Berufsverbot und Pressefreiheit," *Juristische Zeitschrift* (1963): 494ff.

80. U. Lohmar, *Innerparteiliche Demokratie* (Stuttgart, 1963); on this, W. Abendroth, "Innerparteiliche und innerverbandliche Demokratie als Voraussetzung der poli-tischen Demokratie," *Politische Vierteljahreschrift* 5 (1964): 307ff.

81. Ridder, *Stellung der Gewerkschaften*, 26f.

82. Kitzinger, 67f.

83. See my essay on the concept of political participation in Habermas, von Friedeburg, et al., *Student und Politik*, 13ff.

84. *Public Opinion Quarterly* 16 (Fall 1952): 329.

85. See the collections: Burdick and Brodbeck, *American Voting Behavior* (Glencoe, 1959); Eulau, Eldersveld, and Janowitz, *Political Behavior* (Glencoe, 1956); further, the studies of Lazarsfeld, Berelson, and McPhee, *Voting* (Chicago, 1954); Campbell, Gurie, and Miller, *The Voters Decide* (Evanston, 1954); Lazarsfeld, Berelson, and Gaudet, *The People's Choice* (New York, 1944). The voting behavior of populations in England, France, and Germany, as comparable studies in these countries show, is by and large similar to that in America: McCallum and Readman, *The British General Election of 1945* (London, 1947); H. G. Nicholas, *The British General Election of 1950* (London, 1951); D. E. Butler, *The British General Election of 1955* (London, 1955); Nicholas and Williams, "The French Election of 1956," *Political Studies* 4 (1956); Harrison and Kitzinger, "The French Election of 1958," *Political Studies* 7 (1959): 147ff; M. Duverger, *La participation des femmes à la vie politique* (Paris, 1955); Hirsch-Weber, *Wähler und Gewählte* (Berlin, 1957). Many of these findings have been interpreted in S. M. Lipset, *Political Man* (New York, 1960); cf. especially pt. 2, "Voting in Western Democracies."

86. J. Linz, *The Social Basis of German Politics* (Ph.D. diss., Columbia University, 1958); 208f., according to Lipset, *Political Man*, 196.

87. E. Katz and P. Lazarsfeld, *Personal Influence* (Glencoe, 1955).

88. Berelson, *Voting*, 319: "In most campaigns, whether political or informational, the people best informed on the issue are the ones least likely to change their minds. Much of this represents attitudinal stability; some of it may represent rigidity."

89. M. Janowitz and D. Marvick, *Competition, Pressure, and Democratic Consent* (Michigan, 1956).

90. Lipset, *Political Man*, 270ff., on the historical background of voting patterns.

91. S. A. Stouffer, *Communism, Conformity, and Civil Liberties* (New York, 1955), 83ff.; H. H. Field, "The Non-Voter," *Public Opinion Quarterly* 8 (1944): 175ff.; F. H. Stanford, *Authoritarianism and Liberty* (Philadelphia, 1950).

92. Janowitz, *Political Behavior*, Eulau et al., 279.

93. C. Harris, "Election, Polling, and Research," *Public Opinion Quarterly* 21 (1957): 109.

94. Janowitz, *Political Behavior*, 280.

95. *Ibid.*

96. R. Aron, "Fin de l'Age Ideologique?" *Sociologica* (Frankfurt, 1955); see also O. Brunner, "Das Zeitalter der Ideologien," *Neue Wege der Sozialgeschichte* (Göttingen, 1956), esp. 200ff.

97. T. W. Adorno, "Beitrag zur Ideologienlehre," *Gesammelte Schriften*, vol. 8 (Frankfurt, 1972) 457–77; see 476–77; cf. also Horkheimer and Adorno, "The Culture

Industry: Enlightenment as Mass Deception," *Dialectic of Enlightenment*, trans. J. Cumming (New York, 1972), 120–67.

98. H. H. Flöter, "Der manipulierte Mensch und seine Freiheit," *Die Neue Gesellschaft* (1958): Heft 4, p. 272.

99. Characteristic of this was the discussion within the SPD after its election setback of 1957; see the controversy in *Die Neue Gesellschaft* (1958): Heft 1: Willi Eichler, "Wählermanipulierung oder sozialistische Politik?", 27ff. and Jens Feddersen, "Politik muss verkauft werden," 21ff.

100. Riesman, *The Lonely Crowd*, 189–90.

101. G. Schmidtchen, *Die befragte Nation* (Freiburg, 1959), 139.

102. It is no accident that Schmidtchen, *Ibid.*, 173, presented the following case as an example for governmental behavior based on empirical findings: "The reaction of the press to certain efforts or decisions of the government may turn out to be unfavorable. At the same time a survey shows that the population has formed much more positive ideas about these events. If the government were to base its publicity work on the opinions of the press, an information campaign could cause more confusion than clarity, because for the most part its argumentation would have to appear incomprehensible to the population."

103. Kirchheimer, "Majoritäten und Minoritäten," 265.

104. Schmidtchen, *Die befragte Nation*, 166; see also his "Die Bedeutung repräsentativer Bevölkerungsumfragen für die offene Gesellschaft," *Politische Vierteljahresschrift* 4 (1963): 168ff.

105. This empirically falsified assumption lies at the basis of most of the critiques of the function of opinion research within a democracy. It leads, so the contention goes, to a disappearance of the willingness to assume leadership; see J. C. Ramney, "Do the Polls Serve Democracy?" *Public Opinion and Communication*, ed. Berelson and Janowitz, 132ff.; also R. Fröhner, "Trägt die Meinungsforschung zur Entdemokratisierung bei?" *Publizistik* 3 (1958): 323ff.; and more recently, the controversy between K. Sontheimer and G. Schmidtchen, "Meinungsforschung und Politik," *Der Monat* 16 (April and May 1964).

106. Above all, see the studies of Schmidtchen and Kitzinger that cannot be suspected of partisan political affiliations; for an interpretation of the manipulative content of the scientifically managed Bundestag election campaign, cf. L. von Friedeburg, "Zum politischen Potential der Umfrageforschung," *Kölner Zeitschrift für Soziologie und Sozialpsychologie* 13 (1961); 201–16; for a sociological analysis of particular categories of voters, see Hartenstein, Liepelt, and Schubert, "Die Septemberdemokratie," *Die Neue Gesellschaft* (1958); Heft 1; H. Faul, ed. *Wahlen und Wähler in Deustschland* (Hamburg, 1961); V. Graf Blücher, ed., *Der Prozess der Meinungsbildung, dargestellt am Beispiel der Bundestagswahl 1961* (Bielefeld, 1962).

107. Concerning this term, see above p. 80, n. 54.

108. See above, sect. 11.

109. In this sense, Ramm, *Die Freiheit der Willensbildung*, 54, stressed "that the civil law in its concrete formation and articulation was itself an outcome of human and civil rights."

110. Ridder, *Stellung der Gewerkschaften*, 16ff.

111. See above p. 178 n. 88; also Forsthoff, *Begriff und Wesen des sozialen Rechtsstaats*, 27f.: "With the elimination of the dualism of state and society, to which corresponded in the realm of administration an interventionist administration, society-shaping tasks have accrued to legislation and administration the accomplishment of which can no longer be assessed by means of a merely formal legal standard. For these society-shaping functions it no longer suffices that they remain within the confines of the constitution and the laws; but they must be regulated and performed in a manner just in a substantive sense." Cf. also Forsthoff, *Verwaltungsrecht*, 1:57.

112. H. P. Ipsen, *Das Grundgesetz* (Hamburg, 1950). For a survey of the literature on the discussion in constitutional law, see Gerber, "Die Sozialstaatsklausel des Grundgesetzes," *Archiv für öffentliches Recht* 81 (Tübingen, 1956).

113. Ridder, *Stellung der Gewerkschaften*, 10.

114. Art. 10 (the ordering of economic life in accord with the principles of justice and with the goal of providing everyone with an existence compatible with human dignity); art. 155 (distribution and use of land under conditions preventing their abuse); art. 156 (socialization of private enterprises and promotion of cooperative societies); art. 157 (guarantee of labor law); art. 163 (duty to work and right to work); art. 164 (employees' right to participation).

115. Arts. 22–27 (right to social security, to work, to adequate leisure, to a minimum standard of living and health care, to education and culture, and to a share in cultural goods in general). To be sure, articles concerning social policy can be found in the constitutions of many German *Länder*: Hessian Constitution, arts. 27–47; Bavarian Constitution, arts. 151ff.; Constitution of Rhineland-Palatinate, arts. 23ff.; Constitution of Bremen, arts. 37ff.; Constitution of Northrhine-Westphalia, arts. 5ff, 24ff.

116. Fortsthoff, *Sozialer Rechtstaat*, 19.

117. W. Abendroth, *Veröffentlichungen des Vereins der deutschen Staatsrechtslehrer*, Heft 12, pp. 87ff.

118. H. Ridder, "Meinungsfreiheit," *Die Grundrechte*, ed. Neumann, Nipperdey, and Scheuner, 2:342ff.

119. *Ibid.*, 258.

120. *Ibid.*, 259. To be sure, besides the "public freedom of opinion" relating to publicist institutions, Ridder allowed for the classical freedom of expression of opinion relating to private individuals without expressly stating that the latter became dependent upon the former and hence lost the character of a liberal basic right itself.

121. The pertinent decisions of the Bundesverfassungsgericht (Federal Constitutional Court) can be interpreted in the same sense, especially the Loth/Harlan decision of 1958, the Northrhine-Westphalia press decision of 1959, the Schmidt/*Spiegel* decision of 1961, and the television decision of 1961. For a summary, see A. Arndt, "Begriff und Wesen der öffentlichen Meinung," *Die öffentliche Meinung*, ed. Löffler (München, 1962), 1ff., esp. 11ff.; H. Lenz, "Rundfunksorganisation und öffentliche Meinungsbildungsfreiheit," *Juristische Zeitschrift* (1963): 338ff.

122. On the freedom of parties in accord with the provisions of the *Grundgesetz*, see von der Heyde, *Grundrechte*, 2:547ff.

123. Nipperdey, "Das Recht auf die freie Entfaltung der Persönlichkeit," *Grundrechte*, 3:1ff.

124. W. Abendroth, "Zum Begriff des demokratischen und sozialen Rechtsstaats im Grundgesetz der Bundesrepublik Deutschland," *Bürokratischer Verwaltungsstaat und soziale Demokratie*, ed. Sultan and Abendroth (Hannover, Frankfurt, 1955), 97ff.

125. Forsthoff, *Sozialer Rechtsstaat*, 32.

126. The antagonism between critical publicity and manipulative publicity does not extend merely to the politically relevant process of the exercise and equilibration of power; rather, within the intraorganizational public sphere of consumer associations we find the beginnings of a publicist control of the market of consumer goods, the transparency of which is shrouded over by the manipulative publicity of monopolistic competition (see above, sect. 20). The leveling of the threshold between the public and private spheres, within the private realm itself, not only leads to the employment of the public sphere for purposes of advertising but in principle makes possible, conversely, the critical-publicist penetration of the sphere of the market. These in general very weak efforts have been most successful in the United States, where the Consumer Union has about one million members and publishes monthly the extraordinarily informative *Consumer Reports*. More on this in the anniversary volume upon the occasion of the twenty-fifth anniversary of the founding of this organization: *Consumer Reports* (May 1961): 258ff.

127. See above, 129ff.

128. See especially Max Weber, "Parliament and Government in a Reconstructed Germany." The problem has taken on an even more complicated complexion today in view of a scientifically managed political economy. Nevertheless, the antinomies of decision and discussion, of bureaucracy and democratic control, although aggravated by this, are not insoluble. See F. Neumark, "Antinomien interventionistischer Wirtschaftspolitik," *Zeitschrift für die gesamte Staatswissenschaft* 108 (1952): 576–93.

129. H. Sultan, "Bürokratie und politische Machtbildung," *Bürokratischer Verwaltungsstaat und soziale Demokratie*, 32; see also C. J. Friedrich, *Der Verfassungsstaat der Neuzeit* (Berlin, 1953), 57f.

130. The model of the technocratic state (*Verwaltungsstaat*) at one time developed by C. Schmitt, the technical conditions for the functioning of which were at odds with a possible democratization, has recently been included in a sociological analysis by H. Schelsky, "Der Mensch in der wissenschaftlichen Zivilisation," *Arbeitsgemeinschaft für Forschung, Nordrhein-Westfalen*, (Köln-Opladen, 1961) Heft 96, esp 20–32; for a critical discussion of this, cf. H. P. Bahrdt, "Helmut Schelskys technischer Staat," *Atomzeitalter* 9 (1961): 195ff.

131. See K. Renner, *Wandlungen der modernen Gesellschaft* (Wien, 1953), esp. 223ff.; and K. Mannheim, *Freedom, Power, and Democratic Planning* (Oxford, 1950), 41–76.

132. Naturally, today this problem only exists within the international framework of a competition between total social systems of industrial development; see F. Perroux, *Feindliche Koexistenz* (Stuttgart, 1961).

133. The functions of the public sphere were the same for the legal relationship between states as for the legal order inside a state. Ever since Wilson attached high-flown hopes to international public opinion as a sanction at the disposal of the League of Nations, governments have actually been increasingly forced to have at least a

propagandistic regard for the world public. "Peace," however defined, seems to have become a central topic of an international public opinion in the same manner as the slogans of the French Revolution did on the national level; on this see Ernst Fraenkel, "Öffentliche Meinung und internationale Politik," *Recht und Staat* 255/256 (Tübingen, 1962). Publicity has become relevant as a principle in international relations in another respect: in relation to the question of effective arms control. Years ago, in letters to the United Nations, Niels Bohr proclaimed the principle of an "Open World"; Oskar Morgenstern demonstrated the connection between publicity concerning technical-military advances and the requirements of strategy in the atomic age; see O. Morgenstern, *Strategie heute* (Frankfurt, 1962), esp. 292ff. Hanno Kesting, in "Der eschatologische Zwang zur Rationalität," *Merkur*, Heft 179 (1963): 71ff, has the merit of being aware of the continuity, on the level of the philosophy of history, that stretches from Kant to Morgenstern. Today as then, the idea of peace is connected to the principle of publicity—formerly in the expectation of a morally responsible legalization, today with that of a strategically imposed reduction of international tension. The goal however has remained the same—the liquidation of the state of nature between nations that has become ever more precarious. See R. Aron, *Peace and War: A Theory of International Relations* (Garden City, NY: 1966).

134. At this point I neglect the new forms of communication between politics and science. In this connection the task of controlling technological progress accrues to a democratic public sphere; see H. Krauch, "Technische Information und öffentliches Bewusstsein," *Atomzeitalter* (1963): 235ff.; also, J. Habermas, "The Scientization of Politics and Public Opinion," *Toward a Rational Society: Student Protest, Science, and Politics*, trans O. Shapiro (Boston, 1970), 62–80; and *idem.*, "Wissenschaft und Politik," *Offene Welt*, no. 86 (1964): 413ff.

VII On the Concept of Public Opinion

1. S. Landshut, "Volkssouveränität und öffentliche Meinung," *Gegenwartsprobleme des internationalen Rechtes und der Rechtsphilosophie. Festschrift für Rudolf Laun zu seinem 70. Geburtstag*, ed. D. S. Constantopoulos and H. Wehberg (Hamburg, 1953), 583; also H. Huber,"Öffentliche Meinung und Demokratie," *Festgabe für Karl Weber zum siebzigsten Geburtstag 23. Februar 1950* (Zürich, 1950), 34ff.; K. Lohmann, "Parlamentarismus und Publizistik," *Tymbos für Wilhelm Ahlmann* (Berlin, 1951), 198ff.

2. Landshut, "Volkssouveränität und öffentliche Meinung," 586.

3. Of course, "public opinion" itself is not an enacted norm and to that extent not a legal concept; but the system of norms presupposed it implictly as a social entity, which predictably functions in the sense of certain constitutional guarantees and individual prescriptions for publicity.

4. Thus A. Sauvy, "Vom Einfluss der Meinung auf die Macht," *Diogenes*, Heft 14/15 (1957): 253: "It appears that the least discomfitting coercive power of truth would be the coercive power of illumination, which is to say control by way of an entirely enlightened public opinion." The idea of rationalizing political domination is preserved; the suggested system of complete publicity "goes farther than the classical division of powers because it divides and spreads the power itself." This rationalist concept, however, remains naive in relation to the material presuppositions of a critically reflecting public.

5. W. Hennis, "Meinungsforschung und repräsentative Demokratie," *Recht und Staat*, Heft 200/201 (Tübingen, 1957): 56f.

6. *Ibid.*, 25.

7. F. G. Wilson, "Public Opinion and the Middle Class," *The Review of Politics* 17 (1955): 486–510.

8. E. Fraenkel, "Parlament und öffentliche Meinung," *Zur Geschichte und Problematik der Demokratie. Festgabe für Hans Herzfeld*, ed. W. Berges (Berlin, 1957), 182.

9. Leibholz, "Strukturwandel der modernen Demokratie," 94.

10. F. von Holtzendorff, *Wesen und Wert der öffentlichen Meinung* (München, 1879), 91f.; see E. Holzen, *Wandel und Begriff der öffentlichen Meinung im 19. Jahrhundert*, (Ph.D. diss., Hamburg, 1958).

11. A. Schäffle, *Bau und Leben des sozialen Körpers*, 2nd ed. (Tübingen, 1896), 5:191.

12. G. Tarde, *L'Opinion et la Foule* (Paris, 1901).

13. A. V. Dicey, *Law and Public Opinion in England* (London, 1905); J. Bryce, *The American Commonwealth*, 2 vols. (1889); A. L. Lowell's famous study *Public Opinion and Popular Government* (New York, 1913) stands in Bryce's tradition; he also emphasized: "Public opinion to be worthy of the name, to be the proper motive in a democracy, must be really public; and popular government is based upon the assumption of a public opinion of that kind," (p. 5).

14. Cited after P. A. Palmer, "The Concept of Public Opinion in Political Theory," *Public Opinion and Communication*, ed. Berelson and Janowitz, 11.

15. L. W. Doob, *Public Opinion and Propaganda* (New York, 1948), 35; similarly, N. J. Powell, *Anatomy of Public Opinion* (New York, 1951), 1ff.

16. W. Albig, *Public Opinion* (New York, 1938), 3.

17. M. B. Ogle, *Public Opinion and Political Dynamics* (Boston, 1950), 48.

18. Doob, *Public Opinion and Propaganda*, 35: "In this sense it might appear as though public opinion exists whenever people have attitudes."

19. H. L. Child, cited after Powell, *Anatomy of Public Opinion*, 4.

20. H. Hyman, "Towards a Theory of Public Opinion," *Public Opinion Quarterly* 21, no. 1 (Spring 1957): 58.

21. P. R. Hofstatter, *Psychologie der öffentlichen Meinung* (Wien, 1949), 53ff.

22. See D. W. Miner, "Public Opinion in the Perspective of Political Theory," *Western Political Quarterly* 13 (1960): 31–34.

23. Lazarsfeld, "Public Opinion and Classical Tradition," 39ff.

24. For a summary, see the essay of the same title by E. Katz, *Public Opinion Quarterly* 21, no.1 (Spring 1957): 61ff.; see too Katz and Lazarsfeld, *Personal Influence* (Glencoe, 1955).

25. Schmidtchen, *Die befragte Nation*, 225.

26. See H. Schelsky, "Gedanken zur Rolle der Publizistik in der modernen Gesell-schaft," *Auf der Suche nach Wirklichkeit* (Düsseldorf, 1965), 310ff.

27. Schmidtchen, *Die befragte Nation*, 257.

28. *Ibid.*, 149.

29. *Ibid.*, 149ff.

30. *Ibid.*, 265.

31. In this sense, see E. Noelle, "Die Träger der öffentlichen Meinung," *Die öffentliche Meinung*, 25ff.; see in particular the example on 29.

32. For a critical assessment of this conception, see F. Zweig, "A Note on Public Opinion Research," *Kyklos* 10 (1957): 147ff.

33. See above, pp. 231ff.

34. For another differentiation of "qualities of opinion" see K. Riezler. "What is Public Opinion?" *Social Research* 11 (1944).

35. W. Mangold, *Gegenstand und Methode des Gruppendiskussionsverfahrens* (Frankfurt, 1960).

36. C. W. Mills, *The Power Elite* (New York, 1956), 303–4.

37. On the political sociology of the "mass" see the study of W. Kornhauser, *The Politics of Mass Society* (Glencoe, 1959).

38. Mills, *The Power Elite*, 304; and *idem.*, *The Sociological Imagination* (New York, 1959), 81ff.

39. H. Blumer, "The Mass, the Public, and Public Opinion," *Public Opinion and Prop-aganda*, ed. Berelson and Janowitz, 34ff.

Index

Studies in Contemporary German Social Thought

Thomas McCarthy, General Editor

Theodor W. Adorno, *Against Epistemology: A Metacritique*

Theodor W. Adorno, *Prisms*

Karl-Otto Apel, *Understanding and Explanation: A Transcendental-Pragmatic Perspective*

Richard J. Bernstein, editor, *Habermas and Modernity*

Ernst Bloch, *Natural Law and Human Dignity*

Ernst Bloch, *The Principle of Hope*

Ernst Bloch, *The Utopian Function of Art and Literature: Selected Essays*

Hans Blumenberg, *The Genesis of the Copernican World*

Hans Blumenberg, *The Legitimacy of the Modern Age*

Hans Blumenberg, *Work on Myth*

Helmut Dubiel, *Theory and Politics: Studies in the Development of Critical Theory*

John Forester, editor, *Critical Theory and Public Life*

David Frisby, *Fragments of Modernity: Theories of Modernity in the Work of Simmel, Kracauer and Benjamin*

Hans-Georg Gadamer, *Philosophical Apprenticeships*

Hans-Georg Gadamer, *Reason in the Age of Science*

Jürgen Habermas, *On the Logic of the Social Sciences*

Jürgen Habermas, *The Philosophical Discourse of Modernity: Twelve Lectures*

Jürgen Habermas, *Philosophical-Political Profiles*

Jürgen Habermas, editor, *Observations on "The Spiritual Situation of the Age"*

Jürgen Habermas, *The Structural Transformation of the Public Sphere: An Inquiry into a Category of Bourgeois Society*

Hans Joas, *G. H. Mead: A Contemporary Re-examination of His Thought*

Reinhart Koselleck, *Critique and Crisis: Enlightenment and the Pathogenesis of Modern Society*

Reinhart Koselleck, *Futures Past: On the Semantics of Historical Time*

Harry Liebersohn, *Fate and Utopia in German Sociology, 1887–1923*

Herbert Marcuse, *Hegel's Ontology and the Theory of Historicity*

Guy Oakes, *Weber and Rickert: Concept Formation in the Cultural Sciences*

Claus Offe, *Contradictions of the Welfare State*

Claus Offe, *Disorganized Capitalism: Contemporary Transformations of Work and Politics*

Helmut Peukert, *Science, Action, and Fundamental Theology: Toward a Theology of Communicative Action*

Joachim Ritter, *Hegel and the French Revolution: Essays on the Philosophy of Right*